MEMOIRS
OF
GREGORIO PANZANI

JOSEPH BERINGTON

THE MEMOIRS OF GREGORIO PANZANI

Birmingham 1793

With an introduction by
T. A. BIRRELL

1970
GREGG INTERNATIONAL PUBLISHERS LIMITED
ENGLAND

© Editorial matter Gregg International Publishers Ltd.

All rights reserved. No part of this publication may be reproduced, stored in a retrieval system, or transmitted, in any form or by any means, electronic, mechanical, photocopying, recording, or otherwise without the prior permission of Gregg International Publishers Limited

S.B.N. – 0.576.78531.8

Republished in 1970 by Gregg International Publishers Limited
Westmead, Farnborough, Hants., England

Printed in offset by Anton Hain KG, Meisenheim/Glan
Western Germany

INTRODUCTION

"When I succeeded, many years ago, in obtaining a copy of this remarkable book (of which I made great use in *John Ingelsant*) I had so much difficulty in obtaining it, that I suspected the Romanists of destroying copies. ... Reading it now, you would suppose it was written by a rabid Protestant" (*Life and Letters of J. H. Shorthouse,* London 1905, p. 365). Berington's *Memoirs of Panzani,* though not rabidly Protestant, is certainly the most succinct example of what one might call the Cisalpine view of English Catholic history. It is a view expressed in Charles Dodd's *Church History* (1737), in Charles Butler's *Historical Memoirs* (1822), in M. A. Tierney's revision of Dodd (1839) and *passim* in the writings and correspondence of Lord Acton. It is a view which rests on the following propositions: (i) that under Henry VIII the breach with Rome would never have occurred but for the intransigence of the Court of Rome; (ii) that under Elizabeth I a reasonable toleration for Catholics might have been obtained but for the papal bull *Regnans in Excelsis*; (iii) that under James I toleration was prevented by the papal condemnation of the Oath of Allegiance and by Jesuit involvement in the Gunpowder Plot; (iv) that under Charles I attempts at a reunion between the Anglican and Roman Churches were frustrated by Jesuit and Papal intransigence; and (v) that at the end of the 18th century, the chief obstacles to Catholic Emancipation were the continued refusal of the papacy to countenance an Oath of Allegiance, and the continued presence in England of the Society of Jesus. Berington's book must be seen as a manifesto on behalf of a group of English Roman Catholic gentry in the Emancipation campaign, and as such must be used with great caution, and tested against the facts of history.

Joseph Berington (1743–1827) was that rare phenomenon, an English Catholic priest of the "Enlightenment". He was a scholar of wide attainments and considerable polish, in marked contrast to the majority of the English

Catholic clergy of the time. Some of his historical works, written with Gibbonian irony and suavity, and heavily condescending towards mediaeval superstition, acquired a wide circulation. For a great part of his life he resided at Buckland, Herts., as chaplain to his friend and protector, Sir John Courtenay Throckmorton, Bart. (1753—1819), one of the leaders of the Cisalpine party in the Catholic Emancipation movement in England.[1]

Berington's first work on English Catholic history was *The State and Behaviour of English Catholics from the Reformation to the year 1780, with a view of their present Number, Wealth, Character,* London 1780, revised edition 1781. Then in 1793, he published *The Memoirs of Gregorio Panzani,* and this was reprinted in 1813 under the more striking title of *The History of the Decline and Fall of the Roman Catholic Religion in England ... from the reign of Elizabeth to the present time, including the Memoirs of G. Panzani.* It is this book which is reprinted in the present volume.

In *The Memoirs of Panzani* Berington makes the mission of Panzani to England 1634—36 the centre-piece of the survey of English Catholic history which he had already adumbrated in *The State and Behaviour of English Catholics* in 1780. It would be far beyond the scope of this introduction to comment much on Berington's account of English Catholic history in its entirety, but in view of the fact that so much stress is laid on Panzani's mission, and on his *Relazione* of 1637, it may not be amiss to put this in its true historical perspective. Panzani's report was important to Berington, and to the Cisalpines, because it seemed to represent the report of an Italian emissary from the Roman Court who was favourable to the English secular clergy Chapter, hostile to the Jesuits, and hopeful of reconciliation between English Catholics and the Roman Court, if Rome were willing to make concessions on the oath of allegiance — and hopeful

1. cf. Bernard Ward, *The Dawn of the Catholic Revival in England,* London 1909.

even of reunion between the Roman and Anglican churches if certain concessions were made.

The first question is the authenticity of Berington's text. It is certainly not a forgery, but it is a distinctly garbled version of Panzani's *Relazione*. Pages 114–132 of Berington follow Panzani fairly closely, with some omissions, but from there onwards his use of the original is eclectic, and interspersed with some of Panzani's letters to Barberini.[2] But a true understanding of the significance of Panzani's mission can only be obtained by an examination of all the correspondence between Panzani and Barberini[3] and, especially, of Panzani's day-to-day diary of his mission.[4] Furthermore, the attitudes of the English secular clergy may be followed in the archives of the Archdiocese of Westminster, and the policy of Windebank and the government are clearly expressed in the Clarendon State Papers (published Oxford 1767) which Berington had at his disposal.

Gregorio Panzani was an Italian priest attached to the Oratory, sent to England on a purely exploratory mission. His task was to ascertain the situation in England, particularly with regard to the question of the possible appointment of a bishop. With Henrietta Maria as Catholic Queen, the possibility of a mutual agency between her court and the Court of Rome was to be investigated, and this depended on the attitude of the King and his ministers towards Catholicism.

The chief trouble lay in the personality of Panzani and in the circumstances in which he found himself. He knew no

2. For a full transcript of the *Relazione* see BM, MS Add. 15 389. A translation of parts of this may be found in W.M. Brady, *The Episcopal Succession,* Rome 1876, vol. III, and compared with Berington.

3. Public Record Office, Roman Transcripts.

4. Vatican Archives, Nunziatura d'Inghilterra 3A. Though Gordon Albion refers to this in *Charles I and the Court of Rome,* London 1935, he does not make much use of it.

English and his French was so weak that he had to have French lessons even during the period of his agency. He was a vain and credulous man (his successor, the Scotsman George Conn calls him a "pazzo", a madman), who continually exceeded his instructions to act as an observer, and tried to engineer diplomatic *coups*. At an early stage he became a partisan of the opinions and policy of certain members of the English secular clergy. And most important of all was his failure to understand the realities of government policy: in his constant optimism in the teeth of the facts he appears, in his letters to Barberini, like a sort of diplomatic Micawber, hoping for something to turn up.

At an early stage in his agency he became involved in a government intrigue. For many years Thomas Preston OSB had written in defence of the Oath of Allegiance, with the active encouragement of Abbot, the Archbishop of Canterbury. On the death of Abbot, in 1633, Preston found a new patron in his successor, Laud, and in Laud's henchman Windebank, the Secretary of State. In 1634 there appeared a further defence of the Oath, *A Pattern of Christian Loyalty* under the name of William Howard, Windebank's secretary, but in fact written by Preston. A young Jesuit, Edward Courtney, was induced to write an answer, the manuscript was delated to Windebank, and Courtney was imprisoned at the end of October. The government were now able to claim that it was the Jesuits who opposed the Oath of Allegiance. Panzani arrived in London on 15 December 1634 (o. s.). On 22 December he was visited by Preston who brought with him William Howard. Howard called again on 31 December to suggest talks with Windebank concerning the Oath. Panzani consulted the Queen as to the advisability of talks; the Queen was doubtful, but Panzani overruled her. It was in this setting that the talks with Windebank began.

At the first meeting, on 7 January 1635, Panzani made it clear that he had come on account of the controversy over a bishop and that he had no instructions on the question of the Oath. Windebank replied that the country would never have a Catholic bishop with jurisdiction, and urged Rome to mitigate its condemnation of the Oath and to formulate a new one. On 14 January Windebank repeated that "for the present the King did not see that it was possible to admit a Bishop without prejudice to the State" and asked that the Pope should do what he could to assist in the marriage of the daughter of the Prince Palatine and the King of Poland's brother. On 7 February Father Robert Philip, the Queen's chaplain, informed Panzani that the King had informed the Queen that a bishop could not be tolerated in England and that "if a Bishop should come here he could not do less than make a severe demonstration". Panzani did his best to keep this unequivocal statement secret. Despite this clear information concerning the major part of his mission, Panzani continued the conversations with Windebank, who seems to have adopted a policy of stringing Panzani along.[5] On 24 February Windebank brings up the question of reunion. On 28 February he suggests that the Jesuits should be removed, or at least that their numbers should be diminished, for whenever one wished to arrive at a decision, they would join with the Puritans. Panzani replied that "it was necessary to do something for the Pope, that he on his side might be animated also." In other words Panzani patently encouraged Windebank in the idea of trying to do a deal with Rome at the expense of the Jesuits. This is quite unpardonable in one who was supposed to be an impartial agent.

The fact was that from the outset of his mission Panzani had yielded a more ready ear to those hostile to the Jesuits, favourable to the Oath (or at least a modified oath) and favourable to a bishop. His diary reveals that his most frequent visitors were the secular clergy, men like George Leyburn (agent of Bishop Smith), John Southcott and

---

5. This is borne out by the interview with Cottington on 26 March; Cottington insisted that a Bishop must not be sent without the consent of the King, but "what is not obtained today, may be obtained tomorrow."

George Muskett. Southcott had prepared a copious dossier of complaints against the Jesuits which was given to Panzani.[6] On 17 November 1635 a "concordat" was signed between representatives of the secular clergy and the religious orders. The Jesuits were left out, but after the *fait accompli* they were invited to sign. The Jesuits rightly refused these terms and stuck to the fact that the disputes between regulars and seculars had already been settled by papal decree, to which they adhered. The whole episode seems to have been engineered to put the Jesuits in a false position.

Panzani's gullibility about English sympathy for Rome was boundless. On 4 July 1635 Lord Herbert of Cherbury called, and, under the seal of secrecy, protested that he reverenced the Roman church as his mother, and offered to submit his books to the Holy See. Less than two months previously Herbert had presented to the King a tract in which he asserted that only a powerful king could be head of the church.[7]

Most serious of all was Panzani's pathetic faith in the sincerity of Windebank. The Clarendon State Papers show clearly Windebank's (and Charles's) cynicism. The Benedictines Preston and Jones and the Franciscan Santa Clara (Christopher Davenport) with their schemes of Oath formulae and reunion, were simply being used to create internal dissensions among the Catholics.[8] When the idea

6. Westminster Archives vol. XXVIII ff. 49—76. A comparison between the correspondence and memoranda of Leyburn, Lovell, Muskett, Boswell and Fitton in Westminster Archives with Panzani's letters and *Relazione* is very instructive. It shows clearly how much of the material that Panzani transmitted to Rome as his own considered opinion was in fact taken over uncritically from the secular clergy sources.

7. Sidney Lee, *The Autobiography of Edward, Lord Herbert of Cherbury*, London, n. d., p. 143—4.

8. W. K. L. Webb, "Thomas Preston", *Biographical Studies*, II (1953/4) 216—268, is excellent. G. Sitwell, "Leander Jones's

of an English agent (ostensibly from the Queen) to the Court of Rome had been decided on, Windebank wrote to the King, on 6 October 1635, giving his idea of the agent's duties. This was to include "endeavouring to discover the correspondences of the Roman Catholick party here in England, and their ways, and ... fomenting their schisms and differences here; *which he must do if he serves your Majesty well"*.[9] Brett's instructions were signed by Charles on 28 October. They included the following points: "Forasmuch as we find that the number of Jesuits increaseth daily here, who, being for the most part practick and overbusy in matters of state, may become dangerous, and yet we are not willing, but upon great necessity, to use remedies which our laws do provide against them; you shall therefore use the best means you can for their revocation, that so this mischief may be prevented quietly, and rather by the hand of that See than by ours, *which must fall more heavily upon them.* In the meantime, *you are to discover what intelligences they hold, both here and there, and diligently observe their ways, and to give advertisement of them hither ...* You shall hold acquaintance and converse chiefly with those that are most moderate, and best affected to us and our state. And yet, if any Jesuits, or others of their party, shall visit you, you may admit them, and use them kindly respectively, ob-

Mission to England 1634–5", *Recusant History*, V (1960), 132–182, is valuable, but rather apologetic in tone, and politically a little naïve. J. B. Dockery, *Christopher Davenport*, London 1960, is the only recent book on the subject of Santa Clara.

9. *State Papers collected by Edward Earl of Clarendon*, Oxford 1767, vol. II, p. 217; italics mine. The whole letter is a protest by Windebank against the appointment of Arthur Brett as agent, on the grounds that he is too much under the influence of Father Robert Philip, the Queen's confessor.

serving well their ends, and advertise them hither; *and you are to make use of them for our service."*[10]

The English government was in fact completely opportunistic on the Catholic question. Discussions of union, toleration, and bishops were encouraged with the sole object of dividing and weakening the Catholic body as a whole: it was the same policy under Elizabeth I, under James I and, for that matter, under George III. The only difference under George III was the numerical weight and general nuisance value of Irish Catholicism — English Catholicism by the time of Berington was something that could be ignored with impunity.[11] The views of Panzani and Berington may be very attractive; the trouble is that they do not square with the facts of history.[12] However, as Maitland

10. *State Papers collected by Edward Earl of Clarendon*, Oxford 1767, vol. II, p. 249–250; italics mine. In *Charles I and the Court of Rome*, London 1935, the ecumenical historian Dr. Gordon Albion makes no mention at all of the letter from Windebank to Charles. Of Charles's instructions to Brett, the only reference is as follows: "Then, giving way to that obsession he had inherited from his father, Charles said he intended to check the daily increase of the English Jesuits who, 'being for the most part practicall and overbusy in matters of state, may become dangerous, and yet [Charles's natural self breaks in here] we are not willing but upon great necessity to use remedies which our laws do provide against them'." (p. 156) Those who read the full quotation may get a better idea of "Charles's natural self" than that provided by Dr. Gordon Albion.

11. T. A. Birrell, "Latter-day Recusants", *Dublin Review*, 1955, 262–274.

12. As a small example of the precariousness of historical truth, we may note the following episode. Panzani's *Diario* reveals the fact that on 7 February 1635 William Howard told him that "John Penruddock, a great friend of the Jesuits, has said that religion would never more be restored except by the sword." In Berington's *Panzani*, (p. 151) this has become

has said, "The essential matter of history is not what happened but what people thought or said about it."

T. A. BIRRELL

"The Jesuits were not willing to hearken to an accommodation on the terms that were commonly proposed. Their usual language was, that the Roman Catholic religion would never be restored in England, but by the sword. This topic was very displeasing to Panzani." This is repeated by Mgr. Nédoncelle in *Trois Aspects du Problème Anglo-Catholique au XVIIe Siècle,* Paris 1951, p. 85–86. Panzani, he maintains, possessed much judgement, a sign of which was the fact that: "il se méfiait surtout des Jésuites qui ne rêvaient, selon lui, qu'à une victoire par l'épée."

THE

MEMOIRS

OF

GREGORIO PANZANI;

GIVING AN ACCOUNT OF HIS

AGENCY IN ENGLAND,

IN THE

Years 1634, 1635, 1636.

Translated from the ITALIAN ORIGINAL, and now First published.

To which are added,

AN

INTRODUCTION and a SUPPLEMENT,

EXHIBITING

The State of the English Catholic Church,

And the Conduct of Parties, before and after that Period, to the present Times.

By the Rev^d. JOSEPH BERINGTON.

BIRMINGHAM:

PRINTED BY SWINNEY & WALKER;

For G. G. J. & J. ROBINSON, and R. FAULDER, *LONDON.*

MDCCXCIII.

S.B.N. – 0.576.78531.8

Republished in 1970 by Gregg International Publishers Limited
Westmead, Farnborough, Hants., England

Printed in offset by Anton Hain KG, Meisenheim/Glan
Western Germany

TO THE

CATHOLIC CLERGY OF THE COUNTY
OF STAFFORD,

THE FRIENDS OF VIRTUE AND OF TRUTH,

WITH WHOM HE HAS HAD THE HONOUR TO THINK AND ACT,

THE FOLLOWING WORK IS HUMBLY INSCRIBED,

BY THEIR FAITHFUL FRIEND AND BROTHER,

THE AUTHOR.

OSCOTT, *May* 1, 1793.

PREFACE.

THE *Memoirs of Panzani*, which I now present to the public, have been long witheld, from motives, I think, of a false delicacy. He was an Italian clergyman sent into England by his holiness Urban VIII. in the year 1634, the ninth of Charles I. To compose certain differences, that had long divided the Catholics, particularly those of the clerical order, was the main object of his mission; in the prosecution of which, however, much incidental matter intervened, in which the court, some of the ministers, and others were personally engaged. Our historians, in general, seem to have known little of the transaction; and they who have said most, have proved themselves most ignorant.* It was natural that a business, in which a papal envoy, on one side, was the

---

* *Pope's Nuncio*, 4to. 1643. *Popish Royal Favourite*, by Will. Prynn, 1643.

principal agent, should, at that suspectful and jealous æra, be guarded with all possible secrecy.

Whether the *Memoirs* were written by Panzani himself, or composed from the materials he supplied, does not appear; nor is it of moment. Suffice it, that they are *authentic*; of which no one can doubt who, from contemporary writers, has examined the minute histories of the times. The transactions with which we are acquainted coincide with the statements of Panzani. Where no extrinsic vouchers appear, there is still ample evidence of their truth; for in matters of secret negociation what more can be required, than the attestation of a creditable witness whom no facts or opposition of testimony contradict?

The original *Memoirs* were written in Italian and never published; of which, by means of " an eminent prelate of singular candour and scrupulosity," then residing at Rome, our historian Dodd, some years ago

PREFACE.

ago, procured an accurate tranflation.* The Italian MS. he obferves, was not in above one or two hands. Of the tranflation Dodd publifhed only fome *extracts*,† from motives of a benevolent tendency, fearing left the publication of the whole memoirs might prejudice the evil-difpofed, as he fays, ftill more againft the memory of the unfortunate Charles, and from a delicate forbearance towards fome focieties of his own communion.‡ The firft confideration, the reader from the perufal will find, bears no weight; and to the fecond, at this time, he will not give a thought. Mr. Dodd, however, was extremely defirous of publifhing thefe memoirs, in which he faw, he thought, many things that were interefting, and which would throw light on a dark and mifreprefented period. He, therefore, brought the principal materials together under a new title, meaning to publifh them as the *Memoirs of Windebank*, the fecretary of ftate, who was much engaged in the tranfaction. I am

---

* See *Remarks* at the end of the *Memoirs*.
† *Records of Panzani*, vol. iii. p. 128.   ‡ Vol. iii. p. 76.

in possession of his MSS. in this form, as also under the original title, of which I avail myself, subjoining to the text a few notes where the subject may seem to want illustration.

I am myself so satisfied of the *authenticity* of the memoirs, that I was not inclined to make any further enquiries; otherwise, by a direct application to Rome, I could have procured, I doubt not, an attested copy of the Italian original. This Mr. Dodd equivalently did; and on his accuracy and honour the most punctilious reader may rely. I will detain him, therefore with no unnecessary observations.

Mr. Dodd, who is not so generally known, to the protestant public, at least, as he merits, was a clergyman of the Roman church, who resided at Harvington, in Worcestershire, an old seat now belonging to the Throckmorton family, where he died about the year 1745. I can speak of his virtues which are recorded, of his talents which were eminent, of his labours in the range of literature which

were

were inceffant and manifold. The work, that has principally given celebrity to his name, is a *Church Hiftory of England*, in three volumes *Folio, from* 1500 *to* 1688, *chiefly with regard to Catholics*. In the compilation of this work he fpent almoft thirty years. It contains much curious matter, collected with great affiduity, and many original *Records*. His ftyle, when the fubject admits expreffion, is pure and unincumbered, his narration eafy, his reflections juft and liberal. I have feldom known a writer, and that writer a churchman, fo free from prejudice and the degrading impreffions of partyzeal. But I am not fure, that his materials are well arranged. Indeed, he was himfelf, for a long time, fo diffatisfied, as, with his own hand, to copy a work fo voluminous, into two or theee different forms. I think, I have feen three. There are many repetitions, which might have been avoided; but its main defect is the want of a copious *Index*. Of this I have had a painful experience.

The *Hiftory*, of which I am fpeaking, for many years was little known; but it has,

has, at length, found its way into the libraries of the curious, and no copies have remained unsold. The reader will see what use I have made of it in the following pages; and I readily acknowledge my obligations.

Not long after the appearance of the two first volumes, a petulant and captious critique, under the title of *A Specimen of Amendments*, was published by *Clerophilus Alethes*, that is, —— Constable a Jesuit, in 1740. It is extremely peevish, and malevolent as peevish, and weak as malevolent. He rebukes the clergyman principally for his commissions and omissions in regard to the fathers of the society. Them, he more than intimates, he should have never blamed; he should have loaded his page, from the pleasant histories of fathers More, Bartoli, and Juvency, with the edifying and wonderful, sometimes miraculous, events of their births, lives, and burials. With such materials as these, he observes, he might have compiled a history truly worthy of the notice of a christian reader!

Dodd.

PREFACE.

Dodd, whose mind, it appears, was irritable, was not pleased, as, I think, he might have been, with this ludicrous attack. He was aware, that the cant of piety, and certain insinuations breathed with unction, might at once, in the estimation of a misjudging public, blast his character and all the fruits of his thirty years labour. He, therefore, in 1741, replied to Constable, in a work entitled *An Apology for the Church History of England*. It is written with uncommon acuteness, keen discrimination, a brevity that impresses, and a ridicule that cuts. I only lament that his conscious superiority should have sometimes descended to asperities of language, and recriminating taunts, which prove that he did not sufficiently despise his adversary. The generous mastiff indignantly passes on, heedless of the curs that aim to annoy and teaze him.

Other works have been ascribed to Mr. Dodd, of which, I believe he was the author, written too acrimoniously against the insidious conduct, as he deemed it, of the Jesuits in their transactions with

the

the secular clergy. He has also left behind him a variety of papers, some complete, some imperfect, on different subjects, all written with his own hand. Few men have been more indefatigable in research, and patient of that toil that wearies most in the walks of literature.

So much for Gregorio Panzani and Charles Dodd, whose name, as the reader is now sensible, is nearly connected with the *Memoirs*.

To the *Memoirs* I have prefixed an *Introduction* and subjoined a *Supplement*, which exhibit the state of the English Catholic church and the general conduct of parties, before and after the short period comprised in the memoirs, down to the present year. Something, I thought, was necessary to *prepare* the mind of the reader; and if, when I had gained his attention, I could lead him forwards to the contemplation of more recent occurrences, he would find, I flattered myself, some things not uninteresting. But I was not sensible that I should say so much, having, a few years before, traversed the
same

PREFACE.

fame ground, and found it barren.* My fources of information, however, were now more copious; and that muft account to the reader for any departures from, or oppofition to, the ftatements I had before given.

I know not that it is at all neceffary, to fpeak of the authors or different records with which I was furnifhed. When I firft quote them, invariably, I believe, I give, in a note, fome account of their authors or contents. The MS. *Letters* of Dr. Allen and of many of his contemporaries, from which I could have drawn fome curious facts, had my plan required it, were copied with an accuracy too minutely fcrupulous, from originals and copies depofited in the library of the Englifh college at Rome. The *Relation of the Regulars*, almoft the whole of which I have given, was tranfcribed from the fame place. The other MS. documents, I occafionally quote, are equally authentic. I wifhed to have obtained a fight of fome papers,

---

* *State and Behaviour of Englifh Catholics*, 8vo. 1780.

papers, preserved, I understood, in the *archives* of our chapter, particularly of a *History of all their Affairs*, compiled by John Ward, their secretary, at the end of the last century. The liberty I requested was refused me, from the generous motives, I once thought, of the peevish animal who, lying in the manger, refused to let the patient ox, whom hunger pressed, feed on the food that was natural to him, and unnatural to the snarling tyrant that did but defile it by his presence. However, I am now told, that the valuable MS. cannot be found. I was, therefore, necessitated to make use of an *Adridgement*, extracted, I doubt not, very faithfully by the learned John Serjeant, and published in 1706.

It may be asked, as I invariably side with the secular clergy in all their controversies with the monastic orders, and as invariably censure the Jesuits, particularly father Parsons, why I have not been honest enough to consult their own authors?—Perhaps, I did consult them. The truth, however, is, that the principal

pal historians of the Jesuits, whose names I have already mentioned, (two of whom are foreigners, and the other is little esteemed) are acknowledged to be extremely partial; and though, as I am ready to admit, a sufficient degree of partiality may be found on the other side, I was yet disposed, as I could not free myself from all party-prepossession, rather to err, if I was to err, in favour of my own inclinations, than against them. But my deviations from the line of historic justice are not great: I am not even conscious that I have deviated at all. What really is the place of truth, in speaking of men and their transactions, I know it to be morally impossible to define. *Les choses de ce monde sont a facette:* look which way you will, some deception will attend you. To approximate to truth is all we can pretend to; and he is the best historian, who, from some accidental impression, perhaps, taking his bias, falls into the fewest errors.—With regard to the regulars, in general, of which corps the Jesuits were members, I have been laudibly candid, giving their own *Relation* of many events. I warned
the

PREFACE.

the reader, indeed, to be on his guard, from the obvious impreſſion on my own mind, that there was little truth in their ſtatements.

I have been ſevere, I admit, on father Parſons, and ſometimes, on the general policy of the regulars. Under this conſciouſneſs, therefore, I have coolly reviewed my obſervations, when the warmth had ſubſided which naturally accompanies compoſition. But I ſee not much to cenſure: ſome things, perhaps, are improperly harſh, though warranted, to my apprehenſion, by the evidence of facts. One reflection only gives me pain, and that is, leſt, from blaming freely, as I always do, what I judge to be reprehenſible in the conduct of individuals, or the policy of certain communities, an inference ſhould be wantonly drawn, that I am an enemy to whole inſtitutes and all their component members. It is the *eſprit de corps* that I condemn, all behaviour dictated by that ſpirit, and the individuals that it ſways. Its influence, I think, has greatly actuated all the monaſtic orders,

as

as it obviously does all other societies of men, whom a common interest binds, whether of worldly politics or of religious economy. Father Parsons, it was evident, could sacrifice to it considerations of the most weighty import: I, therefore, deemed him most blame-worthy, and treated him as such. *De mortuis nil nisi verum* is the motto of historians. Whether with the predominating spirit, I am censuring, can consist real integrity of manners, and moral worth, I chuse not to define: but of this I am certain, that men of party unblushingly do, what, when taken out of that influence, they would reject with horror.

I shall be reproached with speaking too freely of the Roman pontiff, of his court, and of his sacred congregations.*
—I respect

---

* It is in these Congregations, 15, I think, in number, and which answer to our different departments or offices of state, that the business of the Roman court, in her concerns with Catholic Christendom, is transacted. A discipline, which may be termed *modern*, originating in the dark ages, multiplied those concerns to a vast extent. They now diminish. The Congregations *de prop. fide*, and of the *holy Inquisition*, are the two principal offices.—See the 4th and 7th *Discourses* of Fleury, also *Vera Idea della Santa Side*, 8vo.

—I respect the Roman pontiff, his court, and his sacred congregations; but as neither he nor they are privileged from the errors, into which human passions and their politics precipitate the greatest men, I was, surely, at liberty to censure those errors, when they struck my eye with the broad light of noontide. I can excuse, I think, great misconduct, or not treat it very harshly, when it is conceded to proceed from the instigation of resentment, of ambition, or of interest; but when conscience is pleaded, and the sacred duties of religion, and yet such things are done, as the professed politician would blush to acknowledge, my indignation, I own, rises, and I express its strongest feelings. Such was, sometimes, my indignation, and I expressed it, while I traced with pain the hundred arts and domineering policy practised by the Roman court, in their transactions with the small remnant of the ancient British church. It is indecorous, truly, that the vicar of him who was meek and lowly of heart, and the professed descendents of fishermen, should assume the tones of worldly power and the maxims of worldly craft.

PREFACE.

craft. To this, however, I will agree, that if, after having perused my statement of facts, and compared it with the guarded narration of the most devoted papist, the reflecting reader shall say, I have been unduly severe, I will acknowledge my fault, and be disposed (I think, I may be disposed) to write a treatise in favour of the pretensions of the Roman court, and the views of its fifteen congregations. To the jurisdiction of the Roman see and to the supremacy of its first pastor I bow with reverence; but neither with that jurisdiction nor with that supremacy, though they are sometimes sullied by the contact, has the court of Rome and its fifteen congregations any proper concern. These are human; they divine.*

It will be said, that I have dwelt, with a minute detail, on our ecclesiastical proceedings,

---

* I am projecting a work, which, if Providence shall give me life, I hope to be able to execute under the title of *The History of the Rise, the Greatness, and the Decline of the Papal power*. Nor am I sure, that the word *Fall* will not complete the title, if the present politics of Europe be not stemmed in their course, or the chivalry of France be broken. The first pastor, in my eyes, will be more venerable, when the Christian virtues, *Faith* and *Charity*, shall be the sole supporters of his chair.

ceedings, in the appointment of arch-priests, the nomination of bishops, (if so they might be called) the erection of their chapter, the manly conduct of this chapter, the final delegation of vicars apostolic, and the characters and behaviour of these venerable men.—I own it; for it was to trace these various events, with all their concomitant circumstances, which was a part of history, I was aware, little known, that I undertook to disturb the dust of records. When my brethren, I said, shall be informed by what means, and in the face of how dignified an opposition, their present ecclesiastical government was established, they will view it, perhaps, with a less partial eye, and be disposed to reform what is abusive.—With the same motive, I strongly marked, what I conceived to be, the original mistake in erecting houses for foreign education, the evils they gave rise to, and the error of persevering in the measure.

But to complain of evils, and not suggest a practicable remedy, might justly be deemed idly querulous: I, therefore, before

PREFACE.

before I closed my observations, presumed to delineate a sketch of two plans, which, if adopted, would tend to correct the main grievances under which we internally labour. May I request the reader not to throw by my book, till once, twice, and thrice, divesting himself of all party-prepossession, he has maturely weighed those plans?

And here, I think, the curtain might drop; but I am requested to subjoin a few additional observations. They shall be as brief, as possible.

A work has been put into my hands, lately published, entitled, with a motive of charming benevolence, *Ecclesiastical Democracy Detected*. I read it, rather I ran through it, as was natural, when every step was painful. The terms most familiar with the gentle author,* who styles himself *reverend*, are *heretic*, *schismatic*, *impostor*, *hypocrite*, not always broadly spoken, the two last I mean, but palpably

---

* The Rev. John Milner, F. A. S.

implied; and even more than this, for it may be that the curious antiquary (he is a *fellow* of the antiquarian fociety) has found in the vocabulary of the banks of the Thames fomething *aboriginal* on which to feed his appetite. Take a fample. " But "how fhall I follow my adverfary through "all the *glaring inconfiftencies, malicious* "*mifreprefentations*, and *unblufhing falfe-* "*hoods*, which he has heaped together?"* The man that ufes this language is neither a gentleman nor a Chriftian. Whether the water-nymphs, I alluded to, would take him for their chaplain, I know not: fure I am, that communities of a better polifh and of better principles muft be fhocked by his intemperate effufions. And what, after all, was the provocation that inftigated the *fellow* thus to throw about his ftink-pots?

Sir John Throckmorton, a *gentleman* of large fortune, and of amiable manners, a *man* of great mental endowments, a *fcholar* deeply read, a *citizen* devoted to his country,

---

† p. 176.

PREFACE.

country, a *chriſtian* in practice as well as theory, a *Catholic* enlightened in his belief and ſincere in his conviction, Sir John Throckmorton, a few years ago, addreſſed a *letter* to the clergy of his own communion *on the appointment of biſhops*. He had ſeen, with ſome emotion, two recent inſtances, in which, it appeared, the court of Rome had delegated two vicars apoſtolic, at that time, not favoured by the general wiſhes of the diſtricts, they were appointed to govern. Verſed in the maxims and practices of the beſt æra of Chriſtian diſcipline, to the ſtudy of which the circumſtance of his being a member of the Catholic committee had led him; Sir John viewed the extraordinary delegation of the two vicars as a departure from the uſages of venerable antiquity; and, under that impreſſion, it was, that he wrote his *letter*. In it he adviſed the clergy to aſſume, what he deemed, a better ſpirit, and to return to the ways, ſo they ſeemed to him, of their anceſtors. The *letter* was read; was approved and diſapproved;

PREFACE.

proved; and would soon have sunk into oblivion, as is the common fate of such essays.

The *fellow* of the Antiquarian Society came forward: He was *answered* by Sir John: the *fellow* rejoined: was again replied to: and then appeared this masterpiece of good-breeding and Christian forbearance, *Ecclesiastical Democracy Detected.**

The reader need not be told, that, with each new publication, much new matter was collected: for controversy, as the snow-ball, always picks up as it advances. It concerns not my purpose to discuss the merits of the publications, or of the cause in debate: nor am I a competent judge. With the works of Sir John I am acquainted; but of the *fellow*'s I have only tasted the spirit. This told

---

* I have seen a *Pastoral Letter*, which enumerates and solemnly censures the erroneous assertions of the Baronet, to which *letter* this work of the antiquary seems to have been meant as a *prologue*. Can the reader tell, why that *pastoral* brings to one's mind the title of a merry play in Shakespear?

told me, as I obferved, that he was neither a *gentleman* nor a *Chriſtian*. To the firſt character, probably, he does not pretend; but he ſhould, in this æra of the world, ſtrive to be a *Chriſtian*.

There was a fociety of men, of whom we read much in an old book, called the *Teſtament*, with which, as it is *old*, I marvel our antiquarian *fellow* is not better acquainted, that is, from admiration, at leaſt, of the venerable ſtamp with which time has marked it, that he has not imbibed fome portion of its maxims. That fociety of men were called *Phariſees*. They were extremely popular in their day, and they led the faſhions and taſte of their countrymen. But as, in the line of morals and religious belief, they built much on human traditions, on outward forms, on the obfervances of days, on faith unincumbered by works, and on a flattering complacency of judgment, that, for thefe things, they were the chofen friends of heaven and better than other men, when the divine founder of Chriſtianity appeared amongſt them, their cant of holineſs and oſtentatious preſumption,

presumption, so adverse to the native simplicity of truth, roused his warmest indignation. He pointed the keenest shafts of censure against their arrogance, aware that if their maxims could stand, it would be even vain to sow the seeds of a heavenly doctrine. On no occasion, therefore, did he spare these men, and he, who was gentleness and charity, became indignant and irresistible in reproof, to stem the spreading contagion of their lessons. In many passages of the gospels, but particularly in the 23d chapter of St. Matthew, is a whole-length portrait of the Pharisees drawn, to the contemplation of which I refer our *antiquary* and some other modern christians.

For the family of Pharisees is not yet extinct. We have men that sound their own trumpets, that place themselves in the seat of Moses, that make broad their phylacteries and enlarge the borders of their garments, that love to be called masters, that shut up the kingdom of heaven against men, that make long prayer, that compass sea and land to make proselytes, that pay tithe of mint, and

PREFACE.

and anife, and cummin, omitting the weightier matters of the law, that ſtrain at a gnat, and ſwallow a camel, that make clean the outſide of the cup and of the platter, that truſt in themſelves as righteous, and deſpiſe others. We have ſuch men; and I cannot avoid thinking, judging from their fruits which unerringly denote the good and bad tree, that they who talk as the *fellow* of the antiquarian ſociety talks, and he, by no means, talks alone, are the genuine offspring of the Phariſees. They blazon their *faith*, and they make wide their *hope*, but the greateſt of theſe is *charity*, which, evidently, they have not. I am, then, authoriſed to ſay, that they are not *Chriſtians*, for they want the virtue that is *eſſential* to its nature. Can there be a man that is not a *rational* animal; or a brute that is not *ſenſitive?* They ſpeak loudly, it is true, of their *orthodoxy*, that is, they make broad their *phylacteries*; they proclaim their *ſubmiſſion* to authority, that is, they pay tithe of mint, of anife, and cummin; they extol their own *righte-ouſneſs*, that is, they clean the outſide of the cup and of the platter; they talk with
unction

unction of the *love of souls*, that is, they compass sea and land to make proselytes to their own opinions: while the men they despise, whom they call *heretics* and *schismatics*, believe what, on the authority of revelation, is proposed to be believed, and, neglecting the traditions of men, emulate better gifts. I have seen these give meat to the hungry, and drink to the thirsty; take in the stranger, and clothe the naked; visit the sick, and relieve the prisoner. When all nations shall, therefore, be gathered, we know where their place will be, and what their reward.

I have been more serious on the occasion, than, I thought, I could have been; but it is not without motive. And should it be retorted on me, that, by these remarks, I prove myself as *uncharitable* as the men I censure; I beg leave to refer to the *fruits* of the tree, which I have just mentioned, those unerring guides to judgment. " He who knew what was in man, need- " ed not any should inform him concern- " ing man:" and he who hears what the mouth uttereth, may safely pronounce on
the

PREFACE.

the abundance of the heart. I am willing to be thought *uncharitable* with the divine master of *charity*.

The antiquary, some few years back, published *Exclamations of the soul to God, or Meditations of St. Teresa*, prefixing to them an introductory *preface*, full of abuse and scurrility, chiefly poured out on me. The frontispiece, if I remember well, was a pretty device—the Saint, in the brown habit of her order, seated in a chair of Gothic carpentry, the accompaniments all Gothic, with eyes in a fine phrenzy fixed. It was ingenious, surely, to couple with the effusions of real piety the effusions of real rancour: but the *fellow* is ingenious.

He has, likewise, very lately entertained the public (but I have not the title of the book) with something, I am told, like the story of the renowned *St. George and the Dragon*, against the assertions of Edward Gibbon, Esq. Such labours are innocent; and should scurrility load the page, the *dragon*, it must be allowed, is a more proper vehicle for abuse, than the *meditations* of St. Teresa. He may next undertake

undertake the achievements (they will be no difgrace to antiquarian refearch) of *Guy earl of Warwick and the Dun Cow*, and make the champion or the cow porters of fuch other malevolent remarks, as he may then have collected, againſt *heretics* and *fchifmatics*, that is, againſt Sir John Throckmorton and myſelf.*

There

---

* In a Note of his *Democracy*, (by the way, the *fellow* has no *Ariſtocracy* in his manners,) he honours me with obſerving, that I am no orthodox Catholic, that I do not know my religion, that in the *Hiſtory of Henry* II. I have mutilated the *Conſtitutions* of Clarendon, that I am an ever varying and inconſiſtent author, that I degrade my native talents, and difpofitions to do good, by inculcating erroneous opinions: And then, " It " is hoped, he fays, " that when he (I) ferioufly reflects on the " detriment he has done to the fouls of many, by the errors in " queſtion, he will add one more work to the liſt of his publi-" cations, under the title of *Retractations*."

Will the reader kindly look back to my obſervations on the family maxims of the Phariſees? After that, I ſhall only remark that, in what he ſays about the *Conſtitutions* of Clarendon he ſhews himſelf to be a very ignorant *fellow*. An antiquary ſhould know *when* Matthew Paris lived, and, therefore, what is his comparative authority. But it rejoices me to hear that, in *his* eſtimation, " I have done detriment to the fouls of many;" becauſe, in that caſe, I know, I have eſſentially ſerved them; I have opened to them the realms of truth. As to a book of *Retractations;* perhaps, fome years hence, I may write one, to ſhew the progreſs I have made ſince, about twenty years ago, I commenced author.

There is another prieft,* lineally defcended from the fame Jerufalem ftock, and even more true to the principles of his tribe, than the *fellow* I have juft parted from. I would not notice him; but my filence, I am told, would be deemed a rudenefs.—We faw him, fome time ago, rifing, as he more than intimated, " from " the duty of recollection and felf-exami- " nation, at the foot of his crucifix," to fpread from the prefs defamation and abufe. The wits have named him *Tartuffe*, from the refemblance, they noted in him, to that eminent perfonage on the old French ftage. His fanctimonious air and oily diction veil a mind of artifice; and, at a diftance, may be heard the founding brafs and the tinkling cymbal. " Brother," fays he, ftretching out his hand, " let me pull out the mote that is " in thine eye; while the beam that is in " his own eye he confidereth not." I think, without any effort of fancy, I can fee this man pafs by, whilft he, who had

fallen

---

* Rev. Charles Plowden, a *fellow* of the fallen fociety of Jefus.

fallen among thieves, lay wounded on the road between Jerufalem and Jericho. " And by chance there came down *a certain prieſt* that way; and when he faw him, he paffed by on the other fide." It is true, by a laudable anticipation of future days, he might be bufied in preparing a gay pofey of devotion to the *ſacred heart of Mary*,* heedlefs of earthly objects. When I once obferved to *Tartuffe*, that, from fome circumftances, it appeared, he was actuated, in his writings, by a fpirit of refentment. " Such may be the appearances," he anfwered, " but when I took up my pen, I affure you, *I purified my intention*." Reader! doft thou underftand this cafuiftry, the moft apt of all to cover the commiffion of crimes? I know not that they, who fat in the

---

* A modern *devotion*, and which, with many others, to the difgrace of real religion, has been invented in our church from fordid and fuperftitious views. To this day they hold their ground: even the moſt active means are *now* ufed to fpread them. I have feen a forry tale on the advantages of the *Scapular*, unbluſhingly, thruſt into the hands of the multitude. From ſuch *practices*, let me inform certain guardians of the flock, more is to be feared, than from any innocent *theories* that may amufe the learned.

the chair of Mofes, poffeffed an ingenuity that could reach to this commodious latitude. " It is true," fays the affaffin, " I "did cut the man's throat; but I *purified* "*my intention*, as I drew the knife."*

To the antiquary I kindly obferved that, as he had fpoken fo characteriftically, I thought, he might fairly be recommended to the chaplaincy of Billingfgate: And fo I ftill think: but as it might be well to procure the eftablifhment of a fee there dignified with a complete hierarchy, will it be deemed *fchifmatical*, if I propofe his elder brother as the propereft candidate? By a combined influence, they may efcape the crying fin of a popular election; and when the merits of the candidate fhall be detailed (he underftands the method) by the antiquarian orator in perfon, all oppofition, I am fure, will be calmed, and the fifterhood, with the ejaculations of an approving complacency, receive their worthy paftor.

Then

---

* See this doctrine of *Intentions* admirably detailed in the 7th *letter* of Pafcal. Read, at the fame time, *letters* 15 and 16, on the beft arts of *calumny* and *fcandal*.

Then, taking his stand at the corner of some street, while the trumpet sounds before him, he may pray, making broad his phylacteries; and the chaplain, meanwhile, shall draw motes from the eyes of the passengers, or amuse them with straining at gnats, and swallowing camels.

Having completed his *libel* against the gentlemen of our late committee, Tartuffe (the name is patronymical not opprobrious) assailed me in a pamphlet of some length, denouncing all my errors. I have never read it, nor ever shall; but I hear it is written in his best manner. I am not inclined, unnecessarily, to expose my mind's peace, by the perusal of such personal invectives; to draw any benefit from them, is not possible; reply to them I will not. In a word, my religion, I solemnly declare, is not his or that of his admirers: I profess myself the disciple of a better master, of him who was the friend of man, who was the foe of Pharisaical hypocrisy, and who raised the noble fabric of a divine religion on the broad basis of universal charity. Why then has the
officious

officious prieſt obtruded himſelf on me?
I will ſpeak of him in the words of the
amiable Metaſtaſio:

>Se'l moſſe
>Leggerezza; no'l curo:
>Se Follia; lo compiango:
>Se Raggion; gli ſon grato: e ſe in lui ſono
>Impeti di malizia; io gli perdono.*

---

* If levity moved him; I care not: If folly; I pity him: If reaſon, I thank him: And if malice goad the holy breaſt; I forgive him.

ERRATA.

ERRATA.

Page 100 — line —	2 —	for 1644 —	read	1634.
—— 269 ————	7 —	for real	——	zeal.
—— 323 ————	9 —	for Serne	——	Kerne.
—— 331 ————	25 —	for double	——	doubled.
—— 337 ————	28 —	for affected	——	effected.
—— 352 ————	10 —	for Dadde	——	Dadda
—— 400 ————	15 —	for Arnald	——	Arnauld.

CONTENTS.

CONTENTS.

INTRODUCTION.

From the beginning of the reign of Elizabeth, an. 1558, *to the appointment of the archpriest Blackwell, an.* 1598.

THE opening of Elizabeth's Reformation, 1.—Imprudence of Paul IV. 3.—The supremacy of the crown established, 4.—The bishops and some of the clergy refuse the oath and are deprived, 11.—Conduct of others, 15.—Behaviour of the laity, 17.—Many of the clergy retire abroad, 19.—William Allen, 20.—Father Parsons, 24.—Foreign connections the principal cause of our grievances, 29.—Designs of father Parsons, 36.—The clergy, aware of those

those designs, project a plan for their own government, 40.—They are successfully counteracted, 44.—Mr. Blackwell chosen archpriest, 48.

From the appointment of the archpriest Blackwell, an. 1598, to the nomination of the bishop of Chalcedon, an. 1623.

Resentment and proceedings of the clergy, 53.—Their deputies arrive at Rome and are imprisoned, 57.—The pope confirms the appointment of Blackwell, 58.—The deputies are released, 59.—The clergy still discontented appeal to Rome, 60.—Brief from his holiness, 62.—Another Brief, 64.—Reflections, 65.—Protestation of allegiance presented by thirteen priests, 69.—King James's abhorrence of the deposing doctrine, 73.—Oath of allegiance, 75.—Condemned at Rome, 76.—Distress of the Catholics, 77.—Writings for and against the oath, 78.—Blackwell deposed and succeeded by Birket, 79.—Parsons corresponds with Birket, and dies, 81.—Death of Birket, 84.—Priests suffer and die in defence of the papal prerogative, 85.—Dr. Harrison succeeds to Birket, 87.—He aims to free the clergy from the controul of the Jesuits, 87.—The clergy again resolve to apply to Rome for a bishop, 92.—Mr. Bennet presents a strong memorial, 95.—Dr. Bishop is nominated to the see of Chalcedon, 98.

From the nomination of the bishop of Chalcedon, an. 1623, to the agency of Panzani, an. 1634.

Extent and nature of the powers granted to the bifhop, 100.—He is well received and inftitutes his chapter, 102—Reflections on our new hierarchy, 105.—The bifhop of Chalcedon dies, 107.—Dr. Richard Smith is appointed his fucceffor, 107.—Powers of the new bifhop, 109.

MEMOIRS of PANZANI.

Introduction, 113.——Controverfy between Dr. Smith, bifhop of Chalcedon, and the regulars, 119.—The controverfy engages the French divines, 124.—The pope interpofes, 126.—Proceedings againft the bifhop, 128.—He is compelled to withdraw into France, 130.—His holinefs fends Panzani into England, 131.—Panzani defcribes the general ftate of things in a letter to Barberini, 134.—Difputes about the oath of allegiance, 140.—The agent has two interviews with fecretary Windebank, 142.—He treats with the regulars, and projects a plan for a bifhop, 147.—Character of the Jefuits and Regulars, 150.—The puritans difcover Panzani, 153.—The caufe of the Elector Palatine is propofed to him, 154.—Deep policy of Rome exhibited in a letter from Barberini, 155.—The king and Panzani meet, 160.—He confers with Windebank on various matters, 162.—Father Philip

CONTENTS.

Philip discourses with the king on the reunion of the churches, 165.—A work of father Davenport pleasing to the king, gives offence at Rome, 165.—Windebank's opinion of the Jesuits, 168.—Anecdote respecting father Garnet, 170.—The cardinal sends instructions to Panzani in three letters, 171.—Panzani complains to him of the Jesuits, 174.—Is perplexed in a conference with the Secretary, 176.—The king is irritated, 177.—Panzani again complains of the Jesuits, 177.—Converses with Cottington about a bishop, 180.—And discovers the real sentiments of the Catholics on the subject, 181.—New scheme for a bishop, 184.—The king refuses to admit a bishop, 185.—Project of a reciprocal agency, on which father Philip writes to Barberini, 186.—The king comes into the project, 189.—Mr. Montague, 190. —Mazarin is made acquainted with the scheme of the agency, 192.—Barberini sends presents to the queen, 194.—Mr. Brett is appointed agent to Rome, 197.— Conversation between Cottington and Panzani, 200. —Barberini writes to the latter, 202.—Persons proposed for agents to England, 204.—The cardinal's caution, 205.—The king's instructions to Mr. Brett, 206.—Barberini's sentiments respecting the family of the elector Palatine, 207.—Difficulties in the proposed match, 209.—Mr. Brett's death and other obstacles to the agency, 210.—Mr. Montague endeavours to obtain a cardinal's hat for Mr. Conn, 211.— Returns to the English court, 215.—The clergy and regulars are reconciled, 217.—The Jesuits only stand out, 219.—Father Blond's conduct, 221.—Gives offence, 222.—The clergy shew their desire of peace, 225.—Panzani and the Provincial meet, 227.—Behaviour

viour of the Roman court, 228.—Panzani expostulates with the cardinal, and mentions other matters, 229—The cardinal replies, 232.—Mr. Hamilton and Mr. Conn named agents, 233.—The Jesuits particularly are dissatisfied with the agency, 235.—The bishop of Chichester and Panzani confer, 237.—The agent is directed to compliment the bishop, 239.—And receives other instructions, 240.—Has another conference with Montague, 241.—Dissatisfaction of Windebank, 244.—Third conference with the bishop of Chichester, 246.—The pursuivants are dismissed, 249.—Barberini, in acknowledgment, sends other presents to the queen, 250.—Hamilton goes to Rome, and has an audience of his holiness, 252.—And of the cardinal, 253.—Conn comes to England, 255.—Panzani takes leave of their majesties, 255.—

SUPPLEMENT.

From the close of the agency of Panzani, an. 1636, to the appointment of apostolic vicars in the reign of James II.

State of the nation and the English Catholics, 264.—Exemptions of the Regulars, 269.—Rome favourable to them, 273.—Feudal nature of church government, 275.—The Chapter, 276.—Sufferings of many Catholics, 278.—Death of the bishop of Chalcedon, 287.—The chapter assumes jurisdiction, 292.—Mr. White, *alias* Blackloe, 293.—Proceedings of the

the chapter 295.—State of the Catholics under Cromwell, 298.—The chapter continues to apply for an *ordinary*, 301.—Reflections, 307.—Some tranfactions of the reign of Charles II. 308.—The controverfy on the oaths revived, 319.—End of Charles's reign, 326.—Reign of James II. 327.—Particulars of the appointment of the firft *vicar apoſtolic*, 336.—Reflections on that appointment, 343.—Further proceedings of the king, 345.—The pope's nuncio is received at Windfor, 351.—Father Petre, 352.—Dr. Giffard made an apoftolic vicar, 361.—The laſt year of king James, 162.——Two more apoftolic vicars appointed, 365.

From the appointment of vicars apoſtolic in the reign of James II. to the prefent year 1793.

The revolution not unfavourable to the Catholics, 369.—Government of the vicars apoftolic, 372. —King James, 376.—Proceedings of the chapter, 378.—Its jurifdiction fufpended, 387.—Treatment of the vicars by the Roman court, 392.—The 11th of king William, 392.—Reign of Anne, 394.—The fecular clergy accufed of *Janfenifm*, 396.—The college of Douay involved in the fame accufation, 401.— Both acquitted, 404.—Reign of George I. 405.— Rome propofes an oath of allegiance, 405.—Dr. Strickland bifhop of Namur, 408.—Severe treatment of the Catholics, 409.—Reign of George II. 411.— Controverfy between the vicars and regulars, 413.—

Bifhop

Bifhop Stonor, 418.—The other vicars, 419.—Apprehenfions of the clergy, 422.—Oath of allegiance in 1778, 425.—More recent events, 429.—Cafe of Mr. Wilks, 436.—Is fupported by a few of the clergy, 439.—They are oppofed from the weftern diftrict, 441.—The anfwer from the weftern diftrict examined, 442.

CONCLUSION.

Reflections on our prefent fituation, 450.—Education fhould be adapted to it, 452.—A fcheme propofed, 456.—Evils of our church government, 459.—Propofals for its reform, 465.—Character of bifhop Talbot, 468.—Plan for a reform fketched, 469.

INTRODUCTION.

INTRODUCTION.

From the beginning of the reign of Elizabeth an. 1558, to the appointment of the archprieſt Blackwell, an 1598.

THE various changes which the public mind had witneſſed, through the reigns of Henry, Edward, and Mary, had ſo completely, by diſſipating old attachments and weakening the prejudices of early education, prepared the people for any further change, that, on the acceſſion of Elizabeth, without any reluctance, they quitted the religion of their anceſtors, and accepted the new ſettlement that finally cloſed the *Reformation*. The nobility, indeed, and gentry, whom the ſpoils of the church had enriched, were *intereſted* in the event; and the multitude had liſtened, with an increaſing alienation of mind, to the ridicule thrown on their

The opening of Elizabeth's Reformation.

INTRODUCTION.

their former practices, and to the invectives against the Roman fee and the jurisdiction of its pontiff, while the horrors of the last reign had contributed, perhaps, more than any other cause, to produce the general effect I am describing. Many, however, in the higher orders, and in the lower ranks, stood unmoved; and the bishops, with some of the leading and learned clergy, set an example of firmness, which was viewed with amazement by those, who remembered, with what ease, the same order of men, but a few years before, had adopted more violent and irregular innovations.*

The queen, whom no motives of interest or education could have cordially attached to the religion of her late sister,† seemed disposed to listen to the voice of prudence and policy, and to pursue such measures as, agreeing best with the wishes of her people, should hold out the surest prospects of terminating their differences, and of giving stability to her throne. Yet there were many things, we are told,

---

* In the reigns of Henry and Edward.

† She had been treated by her with great severity, being suspected of attachment to the reformed religion, and of having encouraged Wiatt's insurrection. Camden, Heylin.

told, in the old religion which she admired; and could she have foreseen the success of a rising faction, which acquired the name of *Puritans*, and which soon became so troublesome to herself, and at last so fatal to the throne of one of her successors, it may, with reason, be presumed, that, in establishing the reformation, she would either have adopted the tenets of her father Henry, or have departed, probably, even less from the rites, if not from the doctrine, of the Roman church. But, whatever might have been her first sentiments, Paul IV. soon took care to fix her resolution; and to him, perhaps, in the wayward series of human events, may be imputed the defection of England from the communion of Rome.

On the death of her sister, Elizabeth, through the English resident at Rome, Sir Edward Carne, notified to his holiness her accession to the throne. The stern pontiff replied: " That the kingdom of England was " a fief of the holy see; that Elizabeth was a " bastard, and had no right to the succession; " that he could not annul the decrees of " Clement VII. and of Paul III. with regard " to her father's marriage; that it was an act " of signal audacity in her to have assumed " the title of queen, without his participation; " that thus she was undeserving of the smallest " indulgence; yet, if she would renounce her

Impudence of Paul IV.

preten-

INTRODUCTION.

"pretensions, and submit to his free dispo-
"sition, he would treat her with the kindness
"of a father, and do her every service which
"should be compatible with the dignity of
"the vicar of Christ."* — Thus spoke the haughty Paul, true to the maxims of Hildebrand, even after the lapse of five hundred years! And when the answer was reported to Elizabeth, she must have seen that the admission of such a monstrous prerogative could not consist with the safety and independence of her throne. If in high and indignant resentment she then made her choice, and if that choice proved subversive of a religion, the professors of which could suffer their first pastor so to think, or so, at least, to speak, I may be sorry, but I cannot be surprised.

The supremacy of the crown established.

The new parliament met, modelled according to her own desires, and prepared to go all the lengths of those profound and sagacious politicians, the queen's principal advisers, who now came forward on the scene.† The first act recognised her title to the throne; which being followed by some others, with a view to feel

---

* Hey in., p. 275. Dict. des Heresies, t. 1, p. 116.

† Heylin, p. 279.

INTRODUCTION.

feel the difpofitions of parliament on the fubject of religion, both houfes proceeded to the grand queftion of the *Supremacy*, that is, in the language of the ftatute, *To reftore to the crown the ancient jurifdiction over the eftate ecclefiaftical and fpiritual; and to abolifh all foreign powers repugnant to the fame.*—After warm debates and ftrenuous oppofition, efpecially from the bifhops in the upper houfe, the act paffed with its *oath*, repealing whatever the late king Philip and queen Mary, by their parliament, had done in favour of the jurifdiction of Rome, and reviving all fuch laws and ftatutes as her father Henry and his fon Edward, by their parliaments, had enacted for the overthrow of the fame; and thus uniting and annexing to the imperial crown of this realm fuch jurifdictions, privileges, fuperiorities, and preheminences, fpiritual and ecclefiaftical, as by any foreign fpiritual or ecclefiaftical power or authority had heretofore been exercifed or ufed. In the oath the queen's highnefs is ftyled *the only fupreme governour of this realm, as well in all fpiritual and ecclefiaftical things or caufes, as temporal.* Whoever refufed this oath is declared incapable of holding any public office. The act then ftates that whoever denied the queen's fupremacy, as by law now eftablifhed, or attempted to deprive her of that prerogative, fhould, for the firft offence, forfeit all his goods and chattels; for the fecond, be fubjected to the penalty of a

premunire;

INTRODUCTION.

premunire; and for the third, be guilty of high treason.*

This famous act was followed by others of a similar complexion, all tending to strengthen the new powers of the crown, and to give energy to the plan of reformation, when, on the 8th of May 1559, the parliament was prorogued, having, in a single session, without violence or tumult, altered the whole system of religion, in the commencement of a reign, and by the will of a young woman, whose very title to the throne was by many thought liable to objections.

But while the representatives of the people, and the lords were thus busied, both houses of Convocation, called together by the royal summons, had, with anxious expectation, watched the rapid progress of this lay-reform. Their opposition to every act was steady and uniform; and the lower house drew up and signed a *Declaration*, expressive of their orthodox belief in the holy sacrament, in the mass, in the jurisdiction of the successor of St. Peter, and in the authority of the pastors of the church, which was presented to the lord keeper Bacon,

---

* I. Eliz. cap. 1.

INTRODUCTION.

Bacon, by Bonner, prefident of the fynod. At the fame time, both univerfities, under the hand of a public notary, declared their affent to the fame articles. The folemn inftrument, as delivered into parliament, is ftill upon record;* and it muft remain to pofterity a ftanding proof, that fo far, at leaft, the reformation had proceeded *reclamante clero*.

It is not my intention, though the occafion be moft favourable, here to examine the nature and extent of that *fupremacy* which the legiflature annexed to the crown. Suffice it to obferve, that the notions of all men were then indiftinct on the fubject: for fo univerfal and undefined had the power of Rome been, call it ecclefiaftical or fpiritual; fo much had it abforbed within its cognizance all the concerns of life, that the primitive rights of a firft bifhop could with difficulty be traced, and the whole fabric of his jurifdiction feemed rather to be the contrivance of human ambition on the one fide, and of weak conceffions on the other. How then fhould a ftate proceed, now convinced that fuch a paramount jurifdiction was incompatible with its fovereignty, than at once to break down the whole mafs, (confcious,

at

---

* Fuller's Hift. l. 9, p. 54.

INTRODUCTION.

at the fame time, that their decrees would not affect what was really divine and primitive, and that a jurifdiction fo defined could excite no jealoufy,) and commit any ambiguity of expreffion to the interpreters of the law, fhould an interpretation be afterwards deemed neceffary. Under this view, I believe, many moderate men then patronifed the fcheme, and the legiflature of Elizabeth proceeded.

The queen, by a claufe in the act, empowered to name commiffioners, erected the court of *high ecclefiaftical commiffion*, whofe office it was to execute the late decrees of parliament, in the general reformation of the church and clergy. The agents of no popes had poffeffed fuch difcretionary and independent powers. To thefe commiffioners, fourteen in number, (of whom one only was a churchman,) Elizabeth, in virtue of her fupreme ecclefiaftical jurifdiction, entrufted alfo a body of *injunctions*, containing rules of difcipline and of general order, and to which was annexed an *admonition*, defigned to explain the oath and to remove from it every finifter interpretation. The admonition is;

The queen's majefty being informed that, in certain places of this realm, fundry of her native fubjects being called to ecclefiaftical miniftry in the church, be, by finifter perfuafion and perverfe conftruction, induced to find fome fcruple

INTRODUCTION.

scruple in the form of an oath, which, by an act of the last parliament, is prescribed to be required of diverse persons, for the recognition of their allegiance to her majesty, which certainly was neither ever meant, nor by any equity of words or good sense can be thereof gathered: would that all her loving subjects should understand, that nothing was, or is, or shall be meant or intended by the same oath, to have any other duty, allegiance, or bond required by the same oath, than was acknowledged to be due to the most noble kings of famous memory, king Henry VIII. her majesty's father, or king Edward VI. her majesty's brother. And further, her majesty forbiddeth all manner her subjects to give ear or credit to such perverse and malicious persons, which most sinisterly and maliciously labour to notify to her loving subjects, how by the words of the said oath it may be collected, that the kings or queens of this realm, possessors of the crown, may challenge authority and power of ministry of divine offices in the church, wherein her said subjects be much abused by such evil disposed persons. For certainly her majesty neither doth, nor ever will, challenge any other authority, than that was challenged and lately used by the said noble kings of famous memory, king Henry VIII. and king Edward VI. which is and was of ancient time due to the imperial crown of this realm; that is, under God, to have the sovereignty and rule over all manner of persons born within these her realms and dominions and countries, so as no other foreign power, shall, or ought to, have any superiority over them. And if any person that hath conceived any other sense of the form of the said oath,
shall

INTRODUCTION.

shall accept the same oath with this interpretation, sense, or meaning; her majesty is well pleased to accept every such in that behalf as her good and obedient subjects, and shall acquit them of all manner of penalties, contained in the said act, against such as shall peremptorily or obstinately refuse to take the same oath.

This interpretation of the oath was afterwards repeated in the *declaration* enjoined to be read by the ministers of the church, before the thirty-nine articles were framed, and of these articles the thirty-seventh says: *we give not to our princes the ministering either of God's word or of the sacraments, the which thing the injunctions lately set forth by Elizabeth our queen do most plainly testify; but that only prerogative which we see to have been given always to all godly princes in holy scriptures by God himself, that is, that they should rule all estates and degrees committed to their charge by God, whether they be ecclesiastical or temporal, and restrain with the civil sword the stubborn and evil doers.* — The same sense was finally settled by act of parliament in the fifth year of her majesty: *Provided also,* (says the act,) *that the oath expressed in the said act, made in the first year, shall be taken and expounded in such form as is set forth in an* admonition *annexed to the queen majesty's injunctions, published in the first year of her majesty's reign: that is to say, to confess and acknowledge in her majesty, her heirs and successors, none other authority than that was challenged and lately used by the noble king Henry* VIII. *and Edward* VI. *as*

in

INTRODUCTION.

in the said admonition *more plainly appears.** —
But to proceed.

The commissioners began their progress through the nation, tendering, as they advanced, the *oath*, and directing the execution of the laws and of her majesty's *injunctions*.

The number of bishops was then greatly reduced, being no more than fifteen, including Heath, archbishop of York; and when, in the beginning of July, they were required to take the oath as the law directed, all, but Kitchin of Landaff, refused compliance. "He," it is said, "who had formerly submitted to every "*change*, resolved to shew himself no *changling* "in

The bishops and some of the clergy refuse the oath of supremacy and are deprived.

---

* Many works, in defence of the oath, were written in the course of the last century, one of which, a MS, I mean to publish. It will shew, with great accuracy of deduction, what has been the legal acceptation of the oath from its enaction to the end of the reign of Charles II. from which period, I will endeavour to bring down the same series of proof to our own days. The reader will find the subject very ably treated in a work lately published by Mr. Francis Plowden, entitled *Jura Anglorum*, to the perusal of which I strongly recommend him.—Just notions of the *oath of supremacy* are become peculiarly important to *us*, as it alone witholds us from the exercise of our *elective franchise:* and why should we importune government for a further redress of grievances, or complain that we are aggrieved, if the remedy be in our own hands? One bold man, by taking the oath, may dissipate the whole charm of prejudice, and restore us to the most valuable privilege of British citizens.

"in not conforming to the pleasure of the "higher powers."* The bishops were deprived; and their deprivation was accompanied by various fates, which a general lenity, however, softened, as the interest of friends prevailed, or their own inoffensiveness of conduct solicited.—Heath retired to one of his own houses in Surrey, where he lived unmolested, respected by his neighbours, and often visited by the queen. Tunstall of Durham, and Thirlby of Ely were entertained in the palace of Lambeth, and Bourn of Wells in the house of the dean of Exon. White of Winchester, after a short imprisonment in the tower, was suffered to retire among his friends; which indulgence was also allowed to Turberville of Exeter, a gentleman of ancient descent. Watson of Lincoln, after a short restraint, spent his time with the bishops of Rochester and Ely; but being accused of practising against the state, he was finally committed to Wisbich castle. Oglethorp of Carlisle, soon after his deprivation, died of an apoplexy, Bayne of Lichfield of the stone, and Morgan of St. David's of some other disease; but all of them in their beds, and in perfect liberty. Poole of Peterborough resided with his friends, and

---

* Heylin, p. 286.

INTRODUCTION.

and died on one of his own farms; and Chriftopherfon of Chichefter experienced a like indulgence. Bonner of London alone, whofe cruelties in the laft reign had expofed him to general indignation, was doomed to perpetual confinement. Pates of Worcefter, before the oath was tendered to him, had quitted the kingdom, as had Goodwell of St. Afaph's, who retired to Rome.*

The oath was next offered to the deans and dignitaries, and then to the rural clergy; and, as confcience or as particular views directed, they refufed or took it. But for that refufal, or for not conforming to the public liturgy, only 80 rectors and vicars feem to have loft their preferments, 50 prebendaries, 15 heads of colleges, 12 deans and as many archdeacons, the whole number not amounting to 200 perfons.†

Few then remained firm to the old caufe; and of thefe few, as many were placed in elevated ftations, we may, perhaps, be induced to think that a point of honour, rather than conviction of duty, influenced their determination.

---

* The above particulars are taken from Heylin, p. 286.

† Ibid.

nation. Still, when we contemplate the general state of the kingdom, as contemporary writers represent it a few years later, in its universities and various parishes, the warmest admirer of the reformation will be compelled to own that many, even far the major part, of those whom learning signalised, or probity of manners graced, had withdrawn from their stations. "Our universities," says Jewel, the new bishop of Salisbury, "are in a most "lamentable condition."* — "Upon the "Catholic clergy throwing up their prefer- "ments, the necessity of the church required "the admitting of some mechanics into "orders." They are the words of Collier.†
—"There was not," observes Heylin, "a "sufficient number of learned men to supply "the cures, which filled the church with an "ignorant and illiterate clergy. Many were "raised to great preferments, who having "spent their time of exile (in the reign of "Mary) in such foreign churches as followed "the platform of Geneva, returned so dis- "affected to episcopal government, unto the "rites and ceremonies here by law established, "as not long after filled the church with
"most

---

* Ep. ad Bulling.

† Eccle. Hist. vol. 2. p. 465.

INTRODUCTION.

" moſt ſad diſorders. Private opinions not
" regarded, nothing was more conſidered in
" them than their zeal againſt popery, and their
" abilities in learning to confirm that zeal."*

For ſome time, uncertain what might be the event of things, the great body of the clergy conformed exteriorly to the law. The changes of the preceding reigns, which themſelves had witneſſed, prompted this weak compliance. But when the firmneſs of the queen and her miniſters, and the general aſpect of the nation, convinced them, that no further change, favourable to their wiſhes, might be expected, again ſome ſurrendered their livings; others retained *ſine cures*, through the connivance of their neighbours, or the patronage of friends, procuring men who would officiate in their ſtead; many ſerved as chaplains in private families; more, perhaps, (for there is reaſon to believe it,) fearful of penury or the ſeverity of legal proſecution, perſevered in the outward conformity with a ſervice which their minds inwardly rejected; while all, (to their praiſe be it ſpoken,) biſhops and clergy, in ſilent reſignation bowed their heads, conſcious that to ſubmit to laws which,

Conduct of others.

---

* Hiſt. p. 287.

which, while their active ministry permitted, they had laboured to avert, was now become their christian duty. To clamour, when clamour could only irritate; to disturb, by opposition, the peace of society, when endless feuds would be the only fruits; to provoke persecution or the resentment of the law, when a heavier oppression, with more apparent justice, might be then inflicted; in a word, to aim to restore their religion by violence, or to vilify that of their adversaries by reproach, when that divine master, by whose maxims they professed to be governed, had not set them the example—were rules of conduct which the clergy, I am describing, under more than the common irritation of human passions, nobly disdained to follow.*   The

---

* The reader, whose mind will have anticipated the application, may compare with this behaviour of our countrymen that of a neighbouring priesthood, placed in circumstances of some difficulty and of greater oppression. I listen not to any statement of events or motives of action, which resentment has delivered, or the fanaticism of party has too deeply coloured. We must judge with justice. And how superior, even in an age of persecution, will the moderation of our British governors appear to the intolerance of a boasted philosophy, and the despotism of a boasted freedom! If men, aggrieved in their fortunes and harassed in their opinions, have been uniformly consistent, and uniformly free from every imputation, I pretend not to know. This I know, that the treatment they, and others of both sexes, have experienced, marked with deliberate barbarity, has stamped an infamy on the cause (which otherwise was great and noble,) that no success shall efface, till ample reparation be made to innocence, and to virtue, and to justice, and to manhood.

INTRODUCTION.

The conduct of the laity was such as, from circumstances, might be naturally expected. The nobility, in great numbers, adopted the faith of the court, and they were followed by what might be called the nation. I have said, how much the recent progress of changes had prepared the way for this event. Still amongst this nobility and all the subordinate ranks of life, there were many, some of whom remained firm, while more, actuated by the weak policy of their clergy, exteriorly conformed, frequenting the public service of the church. And in this service, it must be allowed, when it came to be regularly organised, there was a decency and a dignity, well adapted to the sedate and philosophic character of the English people. The churches were the same, the orders of the hierarchy remained, and, what was calculated to conciliate the multitude, the communion table was placed where the altar stood, music was retained, all the old festivals, with their eves, were observed; the dress of the officiating ministry only was changed to a less gaudy and garish vesture. The use of the English language also, when the first impression was effaced, greatly contributed to attach the people to it; as did the admission of the laity to the cup.*

Behaviour of the laity.

---

* Heylin, p. 283.

B

INTRODUCTION.

In framing the articles of the public faith, it was, at the fame time, the wifh of the queen, that they fhould depart, as little as might be, from the tenets of former times. To conciliate the minds of men, not to divide them, was the policy of this uncommon woman. The language of the article on the real prefence, a fubject which had excited great controverfies, indicates this conciliatory plan; and it was remarked, that fhe enjoined the facramental bread to be continued round in the form of wafers.*

Of the great numbers who at firft, we are told, from ignorance, or pufillanimity, or policy, were occafional conformifts, many became gradually attached to the new faith, when every profpect of further change had ceafed, and they faw before them not difcouragement only, but the danger of profecution in returning to the religion of their anceftors. It was afterwards more than once publicly declared by Sir Edward Coke, when attorney general, which the queen herfelf had confirmed in a letter to Sir Francis Walfingham, that, for the firft ten years of her reign, the Catholics, without doubt or fcruple, repaired

to

---

* Heylin, p. 283.

to the parish churches.* The assertion is true, if not too generally applied. "I deny not," says father Parsons in reply to Coke, "but that many, throughout the realm, though otherwise Catholics in heart, (as most then were,) did at that time and after, as also now, (an. 1606,) either upon fear, or lack of better instruction, or both, repair to Protestant churches."†

Such was the general state of things.—But men of more ardent minds than the clergy I have described, such principally as, for non-compliance, had been expelled the universities, or were disappointed in their views of preferment; such as a warmer zeal for religion animated, and who could ill brook the growing success of innovation; such as, habituated as they had been in the schools to resist the new doctrines of the reformers, were resolved not silently to quit the field, but to maintain, by every exertion, the war of words they loved, and which finally, they doubted not, must triumph: all these and more, when the measures of the court prevailed, withdrew to the continent. They were received as

Many of the clergy retire abroad.

---

* Heylin, p. 283.

† *Answer to Reportes*, p. 371.

INTRODUCTION.

professors or students in the universities and monasteries, particularly of France, Flanders, and Italy.*

This secession I lament; because had these men remained at home, patient of present evils, and submissive, as far as might be, to the laws; had they continued the practice of their religion in retirement, and distributed, without clamour, instruction to those that claimed it, the rigour of the legislature would soon have relaxed; no jealousy would have been excited; and no penal statutes, we may now pronounce, would have entailed misfortunes upon them and their successors. The entire series of these evils they could not, I will admit, then foresee; but no uncommon share of penetration might, certainly, have taught them, that the measures they were pursuing must accelerate the ruin, not support the religion of their friends, or the interest of their cause.

William Allen.

William Allen, a divine of Oxford, one of the first who relinquished his preferments, soon became the guide of the exiles, (if they might be so called who had voluntarily retired from their country,) and the soul of their plans.

---

* Dodd Church Hist. vol. 2, p. 8.

plans. His manners were gentle, his learning above the ordinary meafure, his prudence in government conftant, and his energy of action unceafing. In 1568, the tenth year of Elizabeth, having matured the weighty fcheme, and drawn together many learned men who had been educated in Oxford and Cambridge, but who now were fcattered on the continent, he laid the foundation of a college or feminary at Douay, a city in Flanders then fubject to the Spanifh crown. This was fucceeded by other eftablifhments, which the activity of the fame man promoted, in Italy, Spain, and France. To perpetuate the fucceffion of a Catholic clergy, and to fupply England with paftors of that perfuafion, as the old priefts fhould die off, was the principal defign of thefe eftablifhments. In a few years, the number of ftudents and refidents in the fingle college of Douay amounted to 150 perfons. But their means of fubfiftence, by private contributions, were fluctuating and precarious. Recourfe therefore was had to Rome; and the holy fee confpiring, as was natural, with the views of Allen and his affociates, contributed liberally to their fupport. Other fuccours afterwards flowed in.*

---

* Dodd paffim: alfo MSS. Letters of Dr- Allen.

Reflections on our foreign establishments

I am difpofed to admit, what the warmeft advocates for thefe eftablifhments can demand, that the views of their founders, when we contemplate the characters of the men and the motives of their actions, originated in a fincere and commendable zeal; but I cannot admit that thofe views were wife. Will it be proved, that fimilar eftablifhments, better adapted to our genius, might not have been formed at home, if, as I have obferved, time had been allowed for the fermentation of the public mind to fubfide; and moderation and forbearance difarming government of all its jealoufies and refentments, had conciliated its good will to the profeffors of the ancient faith? The bifhops of this faith, befides, who furvived the reformation, had they been animated and protected by the abilities and learning of the men who emigrated, would, doubtlefs, themfelves not have favoured only, but have fuggefted and promoted meafures, whereby a regular fucceffion of clergy might have been maintained, and fchemes of education formed. But feeing themfelves deferted, and hearing of foreign plans to which much praife was given, and on which the moft fanguine hopes of fuccefs were founded, they perfevered in the habits of retirement they had chofen, and entertained, it feems, no thoughts of perpetuating their hierarchy, or providing for days to come. It may alfo be remarked that, in 1578, twenty years

years after the reformation, Watson of Lincoln was the only surviving prelate*

Our ancestors then, I have said, were unwise in founding foreign houses of education, not only because they took place of better establishments which, in the course of a few years, we might have formed at home; but also because, (from their views, some real and some imputed by their enemies, on the ground of their foreign connections and their avowed designs against the religion of their country,) they soon excited in the breasts of our governors a suspectful jealousy, which was the source of many evils. Nor will it, I think, be denied that, from too warm an opposition to the doctrines of the reformers who rejected, without cause, *all* jurisdiction in the Roman bishop; from a connection with the court of Rome, begun in circumstances of penury, upheld by the same calls, and strengthened by sentiments which gratitude created; finally, from associating too intimately with the divines of that court, and adopting the maxims of its schools; it will not, I say, be denied that, from the operation of these various causes, our foreign houses soon imbibed an ultramontane spirit which, as it flattered, and by flattering secured

---

* Dodd, ib. p. 104.

INTRODUCTION.

secured the favour of Rome, so did it offend, and by offending draw down on our heads the vengeance of the British government. The doctrine of deposing princes and disposing of their crowns, with other concomitant maxims of a like tendency, were the *pabulum* on which that ultramontane spirit fed; and we may too easily discover, in reading their works, that the divines of our English seminaries had, with a culpable inattention to circumstances, espoused those dangerous tenets.* Their direct application to the princess on the throne and to many events of her reign, proved too evidently that they were not tenets of barren speculation, calculated for the exercise of school disputation only : and if they rendered the men who maintained them obnoxious to the state, exposing them to prosecution and imprisonment, and sometimes even to death, it should not excite our wonder.

Father Parsons

In a few years, the number of those who returned from these seminaries to support the Catholic

---

* See *Further Considerations* by Sir John Throckmorton, a work which, with great accuracy of research, exhibits the opinions of these men. He has been blamed for delineating too faithful a portrait. Our cause then, it seems, stood in need of concealment and the stratagems of artifice. Rather, let us know the errors of our ancestors and avoid them, admire their zeal, imitate their virtues.

INTRODUCTION.

Catholic caufe was confiderable; and had they returned, (as many of them doubtlefs did) actuated by a pure zeal for religion, and with fentiments of an enlightened patriotifm and of allegiance to their fovereign, they might have practifed the duties of their miniftry, unheeded and unmolefted. But father Parfons had, by this time, fet his hand alfo to the work, a man, with the found of whofe name are affociated intrigue, device, ftratagem, and all the crooked policy of the Machiavelian fchool. He left Oxford in 1574; entered among the Jefuits at Rome in 1575; and in 1580, returned into England with father Campian, being the two firft Jefuits who vifited this country. The fociety had been founded in the year 1540. Campian, in the following year, fuffered death, for a fuppofed plot entered into abroad againft the queen and government, when father Parfons thought it advifeable once more to withdraw. In 1587, having fpent the intermediate time in France, he again went to Rome. A few years after this, we find him in Spain, highly favoured by that court, and ufing all its favour in the eftablifhment of various feminaries at Valladolid, Seville, and St. Omer's, for the benefit, as it was efteemed, of the Englifh Catholics. Thefe foundations being completed, he once more repaired to Rome, which would honour him, it was expected, with the purple; but where he was only raifed to the government

ment of the English college in that city, which he retained to his death in 1610.*

To the intriguing spirit of this man (whose whole life was a series of machinations against the sovereignty of his country, the succession of its crown, and the interests of the secular clergy of his own faith) were I to ascribe more than half the odium, under which the English Catholics laboured through the heavy lapse of two centuries, I should only say what has often been said, and what as often has been said with truth. Devoted to the most extravagant pretensions of the Roman court, he strove to give efficacy to those pretensions in propagating, by many efforts, their validity and directing their application :† pensioned by the Spanish monarch, whose pecuniary aids he wanted for the

---

* Dodd, ib. p. 402. Lit. MSS.

† See *Further Considerations* p. 128. —— " I shall signify to " his holiness," he says, " how necessary it is that he seriously " apprehend this business of England, lest, at the queen's death, " the country fall into worse hands and into greater inconve- " niences, should an heretical prince, *whoever he may be*, obtain " the succession. He shall know, that the English Catholics " desire a king truly Catholic, be he an Englishman, a Scotch- " man, or a Spaniard; and that, in this business, they consider " themselves as principally dependent on his holiness." MSS *Letters*. This he wrote to father Holt in 1597, on his journey from Spain to Rome, six years before the death of Elizabeth.

INTRODUCTION.

the fuccefs of his various plans, he unremittingly favoured the views of that ambitious prince, in oppofition to the welfare of his country, and dared to fupport, if he did not firft fuggeft, his idle claim or that of his daughter to the Englifh throne:* wedded to the fociety of which he was a member, he fought her glory and preheminence; and to accomplifh this it was his inceffant endeavour to bring under her jurifdiction all our foreign feminaries, and at home to beat down every intereft, that could impede the aggrandifement of his order.† Thus, having gained an afcendancy over the minds of many, he infufed his fpirit and

---

* See *a Conference about the next Succeffion to the crown of England*, publifhed by R. Doleman 1593. There is fufficient proof that Parfons was the author of this work, written with a view to eftablifh the Spanifh fucceffion againft the claim of the Scottifh king. It appears to have been read in manufcript by Cardinal Allen and many others, who highly approved the contents, fubfcribing to the doctrines, " that, as the *realm of* " *England was a fief of the holy fee,* it principally regarded the " pope to fettle its fucceffion; and that it was never lawful for " a Catholic, under any pretext, to fupport a Proteftant pre- " tender to the throne." Thus wrote Sir Francis Englefield, in 1596, who had been formerly fecretary to queen Mary, but who now refided in Spain, and was the confidential friend of father Parfons. He gives his judgment on the Book of *Succeffion,* affigns the motives for the publication, and replies to objections. *MS Letters.*

† The fequel will illuftrate this.

and fpread his maxims; and to his fucceffors of the fociety, it feems, bequeathed an admiration of his character and a love of imitation, which has helped to perpetuate diffentions, and to make us, to this day, a divided people. — His writings, which were numerous, are an exact tranfcript of his mind, dark, impofing, problematical, feditious.

To confirm the above ftatement and to prove its truth, I felect the following paffage from a contemporary author and an honeft man. "Father Parfons," he fays, "was the
"principal author, the incentor, and the mover
"of all our garboils at home and abroad.
"During the fhort fpace of nearly two years
"that he fpent in England, fo much did he
"irritate, by his actions, the mind of the queen
"and her minifters, that, on that occafion, the
"firft fevere laws were enacted againft the
"minifters of our religion, and thofe who
"fhould harbour them. He, like a daftardly
"foldier, confulting his own fafety, fled. But,
"being himfelf out of the reach of danger, he
"never ceafed, by publications againft the
"firft magiftrates of the republic or by factious
"letters, to provoke their refentment. Of
"thefe letters many were interrupted, which
"talked of the invafion of the realm by foreign
"armies, and which roufed the public expec-
"tation. Incenfed by his work on the *fuccef-*
"*fion,*

INTRODUCTION. 29

"*sion*, and by similar productions on the affairs
"of state, under the semblance of a cause that
"now seemed just, our magistrates rise up in
"vengeance against us, and execute their laws.
"They exclaim, that it is not the concern of
"religion that busies us; but that, under that
"cloak, we are meditating politics and prac-
"tising the ruin of the state. Robert Parsons,
"stationed at his ease, intrepidly, meanwhile,
"conducts his operations; and we, whom the
"press of battle threatens, innocent of any
"crime and ignorant of his dangerous machi-
"nations, undergo the punishment which his
"imprudence and audacity alone merit."
They are the words of John Mush, taken from
a work published by him in Latin, which will
be quoted in a succeeding note, and which, in
the name of the English clergy, was addressed
to Clement VIII.

To ascertain an important point, that the painful situation in which our ancestors were involved, was principally owing to certain opinions of a dangerous tendency imported from abroad, and that, if we had founded no foreign seminaries, we had provoked no penal laws, I wish to observe that, during the first ten years of her majesty's reign, the Catholics experienced no other molestation than what arose from the act of supremacy, and that the severity of that measure was gradually ceasing,

Foreign connections the principal cause of our grievances.

when,

when, in 1569, the Bull of Pius V. was iffued.*
In language irritating and infolent (for he
denominates her *flagitiorum ferva* and *pretenfa
Angliæ regina*) Pius excommunicates the queen,
deprives her of all title to the throne, and
abfolves her fubjects from every tie of allegiance.† In the fame year a rebellion broke
out in the northern provinces, under one
pretence among others, of reftoring the old
religion, but not fomented, it feems, by the
Bull of Pius, of which the rebels, probably,
had not then heard. But the pontiff, in a
letter to the earls who headed the infurrection,
gave his bleffing to their enterprife, which he
calls

---

* " It cannot be denied, but that for the firft ten years of
" her majefty's reign, the ftate of Catholics in England was
" tolerable, and after a fort in fome good quietnefs. Such as
" for their confciences were imprifoned in the beginning of her
" coming to the crown, were very kindly and mercifully ufed,
" the ftate of things then confidered. Some of them were
" appointed to remain with fuch their friends as they them-
" felves made choice of. Others were placed, fome with
" bifhops, fome with deans, and had their diet at their tables,
" with fuch convenient lodgings and walks for their recreation,
" as did well content them. They that were in the ordinary
" prifons, had fuch liberty and other commodities as the places
" would afford, not inconvenient for men that were in their
" cafes."—*Important Confiderations*, p. 31. Thefe *Confiderations*
were drawn up by fome fecular priefts an. 1601, and the view
they give of the ftate of Catholics foon after the Reformation
coincides with what I before faid.

† Dodd, vol. ii. p. 306. Bulla Pii 5.

INTRODUCTION.

calls *holy* and *religious*, and promifed to fupport it with as large a fum of money as was then in his power to fupply. "Our Lord," he fays to them, "hath infpired your minds with a "zeal worthy of your Catholic faith, that you "may attempt to free yourfelves and country "from the fhameful flavery of female lewd- "nefs, and bring it back to its former "obedience to this holy Roman fee."*

Yet thefe attempts againft the dignity of the throne and the peace of the people were not refented by any public act, except what fell immediately on the rebels, till, in 1571, a new parliament met and paffed the law of the 13 Eliz. entituled *An act againft bringing in, and putting in execution Bulls, &c. from the fee of Rome*. Nor till 1577, did any prieft fuffer death, though, in the fpace of the three preceding years, more than fifty of that order had been fent into England from the feminary of Douay. In the two next years they were followed by thirty two more.† But from the period of 1577, laws gradually fucceeded to laws of more minute and rigorous feverity, and proclamation to proclamation, whereby many were apprehended, and many fuffered death. Of

---

* *Further Confiderations* p. 101. where the *Letter* is given.

† *Memoirs of Miffionary Priefts*, Introduc. p. 4.

INTRODUCTION.

Of those who suffered death, in number more than 120, to say that none were guilty of the crimes imputed to them, would be to arraign too severely the justice of my country; and to say that none were innocent, would be to contradict, I am aware, the truth of history. Often have I read the *Memoirs** of the lives and deaths of those unfortunate men, when I was compelled to admire the innocence of their characters, their zeal for religion, their fortitude in the most trying scenes. That these *Memoirs* were compiled with a partiality too strongly marked, I will allow: still, when I see opinions punished which never came into action, and crimes charged which, with the expiring breath, were denied, I must be permitted to say, that the laws, which thus punished, were cruel, and that the spirit of the times was intolerant and bloody. But let the whole truth be spoken:—The tenets these men adopted, (I mean those regarding the papal prerogative,) were, as I have observed, of a most dangerous tendency. These they would not abjure; they maintained them in their interrogatories;† and as they had been educated,

---

* They were compiled about the year 1741, by the late learned and exemplary bishop Challoner, from documents as authentic as could be procured.

† See *Memoirs* as above, passim.

INTRODUCTION.

educated, all of them, I believe, in foreign seminaries, whence books were daily published in support of the same tenets,* and in which seminaries, machinations, some real, some fictitious, were incessantly practised (as it was rumoured,) against the queen and the religion of the state, it was natural that great alarms should be excited, and more danger apprehended, than, in less irritating circumstances, would have provoked resentment, much less the vengeance of the law.

Lord Burleigh in a treatise entitled, *The Execution of Justice in England*, published in 1584, affirms that none had then suffered for religion; and he instances the old clergy and the numerous Catholics who lived unmolested, while the seminary priests only were brought into trouble, who, on their examinations returned evasive answers, indicating too evidently that they admitted the deposing power in the pontiff, and did not reprobate the Bull of Pius.—The positions of this work were controverted, it is true, and many of them denied by Dr. Allen.†

---

* By Doctors Allen, Bristow, Saunders, Parsons and others. See *Further Considerations*, p. 96, under the article, *Conduct of Catholics in the reign of queen Elizabeth*.

† See *A true and modest Defence*.

INTRODUCTION.

This then I infer, (and I have ample grounds for the inference,) that as none of the old clergy suffered, and none of the new who roundly renounced the assumed prerogative of papal despotism, it was not for any *tenet of the Catholic faith* that they were exposed to prosecution.* But their foreign education connecting them with Rome and other hostile courts, itself raised suspicions; and the tenets which all of them held, many most innocently, formed another link which, in the apprehension of a government justly jealous, again connected them with the great events of the times. These were the insurrection of the earls in the north in 1569; the publication of the Bull of Pius in the same year, its renewal by Gregory XIII. in 1580, and again, with expressions of stronger acerbation, in 1588, by Sixtus V.; the attempts to release the unfortunate Mary, during her many years of imprisonment, but principally in 1586; and finally, the Spanish Armada

---

* After the promulgation of the Bull, *six queries* were generally proposed to the priests who were arraigned. They regarded the import of that Bull, the deposition of the queen as pronounced in it, and what should be the conduct of good subjects in reference to both. Few answered, I am sorry to observe, as became loyal Englishmen and faithful citizens. They seemed, rather, to consider themselves as the subjects of a foreign master, whose sovereignty was paramount and whose will was supreme.—Read the *Queries* in *Further Consid.* p. 100.

INTRODUCTION.

Armada in 1588: To which add the various plots of imaginary existence, supposed to be formed in all English houses on the continent. Parsons, in the mean while, and Bristow, and Stapleton, and Dr. Allen, (with all his virtues too much attached to the interests and prerogatives of Rome,) had been the instructors of those men; and with commissions from them and from his holiness, they had returned, under the positive inhibition of the law, to disturb the established faith of the country and to bring it again under the controuling jurisdiction of the Roman bishop.*

I have

---

* In confirmation of these reflections I subjoin the following Extract: "We are fully persuaded in our consciences, and as "men, besides our learning, who have some experience, that "if the Catholics had never sought by indirect means to have "vexed her majesty with their designments against her crown: "If the pope and king of Spain had never plotted with the duke "of Norfolk: If the rebels in the north had never been heard "of: If the Bull of Pius Quintus had never been known: It "the said rebellion had never been justified: If Gregory XIII. "had not renewed the said excommunication: If the Jesuits "had never come into England: If Parsons and the rest of the "Jesuits, with other our countrymen beyond the seas, had "never been agents in those traiterous and bloody design- "ments of Throckmorton, Parry, Williams, Squire and such "like: If they had not by their treatises and writings endea- "voured to defame their sovereign and their own country, "labouring to have many of their books translated into divers "languages, thereby to shew more their own disloyalty: If
"cardinal

INTRODUCTION.

I have introduced, with more detail than, perhaps, was necessary, this general statement, that the reader might be better prepared for the subject to which I wished to lead him.

<small>Designs of father Parsons</small>

I have noticed that the old bishops, whilst they lived, continued to exercise some juris-

---

"cardinal Allen and Parsons had not published the renovation of the said Bull by Sixtus Quintus: If thereunto they had not added their scurrilous and unmanly admonition, or rather most prophane libel agaist her majesty: If they had not sought by false persuasions and ungodly arguments to have allured the hearts of all Catholics from their allegiance: If the pope had never been urged by them to have thrust the king of Spain into that barbarous action against the realm: If they themselves, with all the rest of that generation, had not laboured greatly with the said king for the conquest and invasion of this land by the Spaniards: If, in all their proceedings, they had not from time to time, depraved, irritated, and provoked both her majesty and the state with these and many other such like their most ungodly and unchristian practices—most assuredly the state would have loved us, or at least borne with us: where there is one Catholic, there would have been ten: there had been no speeches amongst us of racks and tortures, nor any cause to have used them; *for none were ever vexed that way simply, for that he was either priest or Catholic, but because they were suspected to have had their hands in some of the same most traiterous designments.*"—*Important Considerations*, p. 55, 56. I know not who the *secular priests* were that published these *Considerations*, an. 1601; but their statement shews what, at that time, was the belief of many, and it shews how inconsistent with the truth of things our own ideas have generally been. Mr. Dodd, vol. 2, p. 379, ascribes the work to William Watson, a clergyman, who, being an accomplice in the mysterious plot of Sir Walter Raleigh, was executed in 1603.

INTRODUCTION.

jurisdiction over the Catholics, but that they appointed no successors to their sees. The last of them, Dr. Watson, who had been a kind of pope's legate over England, died in 1584; and four years before this, bishop Goodwell of St. Asaph's, who had long resided at Rome, came as far as Rheims, intending to return to England, and take upon himself the charge of our religion.* Age and infirmity impeded the accomplishment of his design, which, had it succeeded, might have left us a hierarchy, without that series of anarchy and internal dissentions, which ensued and have continued.

Dr. Allen who, towards the close of his life, had been made cardinal, and then archbishop of Mechlin in Flanders, died in 1594. Held in high estimation by all, revered for his manifold accomplishments, and powerful by an influence which reached from Rome to Douay, and from Douay to England, he, for many years, upheld a general inspection over the concerns of the Catholics. † The misfortune was that, naturally easy and unsuspicious, he permitted the artful Parsons to gain too great an ascendancy over him, an ascendancy

---

* Dodd, vol. 2, p. 132.

† Dodd, ib. p. 469. *The case stated*, &c.

INTRODUCTION.

which the crafty politician took care to cement by rendering his pecuniary services absolutely necessary to Allen.* So great was the number of emigrants daily flocking to Douay, that common aids could not suffice for their maintenance. This pained the generous mind of Allen, and compelled him to implore assistance from whatever quarter it might be procured. Thus was Parsons become the general spring of action. But when the cardinal was no more, every obstacle, it seemed, to the completion of his most sanguine schemes was removed.

Having established his houses, as I have remarked, in Spain and Flanders, through the interest of the Spanish court which was subservient to his wishes, father Parsons had returned to Rome, and was in the plenitude of his power, at the head of the English college there.

---

* Yet before his death he had forfeited the goodwill of the Jesuits. " Beginning to leave the road in which he had long " walked, (while devoted to the society,) the thread of his " designs and of his life was at once cut." Thus writes Agazarius, the Italian rector of the Roman college, to father Parsons, relating similar judgments on others who were alienated from the society. *Letters* MSS.

INTRODUCTION.

there. This college, founded in 1578,* and well endowed for the education of secular clergy, was forced from them within the same year, by a train of dark machinations, and committed to the administration of the Jesuits.† Besides this, the influence of the same body was becoming predominant also in Douay, to which place the English had returned in 1593, after an absence at Rheims of fifteen years.

It should here be observed, that the English Jesuits themselves were not yet formed into a regular society. They received their education among foreigners; were governed by the general of the order and foreign superiors; and in the concerns of the clergy acted as moderators and inspectors. But father Parsons was incessantly at work to establish their independence on a permanent foundation, which was
effected

---

* It had been originally called the *English Hospital*, built and endowed by our kings, during the Saxon heptarchy, for the entertainment of pilgrims and travellers of that nation. Gregory XIII. at the instigation of Dr. Allen, altered its destination, and erected it into a college, adding, at the same time, very liberally to its rents. Dodd, vol. ii. p. 15, 245.

† Dodd, ibid. p. 225, ad p. 245.

effected, soon after his death, in the three houses of Watten, Liege, and Ghent.*

Thus then stood the power of father Parsons. He ruled the colleges of Spain, and that of St. Omer's which was erected in 1594, retaining all the favour of the Spanish court: at Douay, Dr. Barret, the successor of the cardinal, was subservient to his beck:† In Rome, at the head of the college there, he possessed the ear of the pontiff, and was consulted in all matters regarding the English nation. It only remained that, in England itself, where he had many friends among the laity, and many creatures of the ecclesiastical order, either of his own society, or bound to him by the grateful recollection of favours they had experienced from his hands abroad, he should establish an authority over the body of secular clergy that might bring themselves and their concerns under his immediate controul, or under that of the society.

The clergy, aware of those designs, project a plan for their own government.

But that body of men, soured by some recent events and jealous of their independence, proved more untractable than he had expected.
The

---

* Dodd, p. 342, 3.

† Ibid. 68, et alib.

The wresting from them the administration of the Roman college they recollected with resentment.—In the castle of Wisbich, wherein more than thirty priests had been confined since the year 1587, great dissentions had arisen, disgracing the cause for which they suffered, and of which dissentions father Weston, then superior of the Jesuits, was thought to be the principal mover, by endeavouring to establish among the prisoners a form of discipline and economy favourable to the views of his order.* In this quarrel, strange as it may seem, the whole Catholic body, as they were variously affected, took sides. Nor could the clergy forgive an expression of father Garnet's uttered in reference to that quarrel: " why," said he, " may " not the Jesuits govern, and have the pre- " eminence over the secular priests in England, " as they have at Rome over the English semi- " nary."†—The influence the same order had obtained over the establishment at Douay excited also their indignation.—In a word, they had long experienced the indefatigable ardour

of

---

* *A True Relation of the Faction begun at Wisbich,* by Dr. Bagshaw, an. 1601. It is written with much asperity, but contains some curious facts, and developes the growing politics of the Jesuitical faction. Dr. Bagshaw was a secular priest, and himself confined at Wisbich.

† Ibid.

of father Parsons, who now aimed, they saw, at universal domination. But they were without a head, or any system of union, to resist the growing power, the absorbing influence of which was, with reason, dreaded.

It was this consciousness of their own inability, joined to the necessity which was urgent of having a superior amongst them, who, whilst he governed their body by a canonical superintendence, might, at the same time, administer confirmation to the laity, which determined the clergy to apply to Rome for one or more bishops. They were now sensible, when it was too late, how culpable had been their remissness in not having induced the old bishops to leave successors behind them.

Still, it is my opinion that we always had a *church*, incomplete, it is true, since the death of the last bishop, but ever remaining a society of true believers, governed by a succession of inferior pastors, and holding communion with the centre of unity, the Roman see. The words *mission*, then, and *missionaries* have been improperly applied to us, which always designate a society recently converted to christianity, and unprovided with a regular clergy. The origin, however, of those words is obvious, taking their rise from the circumstance, which I have lamented, of ministers being *sent* from our
foreign

foreign eftablifhments to fupply the flocks with paftors. This idea of the *perpetuity* of our church I muft refume, when incidents of greater moment fhall call for it.

The clergy deliberated, and unanimoufly refolved to prefent a fupplication to his holinefs, praying that he would reftore to them an ecclefiaftical hierarchy in the government of bifhops, " which bifhops fhould be elected by " the common confent of the clergy, and " appointed by them to different diftricts."*

Had they deliberated to better purpofe, and confulting their church chofen fuch a number of bifhops as the exigences of the people required, the meafure would have been more confonant with the fpirit of primitive difcipline, while it would have fecured them from a world of difficulties, into which their

too

---

* *Declaratio Motuum*, &c. p. 21, 30: A work written in Latin by John Mufh an. 1601, who will be hereafter mentioned. It relates, with fome elegance and with accuracy, many events of the period in which he was perfonally concerned. From it I extracted the paffage p. 21, which ferved to complete the portrait I had drawn of father Parfons. It fhould alfo be remarked, that the work in queftion was compiled in the name of the Catholic clergy, and in their name addreffed to the pontiff, Clement VIII. This circumftance gives additional weight to its *declarations*.

too subservient attention to the Roman court was soon to precipitate them, and involve their successors. But their foreign education in pontifical colleges, which I cannot too often repeat, had taught them to think too well of a court, the measure of whose policy has generally been what would most tend to its own aggrandisement, and to the support of the prerogative of its supreme head. Even when that court is inclined to proceed on the most laudable motives, it is ever liable to be misled by the interested or sinister views of advisers, to whom, from a want of that knowledge which present inspection can alone supply, it is almost necessitated to give ear. When a cause, (said the honest men of whom I am speaking,) in which the interests of religion are obviously concerned, presents itself to Rome, with the eagerness of a kind parent she will listen to our prayer, and redress our grievances. So they reasoned. They were also aware of the dependent state, into which the benefactions bestowed by Rome on their foreign houses had thrown them: a dependence which gratitude cemented, but which, to the present hour, has operated fatally.

They are successfully counteracted.

The measure on which the clergy had decided, could not be long concealed from those whose interest it was to obstruct its completion.

pletion. Father Parsons was in Spain; but no sooner was the project communicated to him, than he hastened to Rome. This was about the year 1597.—Mean while, to amuse the clergy and to lull them into security, the faction at home loudly applauded their design and wished it success, while secretly they laboured to draw off some of the clergy to their own side. In this they succeeded. Mr. George Blackwell, whose name will often return, "a man of a quicker penne, than "either of wisdome or sinceritie," not only joined them, but consented to write a letter which should be conveyed to Rome, purporting that " for twenty years, there had been " no dissention between the secular priests " and the jesuits; that the reports, stating the " ambition of those fathers, were so far from " the truth, that, on the contrary, the jesuits " were in all places most notable examples of " humility, gentleness, patience, piety, and " charity." The testimonial thus worded was committed to the care of a Mr. Standish, another seduced clergyman, and with him dispatched to Rome.*

Father

---

* *A True Relation*, p. 62. *Declaratio Motuum*, p. 26.

INTRODUCTION.

Father Parsons had now the game in his own hands. On the arrival of Standish, he introduced him, with two other clergymen, then in Rome, equally his own creatures, to his holiness, Clement VIII, as the deputies from the *secular priests* in England. They presented their letter; then entreated his holiness, "that he would kindly deign to appoint a superior over the English church; for so great were the dissentions betwixt the *secular priests* and the *laity*, that many inconveniences must necessarily follow, unless one were placed over them, who, by his authority, might reconcile and reform them,"—Clement seemed surprised: "Doth what you have said," he asked, "proceed from the desire and consent of my loving priests in England?"—Standish replied: "What we have presumed to offer to your holiness, is done by the most assured and unanimous consent of our brethren."*

His holiness, thus deceived, committed the business to cardinal Cajetan, then protector, as the phrase is, of the English nation, and to cardinal Borghese. But the former being familiarly connected with father Parsons,

---

* *A True Relation*, p. 70. *Declaratio Motuum*, p. 31.

as was natural, deemed it moſt proper to entruſt to him the arrangement of the meaſure; and, by his ſuperior authority, overruled his colleague. The whole plan is ſaid to have been previouſly adjuſted between them.*

The wily politician did not long heſitate.—That the wiſhes of the clergy muſt, in part, be complied with, was plain; or they would ſoon be at Rome with the *Supplication* of their body, when the plot of his faction would be detected, and, perhaps, fruſtrated in its whole extent:—But they muſt not have a biſhop for their ſuperior, with ordinary juriſdiction at leaſt, ſuch, he knew, as they requeſted, who would unite all their intereſts, and annul the project he had laid for the elevation of his own order:—If a ſuperior, of a character hitherto unheard of in the church of God, can be obtained, to him, as a Roman delegate, the clergy muſt ſubmit; and, if he be a creature of the Jeſuits, under his auſpices, the views they had formed will be more effectually promoted:—To ſelect a Jeſuit for this ſuperior would be too palpable and revolt numbers: but the way may be opened to the office; for though the conſtitutions of the ſociety exclude them from the mitre, they bar

not

---

* *A True Relation* p. 72.   *Declaratio motuum* p. 32.

Mr. Blackwell chosen arch-priest.

not the access to other ecclesiastical preferments.

In this, or in a manner not unlike it, we may presume, father Parsons reasoned; and he could not be long at a loss on whom to fix his choice. The name of Blackwell was known at Rome, where he had once resided in habits of intimacy with Bellarmin, and to whom, twenty years before, certain powers had been entrusted.* Recently also, as we have just seen, he had merited peculiar favour by a most signal service. Him, therefore, he deemed a proper instrument for his designs; and he recommended him to the cardinals. They approved his choice; and it was determined that Mr. Blackwell should be nominated superior over the clergy of England and Scotland, with the title of *Archpriest*.†

Had the *Presbyterian* idea come from the school of Calvin, it would have raised no surprise: why then be surprised that it originated in a school, wherein the Jesuits Lainez and Salmeron had taught, that the whole ecclesiastical hierarchy was concentered in the pope, and that

---

* Dodd, p. 25. *Breve Greg.* XIII. et p. 380.

† *A True Relation*, p. 72. *Declaratio Motuum* p. 33.

that he was the only bishop *jure divino*?* The sequel will still develope this unseemly doctrine.

An instrument was now prepared, under the form of a *Letter* from cardinal Cajetan, directed to George Blackwell, and dated March 7, 1598. — It states, that satan had lately moved dissentions between the Catholic laity and the secular priests: That in the Roman college peace and harmony *now* prevail: That some subordination among the priests, it was thought, would tend to generate concord, as the reasons just urged by the delegates proved: That, with this view, he nominates him, with the title of *archpriest*, to direct and govern all the secular priests of England and Scotland: That, however, to lighten the heavy charge, he appoints six advisers or *assistants*, whom he mentions by name, empowering him at the same time, to add six more to the number: that harmony and concord must be maintained, and that with the fathers of the society whom he greatly extols, saying that their labours, for the good of their country, in England as elsewhere, were incessant; that they had not, nor pretended to have any jurisdiction over the secular priests, to whom they would cause no uneasiness; and therefore it was the devil's

---

* Fleury, T. xxxiii. p. 616. See also many other writers on the ecclesiastical business of that time.

work, designed to overturn all the benefits of the ministry, if any Catholics excited or practised envies and jealousies against them.*

Such, in a much longer detail, are the contents of this curious instrument, obviously, in every article, fabricated by father Parsons, in a perfect accord with the late stratagem, and to answer the designs he had in view.—It was signed by the cardinal, and dispatched into England, but in company with another instrument, by way of codicil, still more extraordinary.† This was a paper of *Instructions* which prohibited the archpriest, with his twelve assistants, "from determining any matter of "importance, without advising with the supe- "rior of the jesuits, and some others of the "order."‡ Thus was the controuling power ultimately lodged in the hands of the society, whose superior or provincial, at that time, was the distinguished Henry Garnet.

In this manner, were the venerable remains of the British church wantonly insulted!—His holiness does not deign by a *Bull* or *Brief*, (an instrument used on the most common occasions,) to signify his will to them, but commands his chamberlain to do it. This cham-

---

* *Litteræ Card. Cajet.* Dodd, p. 252.
† Ibid. p. 253. *Breve Clem.* viii. p. 263.   ‡ *A True Relation*, p. 73.

chamberlain, calling himself protector of the English nation, commits the business to father Parsons; and he plans and directs the whole. A man is chosen, devoted to his interest, and who had betrayed his brethren; but he is appointed with a title, in its present application, unknown in the christian church; and that the powers annexed to this title may be restrained, he is provided with a council, all of them the creatures of the jesuits, one of them the notorious James Standish; and that powers even thus restricted may be more effectually restricted, the controuling energy of the whole is delegated to the fathers of the society!*

It was on the 7th of March an. 1598, that the Rev. George Blackwell was nominated *archpriest* in the kingdoms of England and Scotland.

---

* In a MS *Relation* presented by the regulars to Benedict XIV. about the year 1750, in my possession, which gives a succinct account of these events, the transaction is thus stated: "That Clement VIII. greatly incensed that the clergy should "have aimed to establish an independent hierarchy among "themselves, and when he knew that the government of "bishops was neither necessary nor useful to the Catholics, "commanded the protector to appoint an archpriest with "assistants." They also observe, that the omission of a pontifical decree or brief was with equal prudence concerted, lest its introduction, contrary to law, might give offence to the English government! I shall quote this *Relation*, when necessary, and the reader may credit it when he can.

INTRODUCTION.

In tracing the diffentions which continued to disturb our internal peace at home, I omitted to mention a train of similar misunderstandings which kept pace with them abroad, particularly among those Catholics who dwelt in Flanders. The number of these, laity and clergy, was considerable, whom the benevolence of the Spanish court principally maintained. Father Holt, a jesuit, resided at Brussels, in whom the government of the country confided, entrusting to him the distribution of their charities; and through his hands also passed such other charities as were collected in England for the support of the emigrants and exiles. In the execution of this delicate office father Holt offended many, and many charges were preferred against him.—About this same time also, the year 1597, a *Memorial* of great length, containing many heads of accusation against the jesuits in general, and the English jesuits, residing in England, in particular, was sent out of Flanders to Rome. The memorial, though signed by few, was supposed to speak the general sentiments of the English clergy and a large portion of the laity, both at home and abroad. Counter-memorials and counter-petitions were, therefore, procured, while father Parsons, at Rome, father Garnet in England, and father Holt at Brussels, strenuously exerted their predominant influence to check the effects of so dangerous an opposition, and to maintain their credit.—Among those in Flanders who signed for father Holt and the society, I find Dr. Stapleton and other dignified ecclesiastics, the officers and colonel of Stanley's legion, (who a few years before, being sent by the queen to garrison the town of Deventer in Holland, had gone over to the Spaniards, saying that their consciences allowed them not to fight for heretics,) nearly 40 gentlemen and some ladies, at the head of whom is the countess of Northumberland. But Dr. Worthington had laboured hard to procure these signatures. They who refused to sign were far less numerous, Dr. Giffard, afterwards archbishop of Reims, the earl of Westmoreland, and 12 others, whose names are recorded.—MSS *Letters* in my hands: See also *A True Relation*, p. 66, which contains the *Memorial* just mentioned.

From

INTRODUCTION.

From the appointment of the archpriest Blackwell an. 1598, to the nomination of the bishop of Chalcedon an. 1623.

THE resentment of the clergy, thus over-reached and insulted, was great, when they understood what had been done at Rome, and when Mr. Blackwell announcing his delegation, declared his title with the extent of its powers, and demanded their submission. The elders came forward, at the head of whom were Mr. Colleton in the south, and in the north Mr. Mush, firm but candid men, admired for their learning, revered for their virtues.* They saw that the *Letter* from the protector was unsupported by any *Brief* from his holiness; and soon the whole transaction was unravelled to them, the perfidy of Blackwell and Standish,

Resentment and proceedings of the clergy.

---

* Dodd, vol. 2, p. 115. Vol. 3, p. 84.—The clergy, at this time, amounted to more than 400; the number of jesuits must have been inconsiderable.

and the shameless declaration of the latter in company with the pretended delegates before the pontiff at Rome. They doubted not but the whole was the contrivance of father Parsons, and that the cardinal and the pope had been both imposed on, which many clauses of the protector's letter sufficiently evinced. Under this conviction, they intreated that they might not be urged to admit the authority of the archpriest, till it should be confirmed by an express *Brief*, or till his holiness's pleasure were signified to them. Besides, they observed, they would not believe that the court of Rome, as the private *instructions* were said to enjoin, would impose on the clergy of England the hard condition of submitting themselves to the dominion of the new order of *Jesuits*.[*]

Blackwell perceived there was no time to be lost: wherefore, in conjunction with father Garnet, he dispatched agents through the kingdom to collect signatures to a *Letter* of thanks to the pope and cardinal, for that excellent form of government they had established over them. The young and ignorant, as yet unapprised of the matter, allured

---

[*] *A True Relation*, p. 73, 74. *Declaratio Motuum*, p. 35, 36.

INTRODUCTION.

allured by promifes, or intimidated by threats, gave their names; and a meffenger fet out for Rome.*

The heads of the clergy, meanwhile, deliberately concerted their plan of oppofition, when it was agreed to depute two of their body, to exhibit their complaints to his holinefs. The two chofen were Dr. Bifhop, (whofe name will often return,) and Mr Charnock; and they took with them a *Remonftrance*, the chief heads of which were, " That
" the government of an archprieft for a whole
" nation feemed unprecedented and extraor-
" dinary; that it did not anfwer the ends of
" the miffion, efpecially as to the facrament
" of confirmation; that the divine inftitution
" required a hierarchy in every national
" church; that the meafures of the appoint-
" ment were taken by mifinformation and
" furreptitious means; that the chief perfons
" among the clergy had neither been advifed
" with, nor had they confented, as the court
" of Rome had been made to believe; that
" the whole derogated from the dignity of
" the clergy; that it was a contrivance of
" father Parfons and the jefuits, who had the
" liberty

---

* *True Relation*, p. 74.

"liberty to nominate both the archprieſt and
"his aſſiſtants; that the cardinal protector's
"letter, without an expreſs bull from his
"holineſs, was not ſufficient to make ſo
"remarkable an alteration in the government
"of the church; that the archprieſt being
"ordered to adviſe with the jeſuits in all
"matters relating to the clergy, was an unbe-
"coming reſtraint upon their body, and
"without a precedent. For theſe, and ſuch
"like reaſons, they beg leave to demur in
"their obedience to the archprieſt, till his
"authority ſhall be more legally eſtabliſhed."*

The Letter of thanks to the Roman court was ſoon followed by leſs pleaſing information, announcing the oppoſition to the archprieſt, and finally ſtating that two agents from the clergy were actually on their way to Rome.† The cardinal received the news with indignation, and inſtantly, by letter, demanded from Blackwell, in the name of his holineſs, a minute detail of all things, with the names and characters of the agents and their refractory aſſociates, and the motives on which their reſiſtance was founded.‡—The letter is dated Nov. 10, 1598.   About

---

* Dodd, vol. 2, p. 26.

† Ep. 2, Cajet. Dodd, ib. p. 254.   ‡ Ibid.

About the beginning of the new year, the deputies being arrived in Rome, prefented themfelves before the cardinals Cajetan and Borghefe. How gracious their reception was, we may conjecture; for at night, they were arrefted in their lodgings, and conducted under a guard of foldiers to the Roman college, where father Parfons prefided. He committed them to feparate rooms, after their papers, under a threat of excommunication if they with-held any, had been taken from them. That reverend father, it is related, and other jefuits had accompanied the Sbirri. They were now feparately examined by this fame inquifitor, while another father, officiating as fecretary, minuted their anfwers; after which, being again admitted to the cardinals, they underwent another interrogatory, and were reconducted to prifon, where they remained four months.* Their deputies arrive at Rome and are imprifoned.

Such, thus far, was the iffue of a folemn deputation from the Catholic clergy of England to his holinefs Clement VIII. !

But

---

* *Declaratio Motuum*, p. 41, 2, 3, 4. Where is given a minute detail of this extraordinary tranfaction.

The pope confirms the appointment of Blackwell.

But Clement was now fenfible, it feems, either from fomething that had fallen from the delegates, or from their *Remonftrance*, which he muft have feen, that, in authorifing the cardinal protector to appoint an archprieft, he had departed from precedent, and that the meafure muft be amended.—Had he reafoned, that, as the office was unprecedented, a mode of appointment equally unprecedented comported with it beft, I prefume to think, it would have been more confiftent.—He therefore iffued a *Brief*, dated April 6, an. 1599.* Its language is dictatorial and indignant, confirming whatever the cardinal had enacted, and fuperadding the ufual mandates of a papal decree.

While this was doing at Rome, hoftilities, with an increafing acrimony, were waged between the parties in England. Books were publifhed: the non-complying clergy were diftinguifhed by the name of *appellants:* and a father Lifter, in a *Treatife on Schifm*, endeavoured to faften on them the more odious appellation of *fchifmatics*. The clergy drew up their cafe, and propofed it to the faculty of Sorbonne, which returned an anfwer in their favour. Mr.

---

* *Breve Clem.* VIII. Dodd, p. 264.

INTRODUCTION.

Mr. Blackwell, who, during the dispute, behaved with an indecent partiality, issued a decree against the determination of Sorbonne; threatened the clergy with the vengeance of his power; and actually proceeded to the suspension of Mush and Colleton.*

But when the *Brief* arrived in England, the clergy submitted to its dictates, and tranquillity for a time was restored.

The delegates still remained immured: for we have a letter of April 21,† written jointly by the cardinals Cajetan and Borghese, to the rector of the Roman college, wherein, after stating that they had examined the cause of the two English priests, for some months detained in his college by his holiness's order, they give it as their opinion, that it is not expedient for the good of the English church, they should immediately return to a country, where, in concert with their brethren, they had practised contentions. Wherefore, in the name of the pontiff and in their own, under pain of censures and the infliction of punishments,

The deputies are released.

---

* Dodd, p. 26. *Sententia Facultatis. A Decree,* ib. p. 256. *Breve Clem.* VIII. ib. p. 259. *A True Relation,* p. 76.

† *Literæ communes,* Dodd, p. 255.

ments, they command the said William Bishop and Robert Charnock, without an express permission from his holiness or the cardinal protector, not to presume to enter the kingdoms of England, Scotland, or Ireland, but to abide peaceably and quietly in those countries which had been prescribed to them. By a strict compliance with these injunctions, they may the sooner be permitted to return. In conclusion, father Parsons is commissioned to signify these orders to his prisoners.

The prisoners, however, were released, and soon made their way to England, one account* says, by the interest of cardinal du Perron, then embassador from France, after they had obtained an audience of his holiness, in which they stated all the motives of their conduct: while another account† mentions, that they rather escaped by flight, taking different routes through Lorraine and Holland.

The clergy still discontented appeal to Rome.

The tranquillity which the *Brief* had restored did not long continue. It forced obedience from the clergy, but it could not reconcile them to all its injunctions. The clause

---

* Racine Hist. Ecclesiast. T. 13, p. 608.

† Dodd, vol. 2, p. 26.

INTRODUCTION.

clause particularly of the private *inſtructions*, which ſubjected their concerns to the jeſuits, was intolerable; and now more than ever, when the treatment of their delegates, in their own college, under the intruſive eye of father Parſons, was detailed to them, they bore more impatiently the unnatural controul. The archprieſt, beſides, though in his private character eſtimable, and endowed with ability and virtue, was harſh and imperious in command, permitting himſelf to be hurried on by the impetuoſity of the men to whom he owed his promotion.

Charges however unfounded often leave a ſtigma, and reproachful appellations are not eaſily removed. Thus it was with the name of *ſchiſmatic*, which the ignorant and malevolent often repeated in the ears of the clergy. Hurt by an imputation which ſhould only have provoked a ſmile, they applied to the archprieſt, requeſting that ſome reparation ſhould be made them. His reply was, " that " their behaviour had merited the reflection, " and that it was rather their duty to make " him ſatisfaction." The intemperate anſwer rouſed again their reſentment, which was daily aggravated by authoritative edicts, by oppreſſion, and by exertions of power which his commiſſion, it ſeems, did not always warrant. Once more, therefore, they reſolved

to

to recur to Rome; and they drew up an *appeal*, in their own names, and in thofe of the other clergy and laity, againft the oppreffion and mal-adminiftration of their fuperior. It is dated November 17, an. 1600, with only 32 fignatures.*

Brief from his holinefs.

This *appeal* drew fome attention from his holinefs; and nine months after, Auguft 17, 1601, he iffued another *Brief*,† addreffed to the archprieft, to the clergy, and to the Catholic world, wherein he ftates the motives which originally induced him to appoint an archprieft, the approbation given by fome to the meafure, the oppofition of others, with the general ftate of the controverfy, which his *Brief* of confirmation, he fays, happily clofed. He mentions the renewal of the former diffentions, imputing it, in a great meafure, to the imprudent expreffions and conduct of the archprieft, which renewal, he obferves, induced the clergy to appeal, whofe appeal he had received and read. But all circumftances maturely weighed, it is obvious, he fays, that the whole is the work of the devil, who divides the

---

* *True Relation*, p. 77, 8, 9. *An Appeal*, Dodd, vol. 2, p. 258.

† *Breve Clem.* VIII. Dodd, p. 259.

INTRODUCTION.

the paftors that he may fcatter the flock. Then, again confirming the office of arch-prieft with all its powers, he opens an addrefs to him, and to the minifters of religion of both parties, conveying fentiments the moft paternal and paftoral. But he refufes to admit the appeal, which would but widen the breach: he impofes filence on the parties, fuppreffes their various publications, and, under pain of excommunication, forbids them to write on the fubject, or to mention the name of fchifmatic. The *Brief* clofes with a fervourous exhortation, from the apoftle, to peace and charity, in which he includes the laity, whom the late diffentions of their paftors may have fcandalifed.

Though the general fentiments of this *Brief* cannot be too much admired, yet, I own, the claufes of authority difguft me, wherein a pope of Rome takes upon himfelf to regulate the civil conduct, as it may certainly be efteemed, of Britifh fubjects in their mode of writing or treating a private matter of controverfy. And, not long before, he had dared to imprifon two delegates deputed to him. But why fend delegates; or why appeal to this diftant court, unlefs in circumftances againft which no private church has a remedy, and for which the canons of general difcipline have not provided?

The

Another *Brief*. The appealing clergy having gained nothing from the laſt *Brief* but good advice, and the archprieſt continuing the ſame arbitrary and oppreſſive conduct, under the guidance of father Garnet and the Jeſuits, again determined, after ſome months, to apply to Rome. It was apparent, indeed, they ſaw from ſome paſſages of the *Brief*, that his holineſs's mind was not quite hardened againſt impreſſion. Delegates were, therefore, ſent, whoſe names are not recorded, who ſo far ſucceeded as to procure the following *Brief* from the pontiff. It is dated October 5, 1602,* and addreſſed to the archprieſt.

It begins with admoniſhing him to uſe his power diſcreetly, and not to exceed his commiſſion, as, in ſome caſes, he ſeemed to have done. It defines more minutely the limits of his juriſdiction, and then adds, in order that, in the execution of his office, peace may be the better ſecured; " In virtue of holy obedi-
" ence we command you, in tranſacting the
" duties of your charge, not to communicate
" or treat with the provincial of the Jeſuits
" or any members of that ſociety—and we
" annul the inſtruction of the late cardinal
" protector

---

* Breve Clem. VIII. Dodd, p. 262.

"protector appertaining to this matter. More-
"over, we order that, in things regarding the
"administration of your church or office, you
"treat not, by letter, or messenger, or by any
"other means, with the religious of that
"society residing at Rome or elsewhere; but
"let all things be referred to us, or to the
"protector." — That this clause, however,
might not be prejudicial to them, Clement
immediately praises their christian zeal, and
says, that the jesuits themselves, for the
establishment of peace, deemed the measure
expedient. — This is followed by another
injunction, namely, that, when any of the
present assistants to the archpriest die, three of
the appellant clergy be successively chosen by
him to succeed them. — He next proceeds
to condemn all books written against the
society, or against any persons of either
party; and by a more extensive comprehension than before, threatens censures and
excommunication against all men, laity, clergy,
and religious, who, in future, shall publish
such works without the approbation and licence
of the cardinal protector, or have them in their
keeping. He then closes, in a style of more
decent supremacy with another apt exhortation
to fraternal charity and concord.

Thus was contention terminated. But *Reflections.*
when parties have been formed in a community,

munity, such as I have stated, and under the influence of such motives, their duration is written on brass. Political feuds can cease; so can those of civil life; religious animosity alone seems interminable.*

It may appear extraordinary that these internal broils should have agitated the Catholics,

---

*The MS. *Relation* of the regulars quoted above, p. 34, thus observes: " That the clergy seduced by the artifices of the "queen, who meditated the ruin of their religion, and grieved "that their hopes of rising to the mitre were frustrated *(se spe* "*episcopatuum esse privatos,)* pretending some oppression from the "archpriest, appealed to Rome: That their delegates to Rome "were furnished with recommendatory letters from the queen "and her privy council to Henry IV. of France, who, on his "side, recommended the same delegates and their cause to his "embassador at the Roman court, and to the French cardinals "there: That, notwithstanding, after mature deliberation "taken and the best advice, it was resolved at Rome, that "*neither bishops, nor the form of an ecclesiastical hierarchy, as* "*established in Catholic countries, should be permitted in England:* "That, on the whole, it merits particular observation, that "when the clergy nauseating, as they did, the nominal "government *(sine ulla jurisdictione regimen,)* of an archpriest, "thought of introducing an ecclesiastical hierarchy, the queen "and the Protestant ministers, with great eagerness, promoted "their design, well-foreseeing that the *establishment of bishops* "would soon generate such discord and dissentions among "Catholics, as would bring down that ruin on them, which "neither the severest laws, nor persecutions, nor torments had "been able to effect."—Of this statement, unsupported by any historical facts, the reader, as I before observed, will believe what he can.

INTRODUCTION.

Catholics, while the penal ftatutes, made againft them in the preceding years, had not ceafed to be executed with extreme feverity. The prifons and caftles were crowded, (for I find more than fifty, at this time, in the fingle caftle of York,) and many fuffered death, that is, 20 priefts, from 1598 to 1602, and more than 10 of the laity.* They were convicted, principally under the ftatute of the 27th of Eliz. by which Britifh fubjects ordained abroad, and returning into England, were made guilty of high treafon. The laity fuffered for aiding and receiving the fame.—In addition alfo to the obfervation I have made of the inveteracy of thofe difputes, it is worth remarking, that the *appeal* laft fent to Rome againft the archprieft, was dated from Wifbich caftle, where many of the appellants then were, and had been long confined.

The general prejudice againft this unfortunate order of men had now been growing for many years, aggravated by a fucceffion of great political events, in which, as a body, they certainly had no concern. But, as I have fufficiently obferved, the circumftance of their foreign education drew fufpicions on

---

* *Memoirs of Mif. Priefts.*

INTRODUCTION.

them; and the agitating Parsons was unceasingly at work. So obnoxious was he to government that, on some of the trials, it was considered by the bench as a criminal act, to have been abroad, and *have treated and conversed with Parsons.** The laws themselves, under an idea that his disciples would escape their application, if described by the common name of priests, distinguish them by the appellation of *jesuits*, as in the act of the 27th Eliz.

To say, if these men had been away, that fewer penal statutes against Catholics would have existed, is a conjecture founded on no light evidence; but to say, in that case, that we should not have been a divided people, and that, before the close of the reign of Elizabeth, the public odium against us would have ceased, is, perhaps, as obvious a truth as history can reveal. By a proclamation of November 7, 1601, the queen banished the jesuits and such priests as espoused their principles and party, forbidding them, under pain of death, ever to return into England; but to such clergy as would give a true profession of their allegiance, she signified her wish

---

* *Memoirs of Mis. Priests*, vol. 1, p. 348.

INTRODUCTION.

wish to shew favour and indulgence.* The circumstance, as an omen portending happiness, was eagerly embraced by some of the leading clergy, and they came forward with a *Protestation of Allegiance*, dated January 31, 1602.

"We acknowledge," say these patriotic men, "First, the queen's majesty to have full sovereignty over us. We protest, that we are most willing to obey her in all cases, as far as ever christian priests within this realm, or in any other, were bound to obey their temporal prince. And this our acknowledgment we think to be so grounded on the word of God, that no authority or pretence can, upon any occasion, be a warrant more to us, than to any Protestant, to disobey her majesty in any civil or temporal matter.—Secondly, whereas for these many years, conspiracies against her majesty's person, and sundry forcible attempts for invading and conquering her dominions, have been made, under we know not what pretences of restoring the Catholic religion by the sword, by reason of which enterprises, her majesty has been moved to ordain and execute severer laws

Protestation of *Allegiance* presented by 13 priests.

---

* Acta pub. xvi. p. 473, 489.

" against

"against Catholics (who, by reason of their
"union with the Roman see in faith and
"religion, were easily supposed to favour
"these conspiracies and invasions,) than,
"perhaps, had ever been enacted, if such
"attempts had not been made;* we, to assure
"our loyalty, do protest that, in every future
"enterprise of this nature, from whatever
"potentate, or under what pretence soever,
"we will defend her majesty's person and her
"dominions from all such assaults and injuries.
"—Thirdly, if upon any excommunications
"denounced, or to be denounced against her
"majesty, upon any such attempts to be
"made, the pope should also excommunicate
"every British subject, that would not forsake
"the foresaid defence, and take part with
"such conspirators or invaders: in these,
"and in all such cases, we do think ourselves
"and all lay-catholics bound in conscience
"not to obey this or any such-like censures.
"— And because it is most certain, that,
"whilst we thus declare our dutiful affection
"and allegiance, there will not want such as
"will

---

* The reader is requested to remark the words of this second clause, which assigns, as the cause of the many severities exercised on Catholics, the enterprises of disaffected men. I said who those disaffected men were, and I noticed their enterprises.

INTRODUCTION.

" will condemn and misconstrue this our lawful act, yea, and by many suggestions and calumnies discredit our doings with the christian world, but chiefly with the pope's holiness, unless we maturely prevent their endeavours therein; we humbly beseech her majesty that in this our recognising and yielding Cesar's due unto her, we may also, by her gracious leave, be permitted to make known by like public act, that, by yielding her right unto her, we depart from no bond of that christian duty, which we owe unto our supreme spiritual pastor: and therefore, *we acknowledge and confess the bishop of Rome to be the successor of St. Peter in that see, and to have as ample, and no more, authority or jurisdiction over us and other Christians, than had that apostle by the gift and commission of Christ our Saviour*; and that we will obey him so far forth, as we are bound by the laws of God to do, which we doubt not will stand well with the performance of our duty to our temporal prince, in such sort as we have before professed. For as we are most ready to spend our blood in the defence of her majesty, and our country, so we will rather lose our lives than infringe the lawful authority of Christ's Catholic church."*

I have,

---

* Dodd, vol. 2, p. 292.

I have, in some passages, abridged this admirable *Protestation*, which, it would have been well, the successors of those enlightened men had made their own, and annually published to the country as the unequivocal expression of their religious and political sentiments.

It was delivered to the lords of the council who testified their satisfaction, signed, indeed, by only 13 out of more than 400 priests then resident in England; but at the head of those thirteen were the names of Dr. Bishop, Colleton, Mush, and Charnock, with whom the reader is, by this time, acquainted. What they had foreseen soon happened. Their act was represented as little less than schismatical: the university of Louvain gravely pronounced, that they had sinned through ignorance and imprudence, but that it was not the sin of absolute heresy;* and Dr. Champney, one of the thirteen, a man of singular endowments, being, some years afterwards, appointed director to a convent of nuns, was compelled to surrender the important charge, on its being

---

* Remonstran. Hibern. p. 32.

being notified to his fair penitents, that he had signed that horrible *Proteftation!**†

In the enfuing year, March 24, an. 1603, queen Elizabeth died.

Had the Catholics in a body, on the accession of king James, waited on him with the *Proteftation of allegiance*, I have juft ftated, as containing their true and loyal fentiments, we fhould, probably, have heared no more of recufancy or penal profecution. His good will to the profeffors of that religion, from the earlieft impreffions, was deeply marked on his heart; he could look, he had reafon to think, for political fupport from them, if the exigences of events might require it: but in the creed of the majority, at leaft of the majority of their minifters, he knew, there was a principle admitted, that of the papal prerogative over the crowns of princes, which could ill accord, truly, with the exalted opinion he himfelf entertained of royal dignity and

King James's abhorrence of the depofing doctrine.

---

* Dodd, vol. 3, p. 82.

† The *Relation* of the regulars fays: "Caft in the hope they "had imprudently conceived (of re-eftablifhing a hierarchy,) "thirteen of thofe appealing clergy fided with the queen, thus "falling from their religion *(a Catholica religione fenfim decidentes.)* "They dared openly to profefs, what their hearts had inwardly "plotted."

and independence. "That arrogant and
"ambitious fupremacy of their pope, (he
"obferved in his firft fpeech to parliament,)
"whereby he not only claims to be fpiritual
"head of all chriftians, but alfo to have an
"imperial civil power over all kings and
"emperors, dethroning and decrowning princes
"with his foot as it pleafeth him, and dif-
"penfing and difpofing of all kingdoms and
"empires at his appetite." For this, he fays,
they are no way fufferable to remain in this
kingdom. He alfo charges them with affaf-
finating and murdering kings, "thinking it
"no fin, but rather a matter of falvation, to
"do all actions of rebellion and hoftility
"againft their natural fovereign, if he be
"once curfed, his fubjects difcharged of their
"fidelity, and his kingdom given a prey, by
"that three crowned monarch, or rather
"monfter, their head."*

This rooted opinion of James, thus ftrongly
expreffed, is the clue that unfolds fome tranfactions of his reign, and particularly accounts
for many acts of feverity againft a fociety of
men whom naturally he loved. He had not
been twelve months on the throne, when he
iffued

---

* Ap. Rapin, vol. 2, p. 165.

INTRODUCTION.

iffued a proclamation for banifhing "all manner of jefuits, feminary priefts, and other priefts whatfoever, having ordination from any authority by the laws of this realm prohibited." — " Confidering," he goes on, " that abfolute fubmiffion to foreign jurifdiction, at their firft taking orders, doth leave fo conditional authority to kings over their fubjects, as the fame power by which they were made, may difpenfe at pleafure with the ftraiteft band of loyalty and love between a king and his people."* — The ftatement is not accurate, but it fhews the conviction of the king, for which I quote the paffage.

I pafs over the gunpowder plot laid for the 5th of November, 1605, the fource of yet unextinguifhed prejudices againft Englifh Catholics; the part fome jefuits are faid to have had in that plot; and the death of father Garnet, executed for mifprifion of treafon.

Nor fhall I dwell on the famous *oath of allegiance*, enacted at the beginning of the following year, about which fo much has been faid and written. Suffice it to fay, that both parliament

marginal note: Oath of allegiance.

---

* *A Proclamation,*. Dodd, p. 436.

parliament and king, aware that some Catholics, from conscientious scruples, objected to the oath of supremacy, and still that there were many whose civil principles were sound and loyal, seriously desired to offer them a political *Test*, which should establish a just discrimination, that is, should shew them who might be safely trusted. In this view, the *oath of allegiance* was framed, to which, it was thought, every Catholic would cheerfully submit, who did not believe the bishop of Rome had power to depose kings, and give away their dominions.

The oath, accordingly, when tendered, was taken by many Catholics, laity and clergy; and a ray of returning happiness gleamed around them. But a cloud soon gathered on the seven hills; for it could not be that a Test, the main object of which was an explicit rejection of the *deposing power*, should not raise vapours there.

<small>Condemned at Rome.</small>

It was conveyed to the hands of father Parsons, and from them to those of the pontiff, then Paul V. the late cardinal Borghese. Parsons (after having, in vain, attempted, by his writings,* to set aside the royal line of Scotland,

---

* *A Conference about the next Succession to the crown*, by R. Doleman, that is, R. Parsons.

INTRODUCTION.

Scotland, and then, in another work,* declared, that he had ever favoured that succession,) had seen, with pain, James ascend the throne, and now only proposing to give relief to the Catholics by an attack on that power, which he had uniformly laboured to exalt. He laid the hateful instrument before the pontiff. Paul deliberated, and condemned it, as *containing many things obviously adverse to faith and salvation*, in a Brief, addressed to the English Catholics, October 23, 1606.†

Many doubted the authenticity of the Brief, knowing the arts which were practised in the Roman court; or suspecting the insidious agency of Parsons, continued to manifest their allegiance. On this, a second Brief followed, September 22, in the ensuing year, which established the validity of the former, and enforced submission.‡

The Catholics were thrown into the utmost confusion; new dissentions arose; controversies were renewed; while the king, the government, and the nation, strengthened in their first

Distress of the Catholics.

---

* Preface to *The three Conversions of England.*

† Ap. Dodd, p. 463.

‡ *Breve alterum*, Dodd, p. 464.

INTRODUCTION.

firſt prejudices, were now authoriſed to declare, that men whoſe *civil conduct* was ſubject to the controul of a foreign court could, with no juſtneſs, claim the common rights of citizens.—The laws of the preceding reign were ordered to be executed, and new ones, additionally ſevere, were enacted.

With what face can it be aſſerted, that the Roman biſhop or his court have conſtantly promoted the beſt intereſts of the Engliſh Catholics, when, as we have juſt ſeen, their religion itſelf was expoſed to danger, and themſelves and their poſterity involved in much miſery, that an ambitious prerogative, (for ſuch, ſurely, is the power of depoſing princes,) might not be curtailed?

Writings for and againſt the oath.

The archprieſt, who, from the beginning had approved of the oath, would not ſurrender his conviction of its propriety. He took it himſelf, and, by a public *letter*, recommended it to his clergy. Many followed his example. Cardinal Bellarmin addreſſed the archprieſt, whom he had formerly known, lamenting his fall, which he compared with that of the venerable Oſius. Blackwell replied. The king himſelf now engaged in the controverſy, publiſhing his *apology for the oath*, againſt the two Briefs and the Letter of the cardinal. Bellarmin returned an *anſwer* to the royal controvertiſt;

INTRODUCTION.

tift; when James reprinted his *apology*, to which in refutation of the charge of his being a perfecutor of the catholics, he annexed a *Preface*, addreffed to all Chriftian princes. At the clofe of this *Preface*, after having enumerated the many benefits and favours he had beftowed on the Catholics, he fays: " In recounting where-
" of, every fcrape of my pen would ferve but as
" a blot of the pope's ingratitude and injuftice,
" in meeting me with fo hard a meafure (the
" condemnation of the oath) for the fame." The cardinal again replied, which brought forward the great champion for the oath, Roger Widdrington, a learned Benedictin monk.

But before this time, the archprieft, by a mandate from Rome, had been depofed. The laft Brief of Clement had releafed him, indeed, from the controul of the Jefuits; but it had alfo cancelled their friendfhip. They viewed him no longer as the inftrument of their policy; and his late behaviour in favour of the oath, which themfelves uniformly refifted, would apologife for their dereliction, and make it an act of fealty to the Roman bifhop. He was depofed in 1608, having governed 10 years.

Blackwell depofed and fucceeded by Birket.

In

INTRODUCTION.

In the two preceding years application had again been made to Rome for Bishops,* but without success :† now, therefore, on the deposition of Blackwell, Mr. George Birket was nominated his Successor, with the same title and jurisdiction. He was a man of great mildness and moderation, and had been one of the original assistants to his predecessor. What had recommended him most, was the opinion

father

---

* Epist. P. August. Dodd, p. 477: a curious letter, which exhibits the state of parties, and delineates many leading characters among the clergy.

† The *Relation* of the regulars thus states it: " The ambition of the clergy aiming at episcopal dignity was not yet satisfied; for though, through the remaining part of the pontificate of Clement VIII. their leaders had seemed to slumber, they now roused on the elevation of Paul V. and dared to attempt the same game. But he versed in business, well acquainted with the concerns of England, and who already by two Briefs had condemned the *oath* of the king, would consent to no change, and resolutely rejected all applications for a bishop and the establishment of an ecclesiastical hierarchy. In this he was directed by the opinions of his nuncios in France and Flanders; who had themselves collected the sense of the English Catholics. One thing alone he added to the established form, which was, " that the apostolic nuncio in France should, in future, be the ordinary of England, and superintend its church in the name of the Roman See." On this the clergy's agents returned to their own country, where all things remained quiet till the death of Paul.—Speaking of the late conduct of Blackwell, the same *Relation* had said: " He, grown sullen and decrepit, and intimidated, perhaps, by the severe edicts lately made against Catholics, took the oath prescribed by the king; and George Birket was saluted archpriest in his stead."

INTRODUCTION.

father Parsons entertained, that, as he was gentle and had long been his friend, it would be in his power to rule him, and through him to regain that afcendency of controul over the concerns of the clergy, which he had been compelled to relinquifh. With this view, he had had the intereft either to get that claufe omitted in the Brief of nomination, which prohibited the archprieft to confult with the Jefuits, or to procure an interpretation of it from his holinefs that amounted to a repeal.*

Mr. Birket, though a friend to peace, was not difpofed to facrifice all manlinefs of character, much lefs the honour and intereft of the Catholic clergy to the infidious friendfhip of a man whofe policy he muft have defpifed. Parfons opened a correfpondence with him, of which the originals, on his fide, are extant, and which (if all that he has befides written had perifhed, with all that has been related of him) would exhibit a perfect tranfcript of the man.†

Parfons correfponds with Birket, and dies.

---

* *Letters of Parfons* ap. Dodd, 2, 14; p. 483.

† *Letters* ib.

INTRODUCTION.

From thefe letters we learn, that Lord Mountague, about two years before, with other Catholics, had fent a petition for a bifhop to his holinefs, which petition father Parfons had thought proper not to prefent;—that Mr. Birket was diffatisfied with his agent at the Roman court, Thomas Fitzherbert, the devoted friend of Parfons, and who afterwards became a Jefuit;—that his holinefs had exprefsly fignified to father Parfons, that he would have no agents fent from England to profecute the petition for bifhops, of which motion, he fays, *he himfelf had ever been a favourer*;—that the clergy, ftill fixed to this point, and refolved to overturn the interference, which the Jefuits practifed in their concerns, were now fending an agent to Rome;—that whatever oaths of allegiance the Englifh Catholics might think of propofing, none would be accepted at Rome, which either directly or indirectly, regarded the authority of the fee apoftolic;—that Dr. Smith, the new agent of the clergy, with his companion Mr. More, were arrived in Rome (June 6, 1609), with whom neither he nor Mr. Fitzherbert were pleafed;—that the agents had obtained from the pope, with his concurrence to the meafure, that the Jefuits fhould have no concern in the government of the clergy;—that Dr. Smith had given offence by advancing thefe two propofitions, *that it was no article of Catholic faith. that the pope had a power of depofing princes*, and

that

that there is no true Catholic church now in England, so long as they have no bishops.

To these letters of Parsons are subjoined some from Fitzherbert, which speak the same language, and breathe the same spirit.*

Dr. Smith returned to England, leaving Mr. More in the agency behind him, having succeeded in some points, one of which I have mentioned. But in his application for a bishop he was effectually countermined by father Parsons,† notwithstanding the declaration, twice repeated in his letters, that he had always been a friend to the measure.

On the 15th of April, 1610, died this extraordinary man, Father Robert Parsons, the calamity of the English Catholics, in his 64th year.‡

Mr.

---

* Dodd p. 491.

† Dodd vol. 3: p. 77.—The statement I quoted from the *Relation* of the Regulars regards principally, I believe, this agency of Dr. Smith.

‡ I will mention a work of some curiosity, *Gathered and set down* by R. P. 1596, entitled *a Memorial for the Reformation of England*. " It contains certain notes and advertisements,
" which might be proposed in the first Parliament, and National
" council of our country, after God, of his mercy, shall restore
" it to the Catholic faith, for the better establishment and pre-

" servation

Death of Birket.

Mr. Birket, mean while, alive only to the welfare of his flock and the interests of the clergy, incessantly belaboured to procure them a bishop, though the measure would have despoiled him of his present pre-eminence, and to re-establish universal harmony. His endeavours in the latter point, were not totally void of success; and he died discharging the same great duty. From his bed he wrote a letter to the Jesuits, dated April 3, 1614, inculcating peace and charity. " I have dealt, he says, with
" the chiefest of my own body, whom, I know,
" you have held in greater jealousy, than there
" is cause. They only desire that, in their
" government, you meddle no further than
" they do in your's. This being done, there
" will be no occasion, but that you will friend-
" ly and charitably set forward this great work
" you have undertaken. I wish you all as well as
" I do my own heart; and I rest from my bed
" your brother in all charity and love."*

The

" servation of the said religion." They are the author's words. He had foreseen this event as likely to happen at no distant period, and, in confidence of his own superior lights, had prepared for it a system of general instruction. His system comprises what may regard the whole body of the people, then the church establishment, and finally the laity, in the king, lords, and commons. But there is little in it that attests any enlargement of mind or just comprehension of the subject. They are the ideas of such a mind as father Parsons will be understood to have possessed, narrow, arrogant, monastic.

* Dodd, vol. 2, p. 498.

INTRODUCTION.

The state of the catholics, particularly of the clerical order, during these last years, had been peculiarly irksome. They who had taken, or took, the oath of allegiance, were harassed by a papal decree, which came in with Birket, whereby they were deprived of all their jurisdiction, and consigned to penury and ignominy. Of these even many voluntarily surrendered themselves into the hands of justice to obtain a scanty maintenance, an act of direful necessity which the men of their own faith could represent as a sinful apostacy from religion.—
" I understand, says father Parsons to Birket,
" that your unfortunate predecessor with his
" company, (confined in the Clink prison)
" have had sent them by my lord archbishop
" twenty pounds a piece, and that he is per-
" mitted to go abroad at his pleasure.—
" It will be good that his holiness be informed
" thereof by you, and of all such things as
" there do pass." On the other hand, the laws of Elizabeth were carried into execution, and many were committed to prison, and some executed. To these the oath of allegiance was tendered: they refused it, and suffered; among whom we may be surprised to find Cadwallader and Drury, two of the thirteen who, at the close of the last reign, had signed the *Protestation* of allegiance. But the Bulls of Paul, it seems, had extinguished all consistency of reason, and inspired them with a love of martyrdom. I venerate

Priests suffer and die in defence of the Papal prerogative.

venerate the virtues and the firmness of these men; but truly it is pitiable to see such virtues and such firmness expended on a cause, at the name of which reason recoiled, and religion blushed. They died, because when called on by the legal authority of their country, they would not declare, that the Roman bishop, styled the vicar of him *whose kingdom is not of this world*, had no right to dethrone princes.* Their foreign education had inspired this strange conception of the papal prerogative.

And Paul himself could sit undisturbed in the Vatican, hearing that men were imprisoned, and that blood was poured out in support of a claim, which had no better origin, surely he knew, than the ambition of his predecessors and the weak concessions of mortals; he could sit and view the scene, and not, in pity at least, wish to redress their sufferings, by releasing them from the injunctions of his decree. Even when thirteen priests, confined in Newgate for having refused the oath, in all humility and with much enthusiasm in his cause, supplicated his holiness to inform them what those things in the oath were, which he had pronounced to be *adverse to faith and salvation*;† we do not hear, that

---

* See *Memoirs of Mis. Priests*, vol. 2. from the year 1607 to 1618.

† *A Supplication*, &c. ap. Dodd, vol. 2. p. 522.

INTRODUCTION.

that he returned them any anfwer. "We are very defirous to know, they fay, becaufe hitherto it has not clearly appeared."

In our church *Confirmation* is held to be a Sacrament that gives peculiar graces, and which, in the circumftances of difficulty and danger to which the faith of the Englifh Catholics was then daily expofed, ought always to be adminiftered. But fince the death of Watfon, a term of at leaft 30 years, no bifhop, the fole minifter of that facrament, had been in England; and the firft paftor, though preffed to it by reiterated petitions, was ftill refolved there fhould be none. One year paffed after the death of Birket, when Dr. Harrifon was nominated archprieft. Agreeable to all parties, to the Jefuits having, at one time, enjoyed the confidence of Father Parfons, to the clergy who knew his virtues and his mind placed above the reach of faction, to the Roman court whofe efteem he had acquired by a late refidence of five years amongft them, Harrifon united the fuffrages of all.*

Dr. Harrifon fucceeds to Birket.

In fpite of every effort to free themfelves from the controul of the Jefuits, the clergy hitherto had not been able to effect it. The decrees

He aims to free the clergy from the controul of the Jefuits.

---

* Dodd, vol. 2 : p. 368.

INTRODUCTION.

decrees of Rome were eluded, often, it is true, with the very sanction of the court which had passed them; and from the circumstance of a large portion of the clergy being attached to the society, it was hardly possible to break down the ascendency they had gained. In the foreign seminaries, originally designed for the education of clergy, they had the principal rule, being the rectors of the houses, the administrators of the funds, and the directors of conscience. Even in Douay, which the clergy, as I have before observed, bore most reluctantly, this economy had long prevailed. In 1612, in consequence of a visitation permitted by Rome, the president of the house, Dr. Worthington, the passive slave of the Jesuits, had been removed;* the administration committed to the strong arm of Dr. Kellison; and those arrangements overturned, which, with a view to their own interest and elevation, the fathers of

---

* It is remarkable that this Dr. Worthington, two years before, by the interest of father Parsons, he was promoted to the presidency of Douay college an. 1599, had, by a special vow bound himself to that holy father. " Now, in all dutiful hu-
" mility, he says, I beseech you, for God's sake, to accept of me
" into your particular charge to direct, command, and govern
" me as your subject." MS Letters in my hands.—He had before made a similar vow to Dr. Allen. No wonder if, the head of it being thus bound to father Parsons, the college of Douay was soon subjected to his controul. Such arts were used to gain ascendency!

INTRODUCTION.

of the fociety had eftablifhed. But the houfe was oppreffed with debts, and diftracted by internal factions: difcipline was relaxed, and learning languifhed.*

Senfible, that all attempts to reform evils at home would be vain, unlefs the fource of them were purified, the archprieft, now poffeffed of power, refolved to fupport Dr. Kellifon and give energy to his exertions. When this were effected, he would proceed, and overturn, if poffible, the irregular government of which himfelf was now the head, and which ferved to foment diffentions, keeping alive the alarms of the clergy, and infpiring the Jefuits with a fanguine hope that their plan of domination might finally prove fuccefsful. Father Parfons was dead; but he had left behind him his mantle, and with it an ample portion of his fpirit.

Dr. Kellifon's endeavours, thus powerfully invigorated, feemed to promife fuccefs. He had eftablifhed able mafters within his own walls, and fhaken off the interference that galled him, when an order unexpectedly came from Rome, that his fcholars fhould frequent the public fchools of the jefuits, as
for

---

* Dodd, p. 388. vol. 3: p. 89.

for some years they had done, and that one of that order should be their spiritual director.*—This it was that drew from Dr. Harrison and his assistants a *memorial*,† which is extant, addressed to Paul V. an. 1619, wherein they state, much at large, the general grievances of the clergy, and pray for redress. " It is a " melancholy reflection," they say, " to see " all things in the utmost confusion amongst " us; and that nothing should be approved " of, either in the seminary, or elsewhere " among the clergy, but what first passes " through the jesuits' hands, and receives a " sanction from them; as if we were destined " to be their slaves." Then, having enumerated a long list of other grievances, they add; " Yet, though the jesuits are masters of five " seminaries, and that of Douay only is in our " hands, it is so influenced by their contri- " vances, than we can scarce call it our own. " They daily endeavour to distress it more " and more; and, as the prophet Nathan said " to David, feast themselves on the one little " lamb, which the poor man had bought and " nourished up." They conclude: " The " whole of the matter, therefore, lies in this " one

---

* Dodd, vol. 2, p. 500.

† Ibid. *The Grievances*, &c.

" one point: That the jefuits may be pro-
" hibited from exercifing any power or jurif-
" diction over the clergy, or their colleges;
" with an injunction not to intermeddle with
" our affairs, no more than we do with
" theirs."

The firmnefs of Dr. Kellifon finally prevailed, and order, and difcipline, and independence were eftablifhed in his college.

Dr. Harrifon, with the leading clergy, now
turned their views to the accomplifhment of
the other part of their plan. But here, probably, they would have been foiled, as always
before they had been, by the ftratagems of a
fuperior faction, if an event of great political
moment had not come into agitation, in the
fuccefs of which the court of Rome deemed
itfelf interefted. I have faid, that the pure
love of religion, detached from human policy,
has feldom feemed to regulate the conduct of
that flow-deciding cabinet. The event I allude
to, was the marriage-treaty between Charles,
prince of Wales, and the Infanta of Spain.

About the beginning of this year, 1621,
the archprieft died.

Unabafhed

The clergy again resolve to apply to Rome for a bishop.

Unabashed by refusals, however often repeated, rather than chuse their own bishops, which their good sense, aided by reading, must have often told them was a measure most consistent, as I have said, with the rules of venerable antiquity, the clergy again applied to Rome. The king's behaviour inspired them with confidence. Buoyed up with the thoughts of the manifold advantages which would accrue from a match with Spain, he had begun to shew great indulgence to the Catholics, being aware that such lenity would recommend him to the Spanish court, and that it would be a means also of securing the good will of the pontiff, from whom it would be necessary, in case of his son's marriage, to obtain a dispensation. He occasionally saw some of the principal clergy, from whom he understood how anxious they were to procure a bishop, to superintend their concerns. The measure was not displeasing to the king, provided they chose a man of moderate principles, and not disagreeable to himself. He knew Dr. Bishop, and sometimes saw Mr. Colleton; and understanding it was agreed on to send an agent immediately to Rome, he recommended to them, what he had most at heart, to promote his son's match, and facilitate, when it should be called for, the necessary dispensation.*

The

---

* Dodd, vol. 2, p. 366, 368, et passim.

INTRODUCTION.

The agent whom the clergy deputed to his holiness, was Mr. John Bennet, accompanied by Mr. William Farrar; and they arrived in Rome about the end of autumn of the year 1621, when Gregory XV. had succeeded to the chair of St. Peter. Being admitted to audience, Mr. Bennet, in an elegant speech which is preserved, declared his commission: He spoke of the favourable dispositions of the English king, of the intended match, of the dispensation that would be implored; and he concluded with a persuasive address, praying that his holiness would listen to the supplication of the afflicted English church, and give them a bishop, or bishops, with canonical and *ordinary jurisdiction*.—He then presented a *Memorial*, the purport of which was to shew that, in lieu of the late *extraordinary* government of archpriests, that of *regular* bishops was absolutely necessary; and this was proved from the primitive institution by Christ, from the practice of the apostles and the perpetual usage of the church, from the authority and decrees of councils and popes, from the nature of the episcopal functions, from the necessity of restoring and preserving the ecclesiastical hierarchy and discipline, finally from the modern example of all Catholic nations.*

This

---

* *Transactions relating to the English secular clergy,* by John Serjeant, an. 1706. It is the *abstract* of a much larger work

never

This *Memorial* was followed by other writings of the same tendency, offered to the pope and principal cardinals; and it began to appear that success would crown the measure: for the consideration, that the king of England might now be gratified, that it might promote the Spanish match, and that the event of that match might ultimately issue in the reunion of a great nation to the apostolic see, weighed, we may be allowed to think, not lightly on the mind of Gregory.

Mr. Bennet, therefore, after some months, was able to inform the clergy, that a *Decree*, similar to those granted to other countries, would be obtained; but that his holiness, unwilling to give his majesty any cause of offence, intended to allow them only one bishop, whose title should be taken from some district in Asia, and not from England; that the *jurisdiction*, however, of this bishop, should be what is usually received, known, and approved in all provinces, and what each particular bishop exercises in his diocese.*

But

---

never published, and preserved, I believe, in the *archives* of the English chapter. This *abstract* I shall often quote, not being in possession of the MS. originals.

* Transactions, p. 19.

But could it be, the reflecting reader will ask, that the thousand obstacles, which had hitherto intervened, should be at once removed, and the measure, in a flow of general approbation, be completed? It was obvious to think that a court, jealous of the plenitude of its power, would not let go any portion of it, unless compelled by some preponderating motive of policy. It would attempt, at least, to satisfy the petitioners with a less valuable boon, with the offer of the *title* of bishop; but that title should possess only *delegated* powers, such as the archpriests had held. A bishop thus restricted would bear the real character of an agent or an emissary, and be, in all things, dependent on the will of his employers.— And would the jesuits, it might again be asked, possessing their usual influence in the Roman court, now permit their enemies to triumph, without a single effort?—Mr. Bennet perceived there was a demur; and he was not at a loss to conjecture, from what quarter and from what motives that demur proceeded. He, therefore, presented another *Memorial* to the same cardinals, in strong and bolder language.

It stated that, after thirteen months deliberation, his holiness had decreed to give a bishop to the English clergy; but that, when the measure seemed completed, a new consultation had been instituted to determine, whether

Mr. Bennet presents a strong memorial.

ther the jurisdiction of that bishop should be *ordinary*. " Truly, it goes on, *the whole purport of our petition was*, that the *delegated* power of the archpriest should be changed into a power, *episcopal* and *ordinary*. — We even shewed by many documents, that, not only the former *delegated* power, but that *any new and unusual jurisdiction*, would be not only *useless*, but, in these times, even *ruinous* to us.—It is objected, that the society of jesuits by this arrangement is aimed at; whence dissentions and feuds will arise.—I answer: It is plain to every one that, publicly and privately, those fathers have exerted all their strength and artifice to oppose this negotiation, and from this only motive, that they are enemies to that *ordinary* jurisdiction, whereby discipline is maintained.—Then we humbly beg that it be considered, whether it be just, that the episcopal order be banished from the church, because the jesuits, in all places or in some places, oppose the institution. Shall it be refused to the faithful of two kingdoms, that their desires may be gratified ? It is finally objected that no *ordinary* jurisdiction is committed to bishops out of the limits of their own dioceses; and therefore that the power now to be conferred, must necessarily be *delegated*.—I answer: The *ordinary* jurisdiction of bishops is more ancient than the division and limits of districts : besides, by the late regulation of Paul V. the Nuncio residing in

France

France was appointed the *ordinary* of England and Scotland."*

The energy of this *Memorial* gained attention; for within a few days, Mr. Bennet was permitted to deliver into the cardinals the names of three gentlemen, Dr. Kellifon, Dr. Bifhop, and Dr. Smith, perfons, he faid, nominated and approved by the clergy. Here was matter for new deliberation, and it confumed more than two months.

They were men of tried virtue and of large endowments; but in the eyes of their adverfaries and of the Roman court, that virtue and thofe endowments were tarnifhed with many ftains.—Dr. Kellifon, the prefident of the college in Douay, had been long labouring to fubvert the Jefuitical controul, which had oppreffed and difgraced his feminary. He was alfo fufpected of not being fufficiently hoftile to the oath of allegiance.—Dr. Bifhop's fins were manifold. He, the reader will recollect, had originally oppofed the archprieft, had come to Rome, where he was immured under the eye of father Parfons, had himfelf penned and figned the *Proteftation* of allegiance to Elizabeth,
and

---

* Tranfact, p. 20.

and was also said not to execrate the oath.— Dr. Smith had been recently at Rome, an agent from the clergy, and his whole behaviour there was fresh upon recollection. "And "truly upon my conscience," had father Parsons said of him, "I never dealt with any man in "my life more heady and resolute in his "opinions than is the doctor."*

<small>Dr. Bishop is nominated to the see of Chalcedon.</small>

On whom of so unworthy a triumvirate shall the lot then fall? — Dr. Bishop was thought to be agreeable to the English court; and besides, he was in his 70th year, when death, it might be presumed, would soon lay his mitre low, and place the English church in its usual state of anarchy. He, therefore, in February 1623 was declared *bishop Elect of Chalcedon*; and a *Bull* for his consecration was issued on the 15th of the ensuing month, which was followed on the 23d, by a *Brief* specifying his destination and commission for England. He was consecrated at Paris, where he had resided some years, and, on the 31st of July, arrived in England.†

---

* Dodd, vol. 2, p. 487.

† Dodd, ib. p. 362.

INTRODUCTION.

With its wonted partiality, as it seems to me, and, in some regards, insincerity of narration, the *Relation* of the Regulars thus represents this event. "Gregory XV." it says, "had just been raised to the pontifical chair, when the English "clergy, whose practice it almost ever is to occupy the first "openings of the new court, as best adapted to their projects, "again sent agents to Rome. The king had suspended the "severe execution of the laws, under the hope, that it would "facilitate a dispensation, should the projected match succeed "between the Infanta and his son. Of this circumstance the "clergy availed themselves to press more warmly their petition "for a bishop. The cardinals were divided in opinion; while "they who were most conversant with the affairs of England, "viewing the present calm as the forerunner of a greater "tempest, opined that nothing should be changed. But "cardinal Bandini, whom letters from the king of England "had drawn over to favour the dispensation, and whose "influence with the pontiff and his nephew Ludovisi was "predominant, was of a contrary opinion; and his advice "prevailed. Wherefore, the long-solicited point was finally "granted, and William Bishop was nominated to the see of "Chalcedon, himself one of the thirteen priests, who, in the "year 1602, had signed that *Protestation* of allegiance so greatly "injurious to the apostolic see."

From the nomination of the bishop of Chalcedon an. 1623, to the agency of Panzani an. 1644.

<small>Extent and nature of the powers granted to the bishop.</small>

THE *Bull** for Dr. Bishop's consecration to the see of Chalcedon was sufficiently ample, conveyed in the usual style of the Roman court, wherein the lowly *servus servorum* soon drops the menial character, and rises to the demeanour and lordly energy of an all-powerful monarch. He is appointed, *post longum mentis nostræ discursum*, to the church of Chalcedon in the ancient Bithynia; but his residence, *speciali gratia*, is dispensed with, so long as that church remain in the hands of infidels. — The *Brief*,† which directs the exercise of his jurisdiction to the kingdoms of England and Scotland, specifies the powers with which he is invested: " When " thou shalt be arrived in those kingdoms, we " grant

---

* Dodd, vol. 2, p. 465.

† Id. vol. 3, p. 7.

"grant unto thee licence, *ad noſtrum et ſedis apoſtolicæ beneplacitum*, freely and lawfully to enjoy and uſe all and each thoſe faculties lately committed by our predeceſſors to the *archprieſts*, as alſo ſuch as *ordinaries* enjoy and exerciſe in their cities and dioceſes."—Theſe two inſtruments were followed by a *Decree*,* enabling him to chuſe a vicar general, and appoint ſuch other officers as he might judge neceſſary; but which terminated with this general clauſe, that the whole of the powers and juriſdiction granted him ſhould ceaſe, whenever England returned to the Catholic faith, and its ſees were filled with regular miniſters.

It is true, as I have ſtated, that the clergy applied for a biſhop with *ordinary juriſdiction*, meaning he ſhould be no Roman *delegate*, as the three archprieſts had recently been: it is likewiſe true, that Dr. Biſhop, as will be ſeen, was received in England as ſuch, that he viewed himſelf as ſuch, and that the general language of the papal inſtruments imported as much; ſtill when we conſider the ſaving clauſe, *ad noſtrum et ſedis apoſtolicæ beneplacitum*, applied to the exerciſe of that juriſdiction which is alone eſſential

---

* Id. vol. 2, p. 466.

essential to bishops, (such as *ordinaries* enjoy and exercise are the words of the *Brief*,) it must be admitted that the power granted was *revocable at will*, that it was therefore a *delegated* power, and that Dr. Bishop was no more than a *vicar apostolic* vested with *ordinary* jurisdiction. The events which soon followed under his successor will evince more clearly the truth of this observation. Thus was the artful policy of the Roman court, which never willingly lets go a power it has once been permitted to exercise, rendered more conspicuous; and the clergy's agent, Mr. Bennet, did but shew how completely his honesty was duped, when, having read the *Brief* of his holiness, in exultation of mind he was heard to exclaim, *rem habemus, verba non moramur!* *

<small>He is well received, and institutes his Chapter.</small>

The bishop was received with great marks of respect by the clergy and laity. The monks of the Benedictin order† also came forward, welcoming him as *ordinary* of England, and promising filial love and reverence; nor do I find that, openly at least, his government was opposed by any.

Those

---

* *Transact.* p. 36.

† Dodd, vol. 2, p. 467, 8.

INTRODUCTION.

Thofe monks, it may be proper to obferve, had been lately formed into an Englifh congregation, having eftablifhed themfelves in different houfes abroad: and about the year 1617, the friars of the order of St. Francis had been founded in Douay. Of thefe orders fome were now in England.

The general ftate of Catholics continued fuch as I have defcribed it, favoured clandeftinely by the king, whofe mind was ftill fixed on the Spanifh match, but daily haraffed by the popular or puritanic party both in and out of parliament. The utter diflike the nation had expreffed of that alliance, ferved to foment the general odium of popery; but the match broke off, and with it vanifhed the brilliant dream the Catholics had indulged of a returning happinefs.

Meanwhile, the bifhop of Chalcedon proceeded in his functions; and to obviate, as far as might be, the repetition of fuch attempts as had often difgraced the Catholic caufe, and to give a permanent fecurity to an eftablifhment, of which he thought himfelf the canonical head, with the advice of many able canonifts, he inftituted a Dean and Chapter, as a ftanding *fenate* and *council* for his own affiftance, and, *fede vacante*,

INTRODUCTION.

vacante, to exercise *Epifcopal ordinary jurifdiction.**
That his power, if truly epifcopal, extended to this, the difcipline of all ages had clearly evinced. But fome doubts feemed to hang on his mind: "What defect," he fays, "may be in my "powers, I fhall fupplicate his holinefs to "make good from the plenitude of his own."†
The number of canons was 19, at the head of whom was Mr. Colleton, the dean, a man whofe firm integrity I have already praifed. At the fame time, for the government of the diftant provinces, our prelate appointed five vicars general, and twenty archdeacons, with a certain number of rural deans.‡

Now,

---

* Dodd, vol. ii. p. 468, 470.

† *Inftrumentum Capituli*, Dodd, p. 468.

‡ The *Relation* of the Regulars thus, in a few words, difpatches the hiftory of this interefting tranfaction: "How "great was the *wonder*, rather the *fcandal* which this unexpected "novelty (the appointment of a bifhop) excited in the minds "of the Englifh Catholics, can hardly be expreffed, particu- "larly when they perceived this bifhop of Chalcedon *ufurp* the "name of *ordinary*, and more than the power of a patriarch, "in erecting a *chapter*, and appointing over it a dean in the "perfon of Colleton, who was another of the 13 priefts that "had figned the *Proteftation*."——How admirably do thefe few lines delineate the genuine fpirit of party.

INTRODUCTION.

Reflections on our new hierarchy.

Now, it seemed to many, that the English Catholic church was re-established in the renovation of her hierarchy. But the fond imagination, I fear, was founded on no truth; or, if it could, at this time, be said that we had a church, there was no period, since the reformation, in which it might not have been asserted with equal propriety. The archpriests, it is allowed, were delegated agents; and such, I have shewn, was the bishop of Chalcedon. His commission was more extensive, but his powers were *revocable* at the will of his employer, *ad nostrum et sedis apostolicæ beneplacitum*. It is not with such a precarious head that any *ordinary* jurisdiction is exercised; that a hierarchy is established; that a church is formed. The Roman pontiff still continued to be, what the clergy of England had, for many years, *permitted* him to be, their only bishop How then, with him at our head, could it, in the estimation of such men, be said, that we were without a church, and a hierarchy of transcendent excellence? He governed us, at one time, by the agency of Dr. Allen, perhaps by that of father Parsons; at another by his archpriests; now by the bishop of Chalcedon; and in after times, as it will appear, by a series of similar delegations. To the pride of some minds such an extraordinary œconomy might be flattering.

But

But the reader will recollect an opinion, which I expressed on better grounds,* namely, that we always had a church, because we always had a priesthood regularly succeeding in the ministry over a believing flock, and united to the common centre of unity. And if the hierarchy, of which this priesthood is a component part, was imperfect, let the blame fall where it should, either on the clergy, who, instructed by venerable antiquity, neglected obvious means to give to themselves and the faithful a regular superintendant pastor, or on the Roman bishop, who, when applied to by reiterated petitions, agreeably to the rules of a more modern discipline, refused compliance, prefering rather to see the remains of the British church unassisted in its spiritual exigencies, than to part from a power which a vain prerogative had established. The title of *universal bishop* which St. Gregory, with the strongest expressions of horror, had rejected from him,† his successors, in later days, seemed fondly to ambition; at least, in their conduct to the British Catholics, they have, to the present hour, retained the proud preeminence, and exercised it. And let it be remarked that, in the face of the bishops
assembled

---

* Page 42.   † Lib. 4. ep. 32. lib. 7. ep. 30.

assembled at Trent, that was the favourite position defended by Lainez and Salmeron, as I before remarked, two jesuits, who, in the principles of their new-born society, dared to think that the divine hierarchy of the church was concentred on the head of him, to whom they had made a special vow of obedience.

The auspicious opening of Dr. Bishop's government, which seemed to promise peace and a reunion of sentiments, was soon clouded over. He died April 16, 1624, aged 71. *The bishop of Chalcedon dies.*

On the decease of the bishop, the chapter he had elected assumed ordinary jurisdiction, as canonically devolved on them, *sede vacante*, and in their own name applied to Rome for a successor. Urban VIII. was then pope. Fortunately, to enforce the supplication of the chapter, a new petitioner came forward. The Spanish match was at an end; and a treaty had commenced between the prince and Henrietta Maria, daughter of Henry IV. of France, and sister of Louis XIII. a few months before the death of the English king. The moment was favourable: for, with a view, doubtless, to obtain more easily from Rome the dispensation, which his sister's marriage, he trusted, would soon render necessary, the French monarch seemed to interest himself much *Dr. Richard Smith is appointed his successor.*

INTRODUCTION.

much in the concerns of the English Catholics. He had even sent the archbishop of Embrun to the English court, privately to negociate for them with the old king a greater toleration.* In the marriage articles which ensued, some indulgence was stipulated in their favour; and by the tenth, the princess was to be allowed a bishop for her almoner. Still, from motives of a distant policy, his holiness reluctantly granted a dispensation, which reluctance he even signified in a letter of some elegance and of much laboured artifice to the princess.† It was the difference of religion in the parties that rendered the dispensation necessary.

Under these circumstances, Dr. Richard Smith was finally elected bishop, and appointed to the same see of Chalcedon, February 4, 1625. The reader will recollect that he had been placed on the former list with Dr. Bishop, and that he was the same who, some years before, deputed to Rome by the clergy, had given offence, by his firmness, to father Parsons and his faction. His behaviour, on that occasion, and his general character conspiring

---

* Rapin, vol. ii. p. 232.

† Dodd, vol. iii. 168.

spiring with it, paved the way for the opposition which ensued. He was at Paris, when the news of his appointment came, where for some time he had resided, in habits, it is said, of intimacy with cardinal Richelieu, the favourite minister of Louis XIII.* †

As the title of the new bishop was the same as that of his predecessor, so likewise were his powers, specified in a similar Bull, and in a Brief of equal import. Only, after stating in the words of the former brief, " *at our and the apostolic see's good pleasure*, that his faculties were those of the late archpriests, joined to those which ordinaries enjoy and exercise," it adds, by way, it should appear, of a more explicit declaration: " *And we delegate thee to all and every one of the premised by the aforesaid authority*

Powers of the new bishop.

---

* Dodd, vol. iii. p. 76, 77, 78.

† The *Relation* of the Regulars thus speaks: " These most foul innovations, *(see the last remark by the same authors on Dr. Bishop,)* which tended to the overthrow of religion, rendered the apostolic see afterwards less tractable, when on the death of Dr. Bishop, application was made for a successor. The matter was long in suspence, till, the match with Spain being broken off, the aid of the Christian king was implored. And to this application, which cardinal Richelieu also enforced, Urban finally gave way, appointing Dr. Smith, the friend of Richelieu, to the see of Chalcedon, with the same powers as his predecessor had enjoyed."

" *rity and tenor.*" To Dr. Bifhop the Brief had faid, which here alfo it repeats; "By apoftolic "authority we give to thee licence and "faculty," to ufe the above powers.

I am, therefore, authorifed to draw the obvious inference which I did before, that Dr. Smith was a Roman *delegate*, or, in other words, an *apoftolic vicar*, furnifhed with ordinary powers, revocable at the will of his holinefs. And that, in the fenfe of the Roman court, he was no more than its agent, will hereafter be manifeft, though he ftyled himfelf, and was ftyled by others, *Ordinarius Angliæ et Scotiæ*. Soon after his confecration he came to England.

As to the general ftate of politics, regarding the Englifh Catholics, at this time, they are too well known to require repetition. To them, as to many others, the reign of Charles opened with a gloomy afpect, notwithftanding the difpofitions of the court and even of the church were favourable: for that court and that church were themfelves menaced; and ruin foon involved them both. Proclamations againft the Catholics were iffued, and the fevereft execution of the laws was called for; but

---

* Dodd vol. iii. p. 7.

but the tolerant spirit of the king still shielded them from harm. They had much, however, to suffer from certain low offices called *Pursuivants*, who, during this reign, enjoyed an almost unlimited power to search their houses, and distress them on the most unprovoked occasions. Yet, under every oppression from their enemies, they still persecuted one another; and the inveteracy of party remained unabated. But the following *Memoirs* will best detail the succession of these events, which finally compelled Dr. Smith, after a residence of four years, to withdraw into France.—Here, therefore, I shall pause.

THE
MEMOIRS OF PANZANI, &c.

WHEN several ages of plenty and ease had corrupted the English church, and wretchedly disposed the whole nation for that remarkable defection which happened in the year 1533, under the illustrious and powerful prince, Henry VIII. the cause of religion, in the succeeding reigns, experienced a various fate. Edward VI. made a further progress in the Reformation; but queen Mary laboured to close the breach, and was on the point of succeeding, when Providence cut her off to make way for Elizabeth, whose long and prosperous reign settled the *Reformation* on a lasting basis.

Towards the end of Mary's reign nearly one half of the Roman Catholic bishops had been swept away, and those that survived her saw not many years of queen Elizabeth; so that, in a little time, the old religion was confined to a small number of the inferior clergy, and it was obvious to think, that, these dying off,

Introduction.

the English nation would soon be unanimous in the profession of the reformed doctrine.— It was this melancholy reflection that roused William Allen,* a graduate of Oxford (and afterwards a cardinal) to provide against the impending evil, by collecting into a body the scattered remains of both universities, who forming a seminary might supply the places of the old clergy, as these should die away. Accordingly a college, for that purpose, was erected by him at Douay in Flanders, under the protection of Phillip II. king of Spain, and of Gregory XIII. bishop of Rome. Success answered his designs: and immediately after the foundation (which was an. 1568, the tenth of Elizabeth) some priests were sent over into England, who inspired new vigour into those who were well disposed to the old religion, confirming some, and reclaiming others. By degrees, other colleges were erected with the same view, at Rome, Valladolid, Seville, St. Omer's, &c. And thus the clergy continued their succession, while the religion of their ancestors was preserved amongst all ranks of people.

Nor was it long before other Englishmen, such as had entered into religious orders in Flanders, France,

---

* See Introduc. p. 20.

France, Italy, and Spain, obtained permission from their respective superiors, to engage in the same work, so that the Jesuits, Benedictins, Franciscans, &c. joining themselves as auxiliaries to the clergy, came into the harvest. The common cause was carried on with success; but the different domestic views of the labourers insensibly generated some confusion, and the clergy proved to be the sufferers. The regulars being bodies incorporate, were better cemented in order to maintain their interest. The clergy acted separately, were unguarded, and without a head to unite them in one common concern. And of this defect they were soon made sensible: for whereas hitherto they had been supported by contributions, which regularly passed through their own hands, these charities now began to turn into other channels, and though originally designed for them, were disposed of to other persons. They were jostled out of their places to make way for others of a more plausible education. Many of their leading men were every day debauched to enrol themselves in other bodies: and what was the source of the greatest evil, the Jesuits being made superiors of the colleges (as in that at Rome particularly) where the clergy received their education, this obliged the latter to live in a state of dependence and unbecoming submission. Much ill blood was the consequence of this heterogeneous education.

Under thefe circumftances, the clergy had but one way left to make their condition tolerable, which was to petition his holinefs, that he would fend a bifhop into England, to infpect and govern the general concerns of religion. Towards the clofe of Elizabeth's reign this fcheme was much preffed, and it feemed to promife fuccefs, when fuddenly the pope was made to believe that the meafure would be extremely prejudicial to the Catholic caufe.* Father Parfons, therefore, propofed a new fcheme, and by his contrivance two clergymen of diftinction were privately difpatched to Rome,† who, in the name of the clergy, (though few of them were acquainted with the defign,) entreated to be governed by an archprieft. To this dignity Mr. George Blackwell was appointed, whofe private inftructions from cardinal Cajetan were, to do nothing without having firft advifed with the jefuits: yet, for form fake, he had twelve clergymen joined with him by way of affiftants, the majority of whom were known to be entirely devoted to the fathers.‡

The

---

* Introduction, p. 45.   † Ibid.

‡ Ibid. p. 49.

The clergy being unthinkingly drawn into this fcheme, were at a lofs how to extricate themfelves. The more intelligent among them were of opinion, that his holinefs (Clement VIII.) was a ftranger to the whole affair; in which they were confirmed by the archprieft's acting folely by the ftrength of the cardinal's conftituent letters, who was himfelf indefatigable in promoting the intereft of the jefuits. Wherefore, to be further fatisfied, fome of the leading men of the clergy deferred paying obedience to the archprieft's orders, till he had brought better and more authentic proofs of the authority faid to be conferred upon him. In the mean time, the jefuits were very loud in their complaints againft the non-complying clergy, and defended the archprieft's power, as if it had been (and as it really was) a fcheme of their own. Father Lifter, in a pamphlet concerning *fchifm*, declared thofe that ftood off to be, *ipfo facto*, deprived of their ecclefiaftical powers, and to be treated no otherwife than as fchifmatics. The clergy, on the other hand, appealed to his holinefs, and were finally liftened to, Clement iffuing a Brief, which, though it confirmed and eftablifhed the fcheme of an archprieft, yet it cleared the appellants from cenfure, forbidding the archprieft, for the future, to advife with the jefuits, with exprefs orders that three of the appealing priests should be made his assistants.*

For several years the clergy continued under this œconomy (from 1598 to 1623) under three archpriests, Blackwell, Birket, and Harrison. This last gentleman, sensible of the many inconveniences which attended the arrangement, resolved, as well from his own inclination, as at the request of all the eminent men among the clergy, once more to try the court of Rome concerning a bishop to govern the mission. Wherefore, some encouragement being given,† in the year 1622, Mr. John Bennet was sent in the quality of agent to Rome, with a common letter, and the names of several candidates for the episcopal dignity, viz. William Bishop, Matthew Kellison, Richard Smith, Edward Bennet, John Boswell, and Cuthbert Trollop. And that the regulars might take no umbrage at this agency, it was rumoured that Mr. Bennet went to Rome in order to facilitate some matters in relation to the match with Spain.

To

---

* Introduction, p. 65.

† Ibid. p. 92.

To this petition of the clergy Rome assented; and Dr. William Bishop was soon afterwards consecrated at Paris with the title of bishop of Chalcedon in Asia minor. He went over into England, where he was kindly received by all the regulars, even by the jesuits, entering on his jurisdiction by appointing seven vicars, and several archdeacons and rural deans. Also, by a power of which he deemed himself possessed, he erected a chapter of 24 canons, purposing to have the plan confirmed and ratified by the court of Rome; and for the greater solemnity gave to this chapter a common seal with an impression of St. Thomas of Canterbury. In a little time, he made up some breaches between the clergy and the Benedictin monks; and was in a fair way of bringing over the jesuits to a like temper.

Dr. Bishop died in 1624; and was, not long after, succeeded by Richard Smith, he being also consecrated at Paris by the pope's nuncio Spada, with the same title of bishop of Chalcedon. In the beginning of April 1625 he went into England, and adopted all his predecessor's measures, confirming what he had done as to the methods of executing his jurisdiction. For two years he peaceably styled himself the *ordinary of England*; only a certain tract written by a jesuit, under the title of
Responsio

Controversy between Dr. Smith, bishop of Chalcedon, and the Regulars.

Responsio ad quemdam magnum Prælatum gave an alarm. It treated of the privileges of regular orders; and is suppofed to have excited the laity to more than a commendable curiofity and inquifitivenefs concerning the bifhop's power.

About this time, in April 1627, there happened a more public and direct occafion of having thefe matters looked into. Benjamin Norton, one of his lordfhip's vicars, having confidered a Bull publifhed by Pius V. *(Romani pontificis,)* which directed that regulars fhould not hear the confeffions of lay perfons without the ordinary's approbation, (the council of Trent being alfo exprefs in requiring the fame,*) was difpofed to believe that the bifhop of Chalcedon ought to proceed according to that order. This difficulty being ftarted, and made known to feveral lay perfons, penitents to the regulars, they reflected fo long upon it, that the fcruple, at laft, grew too big for them. The bifhop himfelf had often privately confidered the point; but, not to difturb the regulars, he fuffered them to proceed conformably with their own principles. Now, however, underftanding that the confciences of many were entangled, he thought it

---

* Sefs. 23. c. 15.

it his duty to declare himself, and accordingly, having called together the superiors of the jesuits and of the Benedictin monks, he frankly opened his mind, and told them, it was his opinion that no regular ought to hear a lay person's confession without the ordinary's approbation. They acquiesced, and for some time requested his approbation. But having more maturely weighed the case among themselves, they flew off, alledging that the pope, being the *universal ordinary* of the whole church, had sufficiently qualified them to hear any one's confession by express faculties granted for the mission; and for the future they were resolved, they said, not to seek the bishop of Chalcedon's approbation. Afterwards, to strengthen their interest, they drew in some leading men of the laity to countenance their practice, among whom were Sir Thomas Brudenal, Sir Basil Brook, Sir Toby Mathews, &c. this last being himself esteemed a jesuit and in priest's orders.* The Benedictin monks were zealous in the same cause. They had a learned man in their body, father Preston,† who busily engaged in the controversy, and by several odious questions

---

* Dodd, vol. iii. p, 59, 155, 156.

† *Alias* Roger Widdrington, Dodd, vol. ii. p. 420.

questions proposed amongst the laity, he made them very uneasy under the jurisdiction claimed by the bishop. Father Preston was seconded by father David, another learned man of the same order, who wrote a Treatise on the subject, and sent the manuscript to Rome. By degrees, a general attack was made on his lordship's pretensions, and several writings were handed about on both sides.

The Bishop, in the mean time, thought it his duty not to be idle. He addressed himself by a *Letter* to the laity, explaining the nature of his jurisdiction, and asserting his claim to ordinary power. This was ill taken by many; and in opposition to it the three lay gentlemen above mentioned drew up an artificial *Remonstrance*, in the name of all the lay Catholics in England. The writing was left at the bishop's lodgings; but he being abroad, it fell into the hands of Mr. Edward Bennet, his vicar general. Copies were dispersed into other hands; and it failed not to have the desired effect with many. But soon the artifice was detected, a great majority of the laity signing a paper of a contrary tendency, in favour of the bishop.— By this time all the regulars were agreed to oppose the bishop; for though the superior of the Dominicans, in the beginning, ordered all under his inspection to submit, yet he afterwards

was

was brought over to the other party. Father Preston, the champion of the cause, was ordered to write a *Letter*, by way of justification of their proceedings, in which the following bold assertions were noticed, viz: That episcopal authority was directly contrary to law; that it was odious to the nation; that it was pernicious, in the present juncture, to the Catholic cause.— The bishop answered this *Letter* by a MS entitled a *Synopsis*. Father Barlow then, president of the monks, in the name of the whole congregation (of monks) published a book an. 1627, under the title of *Mandatum*, &c.* which reflected much both on the bishop and the clergy. He lays it down as a principle that, the council of Trent not being received in England, its decrees could have no binding force in matters of discipline. —This book the bishop judged proper to send to the Inquisition at Rome, enclosing an answer to it in the same packet, with the reasons he went on in adhering to his claim.

The controversy, by this time, was undertaken by several learned men abroad. Among others, Dr. Kellison, president of the English college at Douay, published (an. 1629), his *De Hierarchia Ecclesiastica contra anarchiam Calvini*. The

---

* Dodd, vol. 3. p. 157.

The book, by impartial perfons, was regarded as a modeft performance; but as it feemed to exprefs the neceffity of epifcopal government, and to exclude regulars from the hierarchy of the church, it hugely provoked all of that party, efpecially the Jefuits who decried it with great vehemency. Two anfwers quickly appeared againft it; one entitled *Brevis et modefta difcuffio affertionum Kellifoni*, &c. (an. 1631) under the borrowed name of Nicholas Smith, but really by Edward Knott, fuperior of the Jefuits: The other entitled *Apologia pro modo procedendi Sanctæ fedis apoftolicæ*, &c. (an. 1631) with the name of Daniel a Jefu, but believed *(known)* to be the work of father John Floyd, an Englifh Jefuit. Thefe pieces were firft publifhed in Englifh, and afterwards tranflated into Latin with fome foftening alterations.

The controverfy engages the French Divines.

Very foon the controverfy became public among the French divines, on the following occafion. — Father Knott, defirous that his work fhould appear in the world with fome reputation, fent it to Paris to be reviewed by one father Rivandier, an Auguftine friar and a doctor of Sorbonne; and he, without confulting the univerfity, gave his approbation to it. The faculty of Sorbonne, being made acquainted with the matter, took upon them to examine both the above-mentioned books, and finding feveral things in them deferving

of

of censure, they extracted certain propositions, and condemned them an. 1631. The French bishops, in like manner, censured the doctrine of the said books as highly injurious to the hierarchy of the church and the episcopal order.—And now the jesuits, having fresh work upon their hands, for a while left the bishop of Chalcedon, and turned all their force against the censures of the Sorbonne and of the French bishops. One Hermannus Loemelius, pretending to be a canon of St. Omer's, but in truth father Floyd himself, publishes two pamphlets against the doctors of Sorbonne and the bishops; the one entitled *Spongia*, &c. the other *Querimonia Ecclesiæ Anglicanæ*, &c.—Two other pamphlets were also published of the same tendency, under the name of George White; but these likewise were ascribed to the same hand. Their titles were, *Vindiciæ Nicholai Smithei*, and *Epistola ad Episcopos Galliæ*, prefixed to the Latin copy of Daniel a Jesu.—But among all the works published on these matters, none gave more scandal than a burlesque piece against the censure of Sorbonne, called the *Censure of the Apostles Creed* in Latin, which was also given to John Floyd.* The doctrine of this piece

bore

---

* The author rather appears to have been Theophile Raynaud, a French jesuit. Panzani is mistaken in saying
the

bore so hard on episcopacy, that the archbishop of Canterbury expressed his surprise that any divine of the church of Rome should be the author of it.

Under this provocation, and when the doctors of Sorbonne, and the bishops of France, were thus insulted, three eloquent and learned writers of that nation undertook to defend the censures they had given. These were Francis Hallier, Nicholas le Maitre, and Petrus Aurelius, who, in several learned works (some whereof were printed at the public expence of the French clergy) vigorously and eloquently supported the dignity of the episcopal order.

The pope interposes.

But Urban, acquainted with all the progress of the English Controversy, at last interposed his authority, and commanded silence to both parties; whereon the bishop of Chalcedon, to shew his inclination for peace, without further application, approved, in general terms, of all the

---

the doctrine of this *Censure* bears hard upon episcopacy. It is a profane composition, designed to intimate that the works, which the Sorbonne and French bishops had censured, were truly as orthodox as the creed of the Apostles. The direct tendency of those works was to vilify and overturn the hierarchical order in the church.

Abregé Chron. de l'hist. Eccle. vol. iii. *p.* 434.

the faculties of the regulars. These seemed pleased with the measure at home, as it was a means of quieting the consciences of many of the laity; but at Rome they exclaimed against it, as a derogation from their privileges, and a lessening of the pope's authority. Wherefore his holiness *declared* that the regulars, by virtue of their apostolic mission, were exempted from the canons that required episcopal approbation; but that the bishop of Chalcedon might claim a jurisdiction as to the three parochial sacraments.* To this order the bishop also submitted. Still the regulars continued to complain, that his Lordship was obnoxious, and troublesome upon several other accounts. Father Barlow's book, termed *Mandatum*, was busily handed about, not only among the Catholics, but among the Protestants, till several of the privy council had a sight of it, who, impressed with the idea of the danger of a Catholic bishop by the arguments made use of by that author, acquainted the king with it. A resolution, soon after this, was taken that the bishop of Chalcedon should not be be permitted to remain in the kingdom. The juncture of affairs at that time also seemed to require that
caution:

---

* Dodd, vol. 3, p. 158. The *Brief* here alluded to was never canonically published, and was by many, at the time, deemed spurious or surreptitious. Dodd, vol. 3, p. 13.

caution: for England and France being engaged in, or preparing for a war, it was thought too great a condescension to admit of a Catholic bishop, in compliment to a nation with which they were at enmity.

<small>Proceedings against the bishop.</small>

Nor was it long before a Proclamation was issued out against the bishop, which obliged him to lie concealed; but it had no further effect; and no search was made. This disappointed many, who had hoped that the pope would now have recalled him. Wherefore a second Proclamation came out an 1629,* importing banishment and a reward of a hundred pounds to any one who should seize him. Neither had this any further consequence. No enquiry was made after him: the Catholics were not disturbed on his account: he still performed his functions privately; and what favoured him more, the French and English were now concluding a peace. On the the arrival of an ambassador from France, Monsieur Chateauneuf, the bishop was entertained in his family with great freedom and security, the king himself being privy to it. When Chateauneuf was recalled, and the Marquis de la Fontaine succeeded to him, the bishop continued to enjoy the same privilege of

---

* Dodd, ib. p. 143, 4.

of residing in his family, with every opportunity of exercising his functions.

In the mean time, the regulars, or at least their adherents, were very uneasy; and they drew up a declaration privately,* which signified that the Catholics were generally displeased with the bishop's behaviour. This paper was delivered by a certain nobleman to Don Carlos Colonna, the Spanish embassador, and affirmed to contain the sentiments of all the laity: and that he might not discover the fraud, it was only given into his hands the day before he left London. However, care was taken to disabuse the Roman Catholics at home. The marquis de la Fontaine and other embassadors in London were informed, that the Catholics were not so universally averse to their bishop as was reported: and this was made to appear by a common *subscription*† of the lay gentlemen to another paper, drawn up in English, Latin, and French. La Fontaine, in particular, also signed an attestation, that the number of those who were friendly to an episcopal superior far exceeded the other. Finally the queen herself, an. 1632, wrote to

---

* Dodd, ib. p. 143, 149, 150.

† Ibid, p. 142.

the pope, assuring his holiness, that the case was misrepresented, and that the common voice of the Catholics was in favour of the episcopal order.*

He is compelled to withdraw into France.

During these contests, the bishop of Chalcedon was advised to withdraw himself out of England, at least for a time. He did so.† But his

---

* Dodd, ib. p. 141.

† The order of events, as stated by Panzani, is not accurate.—The contest began, as related, in the year 1627, and on the occasion, as related. Various little publications, on both sides, then appeared, when the bishop, to ease the minds of the laity and to soften the asperity of controversy, publicly signified his approbation of the regulars' powers, *pendente lite*, that is, till his holiness should decide. (Dodd, vol. 3, p. 138.) But his holiness decided against the bishop, and admonished him to drop the appellation of *ordinary of England*, which belonged not to the *bishop of Chalcedon*, whose powers were delegated *ad sedis apostolicæ beneplacitum*. (Dodd, ibid, p. 14.) The contest, however, endured, till government was prevailed on to issue a first and second proclamation, March 29, an. 1629, which compelled Dr. Smith to leave England. Now Dr. Kellison wrote his *Hierarchia*, which was followed by other works, as mentioned by Panzani. The surreptitious *Declaration* against the bishop was procured soon after his departure to the Continent, when his return or the appointment of a successor was apprehended; and the counter-*Memorial*, (Dodd, p. 142,) conveying the just sentiments of attachment of the Catholics to episcopal government appeared in the year 1631. In the same year the Brief *Britannia*, which, by many, I said, was deemed spurious, but which I judge to be genuine, found its way into England through the hands of the Regulars. Dodd, p. 150.

his adverfaries to follow the blow (apprehending another would be fent in his place,) procured a fecond fignature among the Catholics; and in order to induce them to it, they gave it out that the bifhop of Chalcedon's defigns were tyrannical; that he attempted to demand tythes; that he forced his vifits upon them; that he claimed a power of placing and difplacing confeffors at pleafure; that he purpofed erecting a court for the proving of wills. Even they perfuaded Lord Morley, who, for feveral years, on very juft grounds, had lived feparate from his wife, that he would be compelled by the bifhop's orders to recall her.

His holinefs being acquainted with all thefe proceedings, and being fenfible of the common infirmity of mankind, which inclines them to tell their ftory to their own advantage, advifed with his chief minifter, cardinal Barberini,* by what means he could come to a true knowledge of the differences between the clergy and the regulars in England. Himfelf as well as the cardinal had ever fhewn a particular refpect for the Englifh nation, as well from a general wifh of re-uniting them once more to the fee of Rome, as from a certain natural fympathy

marginal note: His holinefs fends Panzani into England.

---

* The pope's nephew.

which seemed to engage their affections. Several inuendoes had been given to them, that the court party was not averse towards keeping up some kind of correspondence. They, therefore, came to a resolution to send over an agent, at once to inform themselves of the true state of affairs among the Catholics, and to feel the pulse of the nation with regard to other concerns. But the person proper for this employment must be a man unprejudiced in the general business of the controversy, and an inoffensive observer in other matters. He that was chosen for this office was Gregory Panzani, of Arrezo, a secular priest of experienced virtue, of singular address, of polite learning, and in all respects well qualified for the business. The queen was first made acquainted with the design; and she communicated it to the king, who gave his tacit consent: but, at the same time, singular care was taken that the matter should not be divulged, among the Catholics or Protestants, who, from different views, might have obstructed its execution. In a little time, a favourable occasion offered for effecting the project. Monsignor Mazarin being deputed Nuncio extraordinary to the court of France, Panzani joined him as an attendant; and having made some stay in Paris, the latter privately passed over into England, under the pretence of satisfying his curiosity with the fashions and
customs

cuftoms of the country, as other ftrangers often did. (This was towards the end of the year 1634.)

Panzani's firft vifit, on his arrival in London, was to the queen, being introduced by father Robert Philip, her majefty's confeffor. He prefented her with a letter from cardinal Barberini. She had expected one from his holinefs; but, through the fecretary's neglect, it had been omitted, and arrived not till the 3d of January, 1635.—At this interview, Panzani acquainted her majefty with the extraordinary refpect, both Urban VIII. and the cardinal entertained for her; and took the liberty to mention fome inftances that had rendered her an object of their efteem, particularly that, by her intereft, eafe had been procured for the Catholics, and the blow averted with which they had been recently threatened. In the cardinal's name he requefted, that fhe would fhew herfelf a parent to that neglected handful of people, and ufe her intereft to bring them to a good underftanding among themfelves, who of late had been unhappily divided.—The queen returned an anfwer fuitable to the occafion: That fhe valued herfelf for the efteem thofe two great perfonages entertained for her; and that it was not the firft time, fhe had been favoured with undeniable proofs of the cardinal's affection.

He is introduced to the queen.

She promifed that nothing fhould be wanting on her part, towards procuring further eafe for the Catholics, as alfo for uniting them amongft themfelves; adding, that the abfence of their bifhop was a great detriment to them, and that fhe, in particular, was fenfibly affected by the lofs. Panzani then acquainted her majefty in general terms, that his holinefs expected the Catholics fhould be exact and fcrupulous in their civil allegiance to the king and government; and that he hoped his majefty would not prefs them beyond the known limits of their duty in matters of religion. He alfo requefted, that his arrival might be notified to the king, with the occafion of it.

When the queen fignified the event to his majefty, his only reply was, that Panzani fhould be cautious, and carry on his bufinefs with fecrecy, and above all things, not to intermeddle in ftate affairs.

Panzani then communicated a common letter to the regulars, which he had brought with him from the cardinal.

Panzani defcribes the general ftate of things in a letter to Barberini.

It may be obferved that, though the Catholics had many enemies in England, yet the court party was very moderate. They had heard many inftances of Urban's good-nature; and the queen's religion was an awe on many. The

The language of the nation was not fo bitter and fcurrilous againſt the pope, as in former times it had been, when parties were debating his jurifdiction. The king himfelf, as he was a perfon of ſtrict virtue and of great benevolence, frequently intimated that he had no averfion to feveral pretenfions of the Roman Catholic party. Of this Panzani takes notice in a letter to cardinal Barberini, dated February 16, 1635, in which he mentions an inſtance of the king's good inclinations, which, fince his coming to England, he had himfelf obferved. — One of the famous preachers, he fays, having bitterly inveighed againſt fchifm in a fermon before the king: his majeſty was heard afterwards to fay, " that he would willingly have " parted with one of his hands, rather than " fuch a fchifm fhould have ever happened." On which one of the courtiers, who was familiar with the king, begged his majeſty to talk foftly, as fuch fpeeches were very dangerous. The king inſtantly replied: " I fay it again : I wifh " I had rather loſt one of my hands."—Some perfons, continues Panzani, were pleafed to underſtand this of the puritanical defection from the church by law eſtabliſhed; but the manner of his delivering himfelf, and the circumſtance of his falling immediately into a panegyric on Urban VIII. were thought by others to be a comment on the words.—In the fame letter, Panzani informs the cardinal of several other mattters, which, though in themselves trivial, plainly demonstrated the people's dispositions: That formerly their churches were distinguished by the name of Peter's, Paul's, Margaret's, &c. but that now they were called St. Peter's, St. Paul's, &c.: that the archbishop of Canterbury had ordered the psalms to be sung in notes according to the Gregorian method used in the church of Rome, and that the king himself made the first essay: that the universities, which formerly made use of the books of the first reformers as containing the only plan of their doctrine, were now enjoined to apply themselves to the ancient fathers and councils.—These, among many others, were the observations which Panzani made, and of which he informed the cardinal, that he might have an idea of the English nation in regard to religious matters.*

But there were still stronger proofs of the complaisance, not to say affection of the court party, towards the Roman see.—It is a privilege of embassadors to be allowed a chapel

for

---

* These observations could only apply to the dignitaries of the established church and the court party, and not to the nation which, as it soon appeared, was more than ever hostile to monarchy, and to popery, in their estimation, essentially connected with it.

for the use of their domestics and attendants; and by the indulgence of the court, not only foreigners, but English Catholics were permitted to frequent these places of worship. The queen enjoyed this privilege to a greater extent. Indeed, by the articles of her marriage, a chapel for herself and servants was allowed her: but, besides this, she had a large handsome church in Somerset-house; and a number of Capucin friars were permitted to wear their habits within the precincts of her court. Her almoner, abbé du Perron, often preached publicly in French; and sometimes English sermons were permitted in the church at Somerset-house. This church was built purposely for the queen, being exquisitely adorned, and furnished with very valuable vestments and plate. The king, from curiosity, sometimes visited it; and it was a satisfaction to him to observe the order and significancy of their ceremonies. How great a respect his majesty had for ceremonies appeared by an occurrence, which happened a little before Panzani came to England.— A small piece of the cross, on which our Saviour suffered, was said to have been found in the tower of London, where it had lain concealed many years. Some of the king's servants took care to have it placed in a kind of open box, on which some pains were bestowed in the workmanship. Their design was

was to have it expofed among other rarities in one of the royal palaces. The queen being informed of it, was much concerned that fo remarkable a relic fhould be lodged with other vulgar curiofities; wherefore acquainting the king with it, fhe defired it might be delivered to her, faying, fhe fhould place it in her chapel at Somerfet-houfe. The king was not pleafed, when he heared in what manner his fervants were going to difpofe of this treafure: he told the queen, no one could have a greater value for things of that nature than himfelf; that he would take care it were made an object neither of derifion nor curiofity. The queen on this withdrew her requeft, extremely pleafed with his majefty's difpofition.

Panzani, in the fame letter, alfo remarked, "That Catholic fchoolmafters were allowed to teach in feveral parts of the city of London; that both the writings and difcourfes of Proteftants were in a different key from what formerly they had been; that the king's preachers often took occafion to run into the praifes of the moderate papifts; that they recommended the ufe of auricular confeffion, extolled the beautifying and adorning of churches, and paying a refpect to the name of Jefus by bowing, &c.; that they difclaimed many
"popular

"popular calumnies fixed on the church of
"Rome, owning her to be the mother church,
"and author of happiness to many nations.
"Altars, images, &c. he said, were mentioned
"with respect; and many, in common con-
"versation, wished for a re-union.* All this
"was attributed, Panzani observed, to the in-
"fluence the court had upon the minds of the
"people, and originally to the queen's reli-
"gion, and to the king's uxorious temper.—
"Providence was dragged in to confirm and
"back every man's conjectures. Some said,
"the prayers of queen Mary of Scotland
"began to be heared with success; that the
"family of Stuart was naturally inclined to
"promote the old religion. Others ascribed
"the whole business to the indefatigable zeal
"of the popish emissaries, and to the easy
"temper of a prince who was entirely governed
"by his wife."

I must now return to the subject of Panzani's agency.

The

---

* The truth of these observations is confirmed by all contemporary writers. Laud, therefore, and others were loudly charged with a design of introducing popery; and their indifference in repelling the imputation rather confirmed the suspicion. The truth, however, is, not that they were friends to the church of Rome, but that they were enemies to the puritans, whose principles they hated, and whose clamour they despised.

Disputes about the oath of allegiance.

The Catholics were divided on two heads: *The neceffity and convenience of a bifhop—and the oath of allegiance.*—His majefty was made fenfible, that it was in vain to prefs them with the *oath of fupremacy*, this being directly oppofite to the tenets of their religion: but he could not be perfuaded they had any colour to refufe the *oath of allegiance*,* which was a civil duty,— However, fome of the King's council intimated to Panzani, that it was not impracticable to have fome of the claufes of the faid oath fo foftened, that it might go down with the moft tender confciences. Father Prefton, a learned Benedictin monk, was the great champion for the oath. He was feconded by father David of the fame order, a perfon of uncommon wit and penetration, though by a mifapplication of his talents, he was unfortunate to the Catholic intereft, being moft factious and fcurrilous.— Father Leander, another monk, appeared for a while in the fame caufe, to which he contributed more by his grave carriage, than by his learning or judgment; however, he forfook the party, and entirely fubmitted himfelf to the pleafure of the fee of Rome. Father Prefton, indeed, was a man equal to the caufe he undertook,

being

---

* This was the oath of James, about which fee introduc. p. 75.

being a profound scholar, and a master of style, which he discovered in a very elaborate work written in defence of the oath.* He was supported by persons of all ranks; many of his own order became his disciples; and several of the laity and clergy struck in with him. But these people, by overacting their part, perplexed and almost ruined the Catholic interest at court. For now the king judged he had a very good pretence to press the oath of allegiance, since so many learned men undertook to justify it: and, accordingly, the oath was urged with such severity, that many who refused it were fined, and imprisoned, and otherwise persecuted as the law directed.

Preston's book remained not long unanswered. Edward Courtney, a Jesuit, undertook it, for which he was soon after imprisoned.—Many Catholics attempted a middle way, pretending the oath might be taken with the king's comment on it, whereby he declared nothing

was

---

* This work was was written many years before this time, an. 1613, when the disputes about the oath, as I stated, were so warmly agitated.—Who father David was, I am not able to investigate, unless he was the unfortunate Benedictin John Barns, who, having written against the temporal power of the pope and the loose casuistry of the Jesuits, was, about this time, decoyed abroad, and for more than 20 years confined with lunatics in the prisons of Rome. Dodd, vol. 3. p. 101.

was intended by it but civil allegiance, without any encroachment on the articles of their religion. But others judged such comments were only a snare, as the obvious sense of the words were of another import. This variety of opinions divided the party, who appeared frequently in print for and against the oath respectively.

The agent has two interviews with secretary Windebank.

As yet Panzani had not made himself known to either of the secretaries of State; and he used the same caution in regard to the embassadors of France and Spain. But father Philip and the abbé du Perron were of opinion, that it was high time, he should have an interview with secretary Windebank, at least in private, to remedy the discords about the oath of allegiance, and to proceed as he should find encouragement. Windebank was a protestant by profession, yet no enemy to the Catholics, and prepared to go all the lengths of the king and the court party. Not long after, Panzani had a conference with him, the particulars whereof are given in a letter to cardinal Barberini dated January 19, 1635*

" First,

---

* The *Letters* in these memoirs are quoted not in the order they were written, but as the subject seemed to call for them.

PANZANI.

"First, he acquaints the secretary with
"the occasion of his coming over, viz. to
"pay a compliment to the queen from the
"Roman see, and to inform himself of some
"matters relating to the Catholic bishop,
"and incidentally, as occasion served, he
"was at liberty to regulate the concerns of
"the oath of allegiance; but having no express
"commission as to the last point, he was at
"a loss how to proceed, but would be directed
"as his holiness and the king of Great Britain
"should agree upon the method.—He further
"assured the secretary, that both the pope
"and cardinal Barberini were disposed to
"give his majesty all the content imaginable, as
"they omitted not to signify upon every occasion
"offered; adding that, if his Catholic subjects
"did not behave themselves with the utmost
"respect to his majesty in all civil matters,
"it was contrary to the knowledge and desire
"of his holiness; and that, on a failure of
"their duty in that regard, they ought to
"be made sensible of it as the law directed.
"—Windebank was well pleased with this
"discourse, and took the liberty to reply:
"That his majesty had always signified the
"great respect he had for Urban VIII. and
"that, as well on his account, as for other
"considerations, he had seldom pressed the
"execution of the laws against the Catholics
"to extremity, only now and then reminded
"them

"them of their state of subjection by pecuniary
"mulcts, and that too very sparingly. He
"added by way of advice; That he thought
"it would be a part of prudence in his
"holiness, either to recall, or moderate the
"*Briefs* * that were in force against such as
"took the oath of allegiance. — To which
"Panzani replied; that, as he had no com-
"mission to act in that affair, so he could
"not pronounce upon it; but it was his
"opinion nothing would be altered in the
"Briefs, unless his majesty would meet his
"holiness half way, and agree to make the
"oath more agreeable to the humour † of the
"see of Rome. — Windebank insisted, that
"several Roman Catholics admitted the oath
"might be taken with the king's comment,
"restraining the sense to civil allegiance.—
"This, said Panzani, may be the opinion of
"some of the party; but, in things of this
"nature, men are to act in concert, and
"govern themselves by an uniform practice.
"All I can say, continued Panzani, is, that
"I know it is the pope's pleasure that the
"Catholics answer all the demands of civil
                                    "allegiance.

---

* Introduction, p. 76.

† How well does that word *humour* explain the whole policy of the Roman court in censuring the *oath!*

" allegiance.—On this Windebank replied:
" Then let the pope draw up the form of an
" oath, and fend it hither.—Panzani promifed
" to write to Rome about the matter, and
" gave the fecretary fome encouragement that
" the defign might have its defired effect, for
" that very lately an affair of the fame nature
" was carrying on in Ireland. The Irifh
" Catholics having refufed the oath of alle-
" giance, the king propofed another to them
" of a fofter nature; but this was alfo quar-
" relled with, as bearing ftill too hard on the
" pope's fpiritual power. However, Panzani
" judged it proper to fend the form of the
" Irifh oath to Rome, as a model for England."

But as it appeared afterwards, Panzani was very much blamed as to this affair of the oath, Barberini taking the liberty to tell him, that he had exceeded his commiffion, and that it was too tender a point to be handled at that time.

" Before they broke up the conference,
" Windebank acquainted Panzani, that his
" majefty was very much difpleafed, when
" he underftood that Prefton's book had been
" cenfured at Rome: But Panzani diverted
" the difcourfe by pretending ignorance, and
" affuring him, it was againft his holinefs's
" mind, that any books were publifhed on
" thofe

" thofe fubjects. — Then Windebank very
" familiarly told Panzani, that it was whif-
" pered in corners, that he would be ordered
" to leave the kingdom: But take no notice,
" faid he, of thofe reports; you may ftay
" without any apprehenfion or hazard. —
" Hence Panzani conceived a favourable opi-
" nion of the court, and imagined they were
" difpofed to enter into a further correfpond-
" ence with the apoftolic fee; which con-
" jecture was more confirmed when Winde-
" bank added, and requefted that his holinefs
" would write an obliging letter to the king:
" For why, faid he, fhould not a common
" father make himfelf familiar with his chil-
" dren? — The fame requeft was made by
" feveral others of the nobility, who were
" of opinion that fuch a letter would be very
" acceptable."

Panzani confidered all thefe things, and took care to fend intelligence of them to Rome. —Afterwards in another conference he had with the fame fecretary, concerning the fubject of a bifhop, Windebank told him very frankly, that the Proteftant clergy would never fuffer a popifh bifhop to exercife jurifdiction in England.—To which Panzani replied: That nothing was determined in Rome as yet in that affair; but in cafe a bifhop fhould be fent over, his authority would not

in

in the least interfere with the Protestants claim of jurisdiction; that he would challenge no power in *foro externo,* either as to tithes, wills, or any thing else that had the appearance of a tribunal;* that his power would be confined to matters purely spiritual, viz. confession, confirmation, and other things belonging to discipline and morals: In fine, that such a person would be pitched upon, with whose conduct the king himself should undoubtedly be pleased. — Windebank seemed not averse from this scheme: He only said, it would be proper that his majesty should be acquainted with the nature of his jurisdiction; and that a list of seven or eight persons should be sent to Rome, that his holiness and the king might agree upon a proper person of approved merit and inoffensive carriage.

The regulars and the laity under their direction were, all this while, very busily employed, and making interest, that another bishop might not be sent over, which Panzani understanding, he endeavoured to convince them of the necessity there was of having Dr. Smith's place supplied; and he took pains to

He treats with the regulars, and projects a plan for a bishop.

---

* The faction that drove Dr. Smith from England had very falsely published, that he was aiming to erect such a tribunal.

to answer all objections raised against it. The Jesuits and Benedictin monks were very frank and open in the attack. They alledged, that episcopal authority in England was inconsistent with their privileges as missioners; that they had superiors of their own to have recourse to: that the presence of a bishop would occasion a persecution, and involve the whole Catholic body in a general calamity.—Panzani returned distinct answers to these objections; and as to what regarded persecution, he convinced them that during the six years the two bishops, Dr. Bishop and Dr. Smith, made their abode in England, the Catholics had never been disturbed on that account; and if bishop Smith was at last become obnoxious, and ordered into banishment by the king's proclamation, it was occasioned by the Catholics themselves, who exposed him, and alarmed the nation by very odd sort of methods. He further told them that, in queen Elizabeth's reign, the Jesuits laid a scheme to have the Catholics of England governed by 3 or 4 bishops,* and that the fear of falling under persecution was then judged to be an objection of no force.

While

---

* I have met with no documents to vouch the truth of this assertion.

While Panzani was endeavouring to prepare the way for a bishop, he was put upon forming a plan, how it could be effected. The occasion whereof arose from a report, that the king designed to order away abbé du Perron, and most of the ecclesiastics and Capucins that attended on the queen at Somerset-house. — His majesty had received frequent complaints that they were too numerous, and some of them too inquisitive about state affairs. From this juncture he devised a scheme which he communicated to cardinal Barberini in a letter dated February 2, 1635.

The substance of the letter was:—" That
" the new bishop should succeed du Perron, as
" almoner to the queen: That the places of
" the French chaplains, Capucins, &c. should
" be supplied by English clergy, who were to
" be vicars, canons, archdeacons, &c. and
" bear all the offices under the bishop: That,
" by this means, they would be under the royal
" protection, and upon that account would be
" cautious how they behaved themselves in re-
" gard to state affairs; and, at the same time,
" would not be suspected of tampering in fa-
" vour of a foreign power: That the queen's
" chapel would be sufficiently provided for by
" this method: That the bishop might exercise
" his jurisdiction, and make his visitations at
" convenient times, and not the less com-
" ply

"ply with all the queen expected from him
"in quality of almoner. He assured the car-
"dinal, this plan would be acceptable to the
"queen, who desired nothing more than that
"a bishop might be sent over. Then he
"goes on to mention the general motives
"which induced him to be so urgent for a
"bishop: It was requisite, he said, on account
"of the regulars and the clergy. For he
"found, by experience, that the regulars,
"especially the Jesuits, were for being sole
"proprietors of the mission; that they daily
"made new conquests, and incorporated
"youths of the best families into their society;
"that the clergy were wormed out of their places
"and obliged to yield to the force of interest
"and money. Besides, added he, many of
"the regulars make themselves popular by
"pretended privileges and ill grounded
"indulgences; and when they were questioned
"and desired to justify these singularities,
"their answer is, that some pope granted them
"*viva voce*. The clergy on the other hand,
"he says, are in an abandoned state, living
"under a kind of anarchy without an imme-
"diate head; and that, every day, irregulari-
"ties were detected among them for want of
"a bishop."

Character of the Jesuits and regulars.

About this time, it was whispered at court that, either liberty of conscience, or some other great matter was in agitation, in favour of of the Catholics; and that the king, from an inclination to their caufe, or out of compliment to the queen, was refolved to make them very eafy: but then it was expected, that the bifhop of Rome fhould defift from fome of his claims. The Jefuits were not willing to hearken to an accommodation on the terms that were commonly propofed. Their ufual language was, that the Roman Catholic religion would never be reftored in England, but by the fword. This topic was very difpleafing to Panzani. He told them very frankly, it had too great an affinity to the deteftable contrivance of the gunpowder plot; but he was fatisfied, their zeal would never tranfport them fo far. Their averfion to an accommodation was ftill more fufpected from a book, publifhed by one of their order, entitled; *Quod libertas confcientiæ non conveniat Anglis pro prefenti rerum ftatu.* Some enemies to the fociety thus paraphrafed on it: That they (the jefuits) judged it a more eligible ftate to remain as they were, than to fee a total converfion of the nation, with the detriment or exclufion of their body: the latter being much talked of: and the firft would certainly happen, if other orders were allowed their ancient claims, and the Jefuits be permitted to languifh without lands, and by confequence without intereft or power; whereas now, by methods peculiar to themfelves, they bore up their heads above all the reft.

With

With all matters of moment, Panzani also, not unfrequently communicated to Barberini his own private thoughts and conjectures. In one of his letters, dated February 23, 1635: he has the following words: " It is but too "true, that some, and I may say many, " both Jesuits and Benedictins, have turned " the mission into a business of profit: of " which abuse I see no other remedy than " to cramp them in their faculties, especially " the Jesuits. By this method, they would " not have so many followers and admirers: " They would traffic less, and attend more " to the cure of souls. Avarice was the only " motive which pushed them on to persecute " the bishop. Some here propose a sharper " remedy, viz. to take the English college " at Rome out of their hands, and restore it " to the clergy, who, it is thought, would " make a much better use of it. The Jesuits " cull the best wits out of it for their own " body: the others are designed only for the " mission. Whereas the clergy, as being " more peculiarly designed for the mission, " would not only reserve the prime wits for " that use, but would take equal pains that " others should be qualified. Things are now " come to that pass, that a good religious man " is one that is most zealous for his order; " and those that are not good attend only to " themselves: and between both the mission
" is

"is very much neglected, and the designs of the see of Rome frustrated. Besides, religious men are not so easily brought to reason when they do amiss, as being more united among themselves, and by consequence more stubborn. A clergyman stands by himself. He is sooner corrected; and when bad, his example is neither of so much weight, nor so infectious as the Jesuits who are one and all. I mention the Jesuits rather, because they are the leaders in the affair of the bishop: and it is the opinion of several Protestants, that the Jesuits, upon I know not what view, do very much oppose an union* at this time."

While Windebank and Panzani were carrying on their conferences, one Cook, a kind of secretary, and by sect a puritan, desired to have an audience of his majesty on a subject, he said, which very much concerned the nation's welfare, he, at the same time, intending to do Windebank a notable disservice, if not to throw him wholly out of the king's favour. Cook being admitted, told his majesty with a great deal of concern, that there was a certain Italian priest,

The puritans discover Panzani.

---

* Union of the two churches, as will be seen.

prieft, named Panzani, fent fecretly by the pope, and who might be of dangerous confequence to the ftate, as well as to his majefty's private affairs. The king fmiled, telling the gentleman that he was no ftranger to Panzani's arrival; that he was a perfon of worth and of unfufpected behaviour; that he had fully explained himfelf as to the reafons which brought him into England, and that he (Cook) needed give himfelf no further trouble on that head.— The king, however, thought it proper, by the means of Windebank, to acquaint Panzani, that, though he was difcovered by the Puritanical party, he might be eafy; that no body fhould moleft him.

<small>The caufe of the Elector Palatine is propofed to him.</small>

But now fecretary Windebank had another game to play, which was, to make ufe of Panzani in favour of the Elector Palatine's family.* He requefted of him, therefore, in the

---

* It may be proper juft to notice, that this was the family of the elector Frederic, married to Elizabeth, daughter of king James. He had liftened to a wild propofal that was to fix on his head the crown of Bohemia; but with this crown he alfo loft his hereditary dominions of the Palatinate. The event embittered the laft years of James, and nearly involved the nation in a continental war. The elector was at this time dead, and his children lived in exile: but one of thofe children was Sophia, deftined to be the mother of our firft George; and Louis, the eldeft fon, in 1648, was reinftated in the Palatinate.

the king's name, that he would use his interest with the king of Poland, the pope, and cardinal Barberini, that a match might be brought about between a daughter of the Elector and the Polish king, insinuating that this would be a handsome preliminary, on which to establish a further correspondence with the see of Rome. Panzani promised to take a proper time to propose this affair; but he was very dilatory in doing it.

He was, however, assiduous enough in sending to Rome the new form of an oath, which he desired the cardinal would remit with his thoughts on it, that the king and ministry might consider it.—It appeared soon after, by Barberini's letters to Panzani, that the court of Rome was very much displeased with the liberty he had taken in declaring himself on the subject of the oath. The cardinal acquainted him, that Rome ought to be very cautious and rather passive in controversies of that nature: " For, said he, should we pretend to " draw up forms of oaths, the English would " pretend to be judges of the qualities of " them, whereas it is our business to act as " judges, where faith is attacked or endan- " gered." He also advised him not to concern

Deep policy of Rome exhibited in a letter from Barberini.

cern himfelf with Courtney's Book* (which Windebank endeavoured to have cenfured at Rome), "for this, he faid, was entering too "far into a thorny matter where he might "prick his fingers. To condemn Courtney "was to appear too openly againft the autho- "rity of the fee of Rome, and to approve of "what he had written was too difobliging on "the other fide."—Nay, even with regard to the bifhop, Panzani was accufed of being lefs cautious, efpecially in being too particular in his reafons, fome of which feemed to require his (the bifhop's) prefence that he might pre- fcribe rules to the regulars, which feemed not to be the intention of the holy fee, which was always tender of the Regulars privileges.—He then privately acquaints him that Prefton's book was actually cenfured at Rome,† as alfo ano- ther by a Francifcan entitled *Deus, Natura, Gratia.*‡

Thefe

---

* In reply to Prefton: See above.

† According to Dodd, vol. 2. p. 481, the works of Prefton, alias Widdrington, in favour of the oath of allegiance and againft the depofing power, had been formally cenfured at Rome as far back as the year 1614. He gives a copy of the cenfure. Prefton appears to have written nothing after the year 1622: Ibid. p. 421.

§ The author was father Davenport, a man highly learned and much efteemed, whom the king and the archbifhop fome- times faw. Dodd, vol. 3. p. 103.

Thefe were the reproofs Panzani received from the cardinal in a letter, directed to him in March 1635, which he thus concludes: "The Englifh are a myfterious people, and "require all your attention. The fea which "you paffed to vifit them is an emblem of "their temper, and a direction how you ought "to fteer. Scarcely were you arrived, but "you began to difpute with yourfelf, whether "it was more advifeable to remain, or to "return back. The curiofities of a place are "fooner known, than either the religion or "politics of its inhabitants. Time is required "to become acquainted with the factions of a "country, and much more time to find out a "remedy, when the diftemper is difcovered. "You are yet a ftranger to the Catholic "churchmen of that country. This is your "main enquiry. We muft know the qualities "and merits of perfons, before we can chufe "a bifhop from among them. This muft be "done gradually. You muft obferve many "things; and endeavour to filence all paft "animofities. I am afraid you aim at too "much. You feem to be engaged in affairs "relating to the queen's family, and lay "fchemes upon the removal of her French "chaplains, and perhaps not to her liking. "I cannot fay, but you acted prudently in "giving no umbrage to the embaffadors of "France and Spain, by making yourfelf
"public;

"public; and I wish you had been as cautious
"in relation to the oath. Father Leander's*
"example might have deterred you. His
"meddling about the oath was very ill taken
"by all parties; but being a person of no
"extraordinary reach, he was not likely to do
"much either way. What will the Catholics
"say who refuse the oath, to see you familiar
"with those who maintain it? It may, per-
"haps, be a stroke of politics, whereby the
"ministers of that court endeavour to draw
"something from you. Such practices are
"very common. It might, perhaps, not have
"been amiss to have mentioned, in general
"terms, something concerning the oath to
"secretary Windebank; but you went too far
"in making proposals. In things of that kind
"it is your business to see, hear, and observe.
"It is a piece of necessary policy not to seem
"to be fully informed of matters. One of
"your character is supposed never to speak
"but to the purpose. It is a pleasure to hear,
"that the king speaks well of the pope; but
"the praises of others are of no account with
"him, unless they be introductory to the main
"point of salvation. It is a comfort to hear,
"the

---

* I know nothing of father Leander, or to what the passage alludes.

" the Catholics are not perfecuted. All forts
" of perils attend perfecution—honour, faith,
" eftate. The foftening of the pope's Brief,
" which Windebank mentioned, was a dan-
" gerous topic. You entered unadvifedly on
" that fubject; yet were in the right to reply,
" that not repealing, but foftening was to be
" the thing infifted on. I wifh, however, you
" had never mentioned any thing of fending
" hither about the form of an oath, fince you
" are not ignorant how much his holinefs
" fuffered on fuch another propofal concerning
" the fovereignty of the Grifons over the
" Valaifins. Should we form an oath here,
" and fend it to the king, they would examine
" it, and cenfure it in England. On the
" whole, it is my advice, that you difengage
" yourfelf as well as you can from this trouble-
" fome affair of the oath. However, what I
" write now is all from myfelf, till I can find
" a fit opportunity to reprefent things to his
" holinefs, that you may have full inftructions
" how to carry yourfelf hereafter. I commend
" your refervednefs in not making any pro-
" mifes of the pope's writing to the king.
" Such things are never done, but when
" princes have drawn a letter from his holinefs
" by writing firft. Befides, a letter to the
" king muft be by way of exhortation on the
" fubject of religion, of which, perhaps, his
" majefty is not yet difpofed to hear. As to
" the

" the queen's family, in my opinion, it were
" better not to be tampering there, nor to
" propose any schemes of a bishop residing
" with her in the manner you speak of."

The king and Panzani meet.

All this while, Panzani and Windebank had frequent opportunities of conferring together. The form of an oath was very often the subject; and Windebank often took occasion to say, that he did not understand there was any inconvenience, or prohibition in our laws against corresponding with his holiness in matters purely civil and temporal. At last, by frequently repeating this argument, they resolved that it should be proposed to the queen and cardinal Barberini, whether a mutual agency between the court of Rome and England would not be very convenient. Windebank[*] seemed so charmed with the beauty of the project,

---

[*] Sir Francis Windebank who, in these memoirs, acts so conspicuous a part, had, in 1632, been made secretary, through the interest of Dr. Laud, himself, the year following, promoted to the see of Canterbury. Windebank was much attached to the Catholic party, (whose extraordinary patron, says Lord Clarendon, indeed he was.) In 1640, for his friendly conduct to that people, articles of impeachment were by parliament prepared against him, when he withdrew into France, was formally reconciled to the church of Rome, and died in that communion, in 1646. Dodd, vol. 3, p. 59. Clarend. vol. 11. p. 178, 80.

project, that he was beforehand with Panzani in communicating it to the queen. He affured her majefty, he would be fecret, cordial, and affiduous in carrying it on, adding, that the king was very curious, and urgent to have a perfonal conference with Panzani, though, for fome reafons, this meeting was to be the confequence of the queen's requeft, and not as if it were a motion of the king himfelf. The queen was rejoiced at the propofal, and went heartily into it: fo that, in a few days, the king and Panzani were brought together, though in a very remote and unfufpected place, the queen alfo being prefent.

The king received him with a very cheerful countenance, taking off his hat, while Panzani kiffed his hand; and then, with a great deal of freedom, the latter gave his majefty an account of his bufinefs in England, with an ample affurance of the great affection his holinefs had for him, and a grateful remembrance of the kind treatment the Catholics had met with under his majefty's mild and prudent reign. He alfo made a proper compliment, in the name of cardinal Barberini. — His majefty returned thefe compliments in a very obliging manner, owning that he had always conceived a very exalted idea of the merits of Urban VIII. and had an uncommon affection for his perfon, adding. that it was a fenfible trouble to him,

him, that the prefent controverfies, and wars in Europe gave his holinefs fo much difturbance: that cardinal Barberini's virtues did give him a fingular preference in his efteem: and as to the Catholics, he was refolved, none of their blood fhould be fpilt during his reign, though things were otherwife reprefented at Rome; but, at the fame time, he could not conceal the high provocations fome of that party had given him, as namely Mr. Courtenay, whom they had recommended to the French court.—Panzani only replied in general, that he knew it to be his holinefs's defire, that the Catholics fhould be punctual in their obedience to his majefty; and that it was expected, or hoped, on the other hand, that they fhould enjoy a reafonable indulgence in the practice of their religion.—Thus ended the conference between his majefty and Panzani.

He confers with Windebank on various matters.

This interview encouraged Windebank to treat more familiarly with Panzani, efpecially on the heads of religion. He told him that, he really looked on himfelf to be a good Catholic; otherwife, that he fhould make no difficulty to bid adieu to all that was dear to him in order to purchafe that name. He then inftanced fome things he boggled at in the church of Rome, and namely, the article of communion in one kind, which he viewed as a fcandalous practice, adding that, if he were to be concerned in in uniting the churches, the Catholics fhould difclaim that article as a preliminary.—Panzani only replied that, in his opinion, the writers of the church of Rome had given full fatisfaction on that head.—Windebank went on to another point: "If," faid he, "we had neither Jefuits "nor Puritans in England, I am confident, an "union might eafily be effected." — "As for "the Jefuits," anfwered Panzani, "though "they have always been regarded as a learned "body, and very ferviceable to the church of "Rome, yet it is not improbable but his holinefs "would facrifice their intereft, on the profpect "of fo fair an acquifition."—This anfwer, as it was unexpected, fo did it feem to pleafe the fecretary much. It was an inftruction to him, that the church of Rome did not depend on the Jefuits, who had always been odious to England, not upon account of their religion, in which they were on the fame footing with the reft of that perfuafion; but becaufe they were reprefented as too bufy in ftate affairs and in temporal matters, and too much concerned in the gunpowder plot; and that the moderate men of the church of Rome had conceived a diflike to them, on account of their averfion to epifcopacy, which they treated with difrefpect, and viewed as inconfiftent with their defigns of always being at the head.

Windebank

Windebank afterwards proceeded further in his difcourfe concerning an union, affuring Panzani, that all the moderate men in church and ftate thirfted after it.—Panzani, on this, defired to know what terms would, probably, be propofed as a plan to go upon.—The fecretary faid he would inform himfelf: but this he knew in the mean time, that it was expected, the church of Rome fhould give up three of her tenets, namely, Communion in one kind, the Latin Liturgy, and the celebacy of the clergy.—Panzani judging thefe points too big for him, only anfwered, that he hoped fuch obftacles might be removed: but, in the interim, to facilitate matters, he thought a decree for liberty of confcience would be a good expedient.—Windebank was of opinion, there would not be much difficulty in obtaining it, provided the Roman Catholics would not incapacitate themfelves by refufing the oath of allegiance.—Panzani obferved, he had already preffed the court of Rome as to that matter. " But why," faid he, " may not his majefty " rely on the obedience of his Catholic fub- " jects without the ceremony of an oath, as " the pope relies on them in the article of his " fpiritual fupremacy?"—And thus they concluded for the prefent.

Father

Father Philip, the queen's confeffor, had incidentally fome difcourfe with the king on matters of the fame tendency, in which he endeavoured to perfuade his majefty, that it was directly oppofite to the whole defign of the gofpel, that there fhould be more churches than one; whence he inferred the neceffity of a re-union. He alfo foftened the article of communion in one kind, telling him, it was only a point of difcipline, alterable with circumftances, and might be compromifed fo as not to be the fubject of a breach; with other fuch like difcourfes in order to level the way, and remove prejudices.

Father Philip difcourfes with the king on the re-union of the churches.

I muft here notice a conteft which happened concerning the book entitled *Deus, Natura, Gratia*, the author whereof was Mr. Davenport, a Francifcan friar, otherwife called Francifcus a Sancta Clara. This book was highly efteemed by his majefty, as being full of complaifance for the Proteftant fyftems in feveral points, and difcovering an inclination of approaching nearer to them by conceffions, where the Catholic caufe would permit it to be done. But the work was far from being liked at the Roman court, where it was confidered as a very dangerous production, far too condefcending to fchifmatics and heretics. The generality alfo of the Englifh Catholics were difpleafed with it. At Rome they proceeded to cenfure it, though the

A work of father Davenport pleafing to the king, gives offence at Rome.

the decree was not made public, the author himfelf being firft fummoned to make his appearance, which he declined on account of infirmity, promifing to give fatisfaction any other way.

This, indeed, was but a private concern, yet it had a public influence, as things then ftood. — It was the opinion of many that the king was inclined to hearken to terms of an union between the two churches; and that he looked on this book of Davenport as a remote difpofition towards it. It was, therefore, deemed an impolitic ftep in Rome, to let their cenfures loofe againft it at this juncture. Father Philip was very induftrious in acquainting the Roman court with the inconveniences of rigorous proceedings. He advifed them to go on flowly; to wink at the author for a time, alledging that he had fubmitted himfelf, and that it would be foon enough to take notice of him, when he perfifted, or affairs would permit a cenfure. — Soon after, care was taken to inform Windebank, that the condemnation was fuppreffed. But it happening that the author, or fome one for him, fet forth another edition, in which no fubmiffion was expreffed, Panzani told the fecretary, he was afraid the court of Rome would proceed to a cenfure, and declare the author contumacious, that the faithful might not be fcandalized. The
account

account gave Windebank great concern; and being acquainted with the author, he conferred with him on the fubject. They agreed in opinion, that a cenfure would irritate the king, and divert him from any thoughts of an union. However, to foften the matter, it was given out, and confidently reported that Mr. Davenport was ftill prepared to fubmit himfelf, and that he had no hand in the fecond edition, it being the bookfeller's contrivance folely for the fake of gain. Windebank alfo preffed Panzani to take care that they were very cautious at Rome, for that it would certainly ruin all their projects, if a work of that pacific tendency were condemned. But notwithftanding all the care which the author and his friends could take to ftifle the cenfure, (which as yet was only privately whifpered at Rome,) the Jefuits were very bufy in publifhing it among their acquaintance in England. Davenport then publifhed an *Apology*, wherein he amply declares himfelf as to the work itfelf, and fubmits himfelf both in that, and all other matters, to the Roman fee. He was not, however, willing to leave England; but rather ftrove to fhelter himfelf under the king's protection, which to fome perfons appeared to be a very odd proceeding, and looked as if he defigned to go on further. Even fome fufpected the worft of him, from his having once been a

member

member of the Englifh church.—In the mean while, Panzani omitted not to advife his court to be cautious, and to compliment the king in favour of Mr. Davenport, as far as the cafe would admit.

Windebank's opinion of the Jefuits.

At another conference between the fecretary and Panzani, the former took a great deal of liberty in railing at the Jefuits, whofe number, he faid, was above 300; and that it was expected, they fhould either all be banifhed or be reduced. He added, it was his opinion that, in cafe his majefty were difpofed to liften to an union, the Jefuits and Puritans would endeavour to obftruct it; that the Jefuits were Spaniards by faction; that an union brought about by a French woman (the queen) would tie France and England together in intereft as in religion; and that the Spaniards muft be fufferers by that event. Again, he fufpected the Jefuits would ruin the project by humouring the king in fome other matters; that it would be as much for their intereft to continue as they were, they being full as expert in raifing their fortunes in a ftorm, as in a calm.—Panzani was very much difpleafed at this invective againft the Jefuits. He told Windebank, that the world laboured under great prejudices in their regard; and that, though fome particular perfons among them might be defervedly cenfured,

censured, the whole body ought not to bear the weight of the charge. — " It is in vain," answered the secretary, " to colour their pro-
" ceedings: England is no stranger to their
" labours and inclinations: we have been
" many years acquainted with their artifices:
" The church may subsist very well without
" them; and why should a nation be pestered
" with them? — " Is it likely," rejoined Panzani, " that the king would send away the Jesuits for refusing the oath, and tolerate the clergy in the same practice? I am informed that, about two years since, his
" majesty was heard publicly to say, that the
" greatest sticklers against the oath were the
" secular priests. Nay, it is well known at
" this day, that the Jesuits are on good terms
" with those that take the oath; nor do they
" drive them from the sacraments, as several
" of the secular priests are known to do."—
This is the substance of what Panzani wrote to the cardinal in a letter dated March 16, 1635, which he concludes thus: " If the
" king will agree to have the controversy
" about the oath determined according to a
" method prescribed by his holiness, it will
" then, perhaps, be thought reasonable to
" humour him in what relates to the Jesuits.
" In the mean time, I do assure you, he is
" very much exasperated against Courtenay,
" not only for declaiming against the oath,
                                            " but

"but becaufe he has fallen foul on the royal
"prerogative, and exprefsly prefers the
"authority of the parliament to that of the
"king."

Anecdote refpecting father Garnet.

I muft not omit to mention an incident which happened during Panzani's agency, in relation to Father Henry Garnet a Jefuit, who was executed for the gunpowder plot, in the beginning of the reign of his majefty's father. Roman Catholics were at liberty to fignify their opinion of that gentleman's innocence, by thinking or acting as they pleafed in private; but his majefty deemed it an infult to his parent's memory, that he fhould be publicly venerated as a faint or martyr, who had juridically been condemned as a traitor. For the king was informed, that the picture of father Garnet was not only expofed in chapels abroad, but alfo that he was beatified, if not canonized as a faint, by Urban VIII. Urban, to difabufe his majefty, as far as either he or the church was concerned, ordered Panzani to fhew two decrees to the king. One imported that no picture or image fhould be expofed in churches without the pope's exprefs licence, which had never been granted in favour of father Garnet: the other was, that no beatification or canonization could be completed, till fifty years after the perfon's deceafe. The king appeared fatisfied with this affurance from his holinefs, and
concluded

concluded that the refpect fhewn to father Garnet was only an inftance of miftaken domeftic zeal.

By this time, Urban had been acquainted with all the particulars relating to Panzani's agency, of which having weighed every point, he ordered Barberini to give him his inftructions. This the cardinal did in a letter dated March 13, 1635, the fubftance whereof was:—" That, for the future, he fhould
"engage himfelf no further in the controverfy
"about the oath, but as he was advifed by
"father Philip, the queen's confeffor:—That
"his chief bufinefs in England was, to enquire
"into the differences between the fecular clergy
"and the regulars:—That he fhould keep the
"conferences he had with fecretary Windebank
"a fecret from the Roman Catholics, who
"would be apt to grow uppifh on the report
"of an union between the two churches, and
"fo break out in impertinences, which after-
"wards, if the defign miffed, would have a
"contrary effect, and draw a perfecution on
"them:—That England would, by that means,
"prove too hot for Panzani himfelf, as fome
"had already fuggefted, he could not remain
"there long:—That, in a little time, he
"would be recalled; for in cafe what was
"hoped for did fucceed, that affair was too
"big for him and muft pafs through other
"hands:—That the method he took to filence
"both

The cardinal fends inftructions to Panzani in three letters.

"both parties about the oath of allegiance,
"was an injury to the right his holinefs claimed
"in that controverfy: — That the court of
"Rome would make a further trial of the
"difpofition of the court of England, before
"they would enter into any further corref-
"pondence concerning an union; for as yet
"there was reafon to fufpect, the king was not
"fufficiently prepared for that nice point, as
"his averfion to fuch as oppofed the oath, and
"his favouring others of a contrary fentiment,
"was a ftrong indication:—That the author
"of the book, *Deus, Natura, Gratia*, fhould forth-
"with difclaim his bold affertions, and leave
"England, for as yet his fault was pardonable,
"and fhould be forgotten: — That Panzani
"fhould content himfelf with affuring the
"king in general, that he fhould have all
"reafonable fatisfaction, of which his holinefs's
"promife to forward the match between the
"king of Poland and a daughter of the
"elector Palatine was a good earneft:—In
"fine, that Panzani would avoid all familiar-
"ality with the archbifhop of Canterbury, left
"it might give occafion to the regulars to
"fufpect, that his holinefs meant to revoke the
"decrees againft the oath of allegiance, as it
"had already been noifed abroad."

In another letter from Barberini dated April 25, 1635, Panzani is inftructed " to feel
" the

" the king's inclinations as to a bishop; but
" that this be done by the queen's means,
" for no suspicion was to be given, as if the
" see of Rome had entered into any such
" consultation. This also was to be kept
" from the regulars, especially the Jesuits, who
" certainly would traverse all such designs.
" In case the king hearkened to the proposal,
" and was afterwards inquisitive about the
" bishop's jurisdiction, that Panzani should
" say nothing as to that point, and seem to
" act in the whole with a commission; yet
" to insinuate, at the same time, as from
" himself, that the see of Rome would grant
" no jurisdiction to a bishop that should be
" prejudicial to the Protestant hierarchy. He
" then exhorts him to carry himself in such
" a manner, as to give the Jesuits no occasion
" of jealousy against him, since his object was
" to bring the clergy and regulars to a good
" understanding: that he should, for the
" future, keep off from those two dangerous
" points, the oath of allegiance and the re-
" union of the churches: in fine, that he
" would never more insinuate about banishing
" the Jesuits, or reducing their number in
" order to please the king."

In another letter from the same cardinal
dated May 9, 1635, he acquaints Panzani,
" That the proposal made by Windebank,
                                    " That

"That the church of Rome should give up
"some of her articles, viz. communion in
"one kind, the celebacy of her clergy, &c."
"would never please at Rome; that the
"English ought to look back upon the breach
"they had made, and attend to the motives
"that induced them to it; and that the
"whole world was against them as to the
"points mentioned."

Panzani complains to him of the Jesuits.

It has been before observed that Panzani, in letters from Rome, had been charged with exceeding his commission in several particulars. The circumstance gave him some uneasiness: wherefore, in a letter to Barberini dated April 11, 1635: "he promises to act more
"warily: yet he cannot, he says, without
"injury to truth and to his character, con-
"ceal the carriage of the Jesuits, against whom
"he makes fresh complaints, viz. That his
"being sent over in England, without their
"being pre-acquainted, was an unpardonble
"fault; that, every day, they gave fresh
"instances of their aversion to bishops, ex-
"citing, by their emissaries, the archbishop
"of Canterbury against the proposal.—They
"published everywhere that Panzani was
"recalled, and that he had offended both
"the king and the ministry by his misbeha-
"viour, and was only a spy upon the nation.
—"The Jesuits, he observes, were exasperated
"against

" against him, thinking their credit much
" weakened by his coming over: that they
" usually made the nation believe, his holiness
" did nothing without their advice, especially
" in matters relating to religion."

In a letter of June the 13th, 1635, he tells Barberini, " that the Jesuits gave out, that he
" was not sent by the pope, but by cardinal
" Richelieu; so much were they perplexed to
" find themselves neglected at Rome on this
" occasion." — This letter concludes with the following words: " Your eminence must not
" be surprised, that I complain so much and
" so often of the Jesuits, because I see plainly,
" they are the only persons that cannot bear a
" bishop; and, questionless, they will excite
" all their penitents against him. Every day
" I hear new complaints of them, and of their
" equivocations; and yet I have given them
" more encouragement and tokens of confi-
" dence than to any others; which they
" requite with spreading idle and personal
" reflections, casting my horoscope, and pre-
" tending to be privy to all the particulars of
" my life. And of late, one father Roberts of
" that order attacked me so briskly on account
" of partiality in their disfavour, that I found
" myself obliged to make use of the strongest
" asseverations to silence him."

Is perplexed in a conference with the fecretary.

Panzani was now confidering what anfwer to return to Windebank on the fubject of the new oath. He had received orders from Rome to draw himfelf out of the affair; which he endeavoured to do in the following manner.— Firft, he fignified that, by his laft accounts from the holy fee, both the pope and cardinal Barberini owned themfelves extremely honoured and fatisfied with his majefty's candour and affurance, that there fhould be fome foftening claufes added to the oath of allegiance, which was a condefcenfion, they admitted, fuitable to his majefty's known clemency and goodnefs. But as for wording an oath, his holinefs thought that part belonged to the Englifh miniftry, as being better capable to judge how far allegiance would be required by the laws of their country and the principles of their religion. —Windebank was at a lofs how to get rid of this compliment; and Panzani had exprefs orders not to meddle with the form of the oath. Wherefore, to divert the difcourfe, he entertains Windebank with fomething relating to the book, *Deus, Natura, Gratia*, particularly remarking that it was prohibited at Rome.—The fecretary appeared much concerned, and begged that prohibition might not be made public in England, adding that the author was very much efteemed, not only among the Roman Catholics, but alfo by the king; that the work contained nothing contrary to the faith of the church of Rome;

Rome; and that father Philip valued the author as a perfon of great virtue, learning, and probity.

It was not poffible to conceal this matter from the king, who was fo irritated when he was truly informed of the fact, that it was fcarcely in the queen's power to pacify him. When he had recovered his temper, he faid: " He hoped the fee of Rome would not proceed to prohibit all other books of the fame tendency; and particularly that he fhould confider it as a fingular affront, if a book againft father Courtenay now in the prefs fhould be cenfured at Rome." Courtenay had afferted the depofing power. He defired the queen to acquaint Panzani with his fentiments, which, if complied with, he might ftill remain in England without moleftation.

The king is irritated.

Cardinal Barberini being informed of this particular, thought it a difhonour to the holy fee, to have a bar put to the execution of its jurifdiction. But to compromife the matter, the anfwer to Courtenay never appeared; and thus the affair ended. And not long after, the defign of a reciprocal agency between the queen and the court of Rome was fet on foot, as will be feen in its proper place.

In the mean time, Panzani in a letter to the cardinal dated July 4, 1635, gives him an account

Panzani again complains of the Jefuits.

count of a scheme which was laid some time before he came into England, and which chiefly related to the controvesy about a bishop. It was this. — One Basil Brook,* a gentleman of account and very zealous in maintaining the privileges of the regulars against episcopal jurisdiction, made Panzani a visit, and left in his hands a *Protestation* against the government of bishops in England, signed by many of the Roman Catholic laity.— The writing was delivered with an intimation, that he was at liberty, if he pleased, to shew it to the secular clergy who might themselves examine the signatures.

Panzani was soon given to understand, that this was a stratagem invented a few years before, when the regulars apprehended that a bishop would be sent to supply the absence of Dr. Smith. The queen was displeased to find the regulars were playing their old game. Besides, Panzani, on enquiry, discovered that several of the subscribers were scarcely Catholics, and that others refused to acknowledge their names, which gave him an ill impression against such proceedings. In the letter above mentioned he has these words: " Does not your eminence
" plainly

---

* Sir Basil: See Dodd, vol. 3, p. 58. and p. 129 the heads of the *Protestation* or Remonstrance here mentioned.

" plainly fee, what tricks Brook and the Jefuits
" play, that I may be difappointed in fpeaking
" to their partizans, and in having the figna-
" tures verified. At my firft appearing in
" London, that their adherents might not come
" near me, they gave out that I was a penfioner
" of France and an agent of cardinal Richelieu;
" again, that a perfecution was at hand, and it
" was not prudent to vifit me. Some patience
" is required to bear thefe men's reproaches.—
" They fpare neither the queen, nor his holi-
" nefs, nor your eminence; and indeed, you
" have affronted them, without meafure, in
" fending me hither without firft having taken
" their advice. One of their capital objections
" againft me is, that I am not an impartial
" perfon, that is, that I am not wholly addicted
" to their domeftic intereft. For as they efteem
" their own proceedings juft and reafonable, fo
" all that fall not into their meafures are want-
" ing in their duty, and are partial. They
" have fpread about another report, viz. that
" I am ordered by your eminence to apply
" myfelf no more to the queen or Windebank;
" but rather to Mr. Cottington, the other fecre-
" tary of ftate, a great friend to the Catholics,
" but particularly addicted to the Jefuits intereft.
" In this they feem to have a double view:
" firft, to fet me at variance with Windebank
" and the archbifhop of Canterbury, (who are
" profeffed adverfaries to the Jefuits); then,

"by Cottington's means, to penetrate into my
"designs. Cottington is their friend, and a
"Spaniard by faction; yet I cannot think, he
"would reveal my secrets to the Jesuits, know-
"ing it would be highly displeasing to the
"king and the primate, and be a certain way
"of throwing himself out of favour."*

<small>Converses with Cottington about a bishop.</small>

The idea Panzani had formed of secretary Cottington, was very just, of which he gives a proof in another letter to the cardinal dated July 11, 1635. "One day," he says, "dif-
"coursing with Cottington concerning a
"bishop, he observed, that it was a nice point.
"If, said he, the pope sends a bishop against
"the king's inclination, the Roman Catholics
"will have reason to apprehend the conse-
"quence; and for the king's inclinations, he
"was satisfied, they were averse to the design
"at present.—Panzani replied that, in his
"opinion, nothing could conduce more to-
"wards keeping the Catholics in a due sub-
"jection

---

* Sir Francis Cottington had been created baron Cottington in the 7th of Charles, and was, at this time, chancellor of the exchequer. "He had the disadvantage of being suspected at "least a favourer of the Papists, (though that religion thought "itself nothing beholding to him,) by which he was in great "umbrage with the people:" says Clarendon, vol. 1, p. 151. He died in Spain, after the restoration, a member of the Catholic church. Dodd, vol, 3, p. 47.

"jection to their prince, than to have a head
" placed over them to inspect their behaviour,
" especially since assurances would be given,
" that the episcopal power granted by the
" pope should not give any annoyance to the
" Protestant clergy.—Cottington seemed not
" to relish the proposal; and as a proof of the
" king's dislike to it, he said, his majesty was
" about to order abbé du Perron to be removed
" from the queen's family on a report that he
" was elected bishop in France."

Before Panzani would make any trial of the king's inclinations in regard to a bishop, he judged it would be well to enquire, how the generality of Catholics stood themselves affected that way. To this purpose, he resolved first to inform himself of the particulars of that Protestation of the laity, lately put into his hands, but which was drawn up in August 1631, before he came into England. He observed that many of the subscribers studiously kept out of the way: but when he insisted, that they ought to appear to justify their signatures, some of them owned they had signed against a bishop, but were persuaded to it. Others said, they had signed only by proxy; and others, that they had opposed a bishop on a misrepresentation of his power, and a belief that it would certainly draw a persecution on them. It was generally believed that the regulars were

And discovers the real sentiments of the Catholics on the subject.

at the bottom of this contrivance, and that the apprehenfion of being cramped in their privileges had made them fo very induftrious.—Now the true ftate of things was this.

The generality of the laity, from the very beginning defired nothing more than to be governed by a bifhop; and many perfons of diftinction among them offered to take the whole concern upon themfelves, not only in providing for his fubfiftence, but in anfwering for his behaviour, and engaging he fhould appear when the king or miniftry required it.—The *Proteftation*, therefore, being detected as furreptitious, in many particulars, the regulars at laft publicly difclaimed it, and cleared themfelves from the afperfion caft upon them on that account. Indeed, there were feveral manifeft proofs of very unfair dealing. For, befides the tricks already mentioned, it was found that, of twelve noblemen named in the paper, few of them had really figned; fome were infants; and fome, in other refpects, had been drawn in.*—On his return to Rome, Panzani made this appear before the congregation *de Propaganda fide*

---

* See Dodd, vol. 3, p, 139, 141, 2. Alfo p. 149, 50: whence it appears what were the real fentiments of the Catholics, and by what means the fignatures to the proteftation were procured.

fide. Now the regulars and such of the laity as were against a bishop, were not so averse to the design, as to wish the clergy were left destitute of a head to inspect them, provided he claimed no authority over the regulars or the laity. They proposed, therefore, to have the scheme of the archpriest revived. On the other hand, the secular clergy insisted, not only on having a bishop according to the divine and primitive institution; but that he should enjoy that power which other bishops claimed in the church of God. They saw no reason, why the Indies should be favoured with bishops, and only England neglected. They alledged, that the queen, and the majority of the nobility and gentry earnestly desired it. That it was to be apprehended, the regulars had human views in opposing it. That the scheme of an archpriest was unusual, and not authorised by the laws of God or the practice of antiquity. That it would not answer the ends of the mission, as they had learned by experience; to say nothing of the indirect means made use of to introduce it amongst them. That the title of a bishop could afford no grounds for a persecution, as was plain in the bishop of Chalcedon's case, who lived undisturbed, till the nation was excited against him by the libels and clamours of their own party. What had the government to apprehend from a bishop more than from an archpriest, or other dignified churchman enjoying the fame jurifdiction? How could it be judged an encroachment on the privileges of regulars to become fubject to a bifhop while ftrolling on the miffion, when even in their monafteries, according to the decrees of the council of Trent and the difcipline of the church, they could not make ufe of their faculties in regard to the laity, without epifcopal approbation?

New fcheme for a bifhop. While the two parties were thus employed in producing arguments in favour of their pretenfions, the embaffador of Spain, with the refident of Flanders, propofed the fcheme formerly hinted at by Panzani, though on the view of a different intereft. They took it for granted, that the greateft part of the Englifh Catholics were Spaniards by faction, and thence inferred, that they would be beft pleafed with a bifhop who fhould refide with the Spanifh embaffador in quality of his excellence's almoner. This propofal was confidered as very favourable to the Englifh Catholics in general, becaufe it would ferve as a precedent for the French embaffador or other foreign agents to expect the fame favour; and the queen herfelf might enjoy the fame privilege. The Jefuits were fuppofed to be at the bottom of this defign, being not yet cured of their apprehenfions, that the bifhop of Chalcedon would make them another vifit.—

Urban

Urban VIII. would not liften to any fuch propofals. Several inconveniences feemed to attend it. The court of England was always jealous of the liberties foreign embaffadors took in admitting Englifh Catholics into their chapels, which would be greatly encreafed when a bifhop had his refidence there. Befides, the Catholics would be divided into factions by adhering to bifhops protected by different nations; and their differences, inftead of being compofed, would break out in new controverfies, and ruin the common caufe.

The king refufes to admit a bifhop.

While perfons of no great intereft were pleafing themfelves with thefe imaginary fchemes, the queen and Panzani were fo far advanced, as to have the queftion propofed to the king, whether he would be content that a bifhop fhould be appointed? The queen folely appeared in it, Panzani having been exprefsly ordered by Rome, not to run the hazard of a refufal himfelf. His majefty's anfwer was very candid: " that it could not be permitted; for that neither the bifhops nor his miniftry would hearken to any fuch propofal, as things now ftood."—Nor was it poffible to move the king from his refolution, he being naturally both fearful and tenacious, and his chief favourite and counfellor, the archbifhop of Canterbury, keeping him clofe to the point.

Project of a reciprocal agency, on which father Philip writes to Barberini.

I mentioned before a reciprocal agency, that was projected between the court of Rome and the queen of England, the defign of which was to make an experiment, how far the two churches could be brought towards a union. The difappointment, as to the king's allowing a bifhop, was no impediment to this fcheme.— Windebank was the firft propofer, and he was careful not to flumber over fo pleafing an idea. Cottington and the cardinal had, in like manner, been acquainted with it, who not only gave their approbation, but went heartily into it. But before they proceeded any further, Barberini ordered father Philip, the queen's confeffor, to deliver his fentiments on the fubject, as to its practicability and method. Father Philip was a perfon of great penetration, who had made it his bufinefs ever fince he came into England, to obferve the religious difpofitions of the nation. The fubftance of the account he fent to the cardinal was this:

"That the king and feveral of his miniftry were far from being adverfe to an union: that it was an undertaking of the moft dangerous confequence, on account of the many and fevere edicts that were in force againft the Roman Catholic religion: that thofe who were moft favourably inclined to the Catholic caufe, were frequently obliged to give proofs of their zeal to the contrary for
"fear

"fear of notice; in which cafe it was difficult
"to form a juft idea of their real fentiments,
"feeing they found themfelves under a neceffity
"of varying from themfelves, and acting inco-
"herently. For inftance, he faid, when there
"was any preffing occafion for money, the
"king was obliged, contrary to his inclination,
"to let the laws loofe againft the Roman Catho-
"lics, otherwife the Puritanical houfe of com-
"mons would make no progrefs in the money
"bills; for the government not being arbitrary,
"no extraordinary levies would be granted
"without the people's confent. That the
"bifhops in like manner, (though feveral of
"them were difpofed to enter into a correfpon-
"dence with Rome) when their temporalities
"were threatened by the Puritanical members,
"(as they had frequently been of late) went
"into the fame perfecuting methods; that fuch
"a conduct as this had fo much of contradiction
"in it, that it was altogether unintelligible to
"thofe who were not perfectly acquainted with
"the infirmities of human nature, and parti-
"cularly with the irrefolution of thefe iflanders.
"Yet, after all, if Windebank's project of a
"reciprocal agency could be fet on foot, there
"might be fome hopes of a reunion."

Then father Philip goes on and acquaints
the cardinal with the qualities of the agents
proper to engage on fuch an undertaking:
particularly

particularly he gives his opinion of the Italian agent, viz. " that he ought to be about 35 years
" of age, youth and old age being neither of
" them capable of that defirable mixture of
" gravity and fpirit requifite in a public mini-
" fter; that he ought to be noble, rich, hand-
" fome, and affable in converfation; a good
" economift, obferving ftrict order in his family;
" grave and referved, yet complaifant, efpecially
" to the ladies of the court, and ftill here very
" guarded, the king and queen being
" ftrictly virtuous, and profeffed enemies to im-
" modefty and gallantry.—Then, as to more
" public qualifications: He muft be fkilled in
" the French language, which will carry him
" through all the bufinefs of the Englifh court ;
" always acceffible, and willing to give full
" fatisfaction to all that addrefs themfelves to
" him; never to blame the king or miniftry for
" the feverities fometimes practifed againft the
" Roman Catholics, but if any reflections be
" made, to take care they be only levelled
" againft the purfuivants and other inferior
" officers; not to appear too zealous to have the
" Catholics relieved from their hardfhips; to
" compliment the fecretaries of ftate with an
" account of what paffed at Rome, and foreign
" courts, yet ftill with due regard to his truft,
" and refpect to his religion. He would have
" the queen now and then pleafured with Italian
" curiofities, and every one accofted in their
" own way and enticed by proper baits."

Then

Then he proceeds to give his opinion how things ought to be managed, after the goodwill of the miniftry and privy council fhall have been fecured; viz. "That none of the laws
"againft Roman Catholics be executed, without
"an exprefs and written order from above to
"every inferior office, which will afford time
"to ward off the blow, and amount to an
"interpretative liberty of confcience; and, at
"the fame time, be an encouragement to
"moderate Proteftants to fpeak their minds
"freely in favour of Roman Catholics. This
"might be followed afterwards by more parti-
"cular allowances for liberty of confcience, and
"fo on gradually, till it became general; and
"then, in a few years, the leading men of both
"houfes might be induced to think of an
"union."

Such was father Philip's plan, of which the cardinal very well approved; and his opinion on the whole was, that the difficulties were not fo great but they might be furmounted, in cafe the king would efpoufe the caufe heartily.

The cardinal on this affured father Philip, that nothing fhould be neglected in order to provide fuch an agent for England as fhould poffefs all thefe neceffary qualifications; and that the bufinefs of Panzani was daily to cultivate the good difpofitions of the two fecretaries.

The king comes into the Project.

It

It required some address to make these gentlemen act in concert; for though they were both zealous in the cause, yet Windebank having been the first proposer of the scheme of the mutual agency, he might perhaps be disgusted, if he were not also a principal actor. But matters were so contrived, that both were equally employed.—The queen now informed his majesty of the particulars, to which he did not object; and he ordered that Cottington should be consulted, being very capable, he said, to advise. This served to unite the secretaries. Secrecy was enjoyned on all hands; and the king requested, he might himself name the person who should be sent to Rome. As to the agent thence to the queen, he desired he might not be in orders; for a lay man would give less jealousy to ministry, nor be considered as a nuncio, and, at the same time, would be the fittest person to terminate the disputes between the clergy and regulars. The matter being thus far settled, Windebank, as the original mover of so promising a work, appeared much delighted.

Mr. Montague.

At this time there was a young nobleman at court, Walter Montague, whose conversion to the church of Rome rendered him highly serviceable in conducting the present projects. His birth, abilities, and other shining qualifications had made him the queen's favourite; nor did they recommend him less to all those who had the

honour

honour of his acquaintance. While he was a Proteftant, his curiofity had led him to vifit Rome, where, on the queen's recommendation, he could not fail of a proper reception. Returning to England, he took Paris in his way, where he ftudioufly expreffed the extraordinary civilities he had received from Urban VIII. whofe carriage and unfeigned affection to the Englifh nation, he faid, had fo charmed him, that he thought there could be no greater happinefs than to ftand at the elbow of fo deferving a prelate. Cardinal Barberini alfo, in imitation of his mafter's example, had fo loaded Mr. Montague with prefents and well-fuited compliments, that thofe two great men were the conftant fubject of his difcourfe and his praifes. By the hands of this gentleman, the cardinal prefented the king of England with a large picture of Bacchus, the work of the celebrated Guido, underftanding that his majefty was a great admirer of fuch curiofities. — Mr. Montague was fo impreffed with a fenfe of religion, from the appearance it made on the countenance of Urban, that, from the firft moment of beholding him, he formed a refolution of becoming a Roman Catholic. On his return to England, he executed this refolution; if he had not done it privately before, as many conjectured. When the king heard of his converfion, he fignified privately to him, that it would give lefs offence to government, if he

abfented

abfented himfelf from court, at leaft for fome time. In obedience to his majefty's orders, Mr. Montague, foon after, once more went abroad, and vifited Paris and Rome.*

Mazarin is made acquainted with the fcheme of the agency.

I have before mentioned that, when Panzani left Italy, he joined himfelf to the retinue of Signor Mazarin who was then going agent to the court of France. This Mazarin was a man of high endowments, and of a remarkable penetration and dexterity in the management of bufinefs. The queen of England, therefore, and the cardinal judged it proper to admit him into the fecret concerning the projected correfpondence between the courts of Rome and England. And in a little while, he was employed in fome remote matters relating to that affair.—The queen had requefted Barberini to ufe his intereft with the famous Bernini, that he would cut two buftoes, one of his majefty and

---

* He was fon of the earl of Manchefter, and brother to Edward Montague Lord Kimbolton. At the breaking out of the civil war, he retired to France, and was made commendatory abbot of the rich monaftery of St. Martin. The name of abbot Montague often occurs in the tranfactions of the Catholics. To their intereft he was greatly devoted, and to the caufe of royalty. He died about the year 1670. Dodd, vol. 3, p. 93, 4.

and the other of herself. Bernini confented.*
Mazarin very much applauded the meafure, as
a means, he thought, which would conciliate
the king of England, as Bernini had lately
refufed a fimilar requeft to cardinal Richelieu.
And the reafons given by Bernini for refufing
the cardinal, not being very confiftent with the
willingnefs he now fhewed to oblige their
Britannic majefties, Mazarin was defired by the
queen to interpofe, fo that it might be no
affront to that great minifter. Though this
may be looked on as a trifling occurrence, yet
Barberini had fuch an idea of it, that he judged
it to be a confiderable ftep towards fettling the
defired correfpondence. We have an account
of fome things relating to it in a letter of the
cardinal to Mazarin, dated October 20, 1635,
which is as follows.

" I am happy to find you concur with me
" as to the affairs of England. I only want
" Mazarin's judgment and good tafte in felect-
" ing the fmall prefents I am fending into
" thofe parts, and his hand to offer them,
" which, I know, would render them accept-

---

* It is related that, while the artift contemplated the original picture of his majefty, which he was to copy, he remarked the melancholy lines of the countenance, that feemed to portend, he faid, fome fatal cataftrophe to that royal perfonage.

" able. You are not ignorant, upon how
" many accounts, I am obliged to employ my
" time for the good of England, it being no
" small honour to me, to have been named its
" protector. My greatest ambition is to enjoy
" that title in its full extent, which the queen,
" in some measure, procures me, by becoming
" a common mother to the distressed Catholics,
" and equally a friend to the clergy and
" regulars. The conduct of that kingdom is,
" of late, very much altered in regard to
" Catholics. They have now both fair words
" and good looks, who not long ago were con-
" tinually frowned upon. Nature has poured
" forth great treasures on their king. It is
" our daily prayer, that he may be as rich in
" grace. I am not able to answer the com-
" pliments, you make me, as to the prospect
" of re-uniting that kingdom: but I refuse
" not the congratulation as to the issue hoped
" for from the mutual agents, we are going to
" establish between the two courts. In this
" concern, I doubt not but Mr. Montague has
" done his part. Fail not to impart to me
" any thing, you may think will contribute to
" the good and happiness of England; for I
" am willing you should come in to rival me
" in that business.— The statues go on pros-
" perously; nor shall I hesitate to rob Rome of
" her most valuable ornaments, if, in exchange,
" we might be so happy, as to have the king
" of

" of England's name stand among those princes
" who submit themselves to the apostolic see.
" It is well known, that his holiness has an
" uncommon affection for that prince; and
" his conversion is the only thing he aims at.
" Yet it is the opinion of his holiness and
" myself, that he is naturally tenacious, and
" not easily removed from the principles in
" which he has been educated. This difficulty
" is daily experienced in those who are less
" tenacious, and in things of less moment.
" Did not Clement VIII. both before, and
" after he was pope, try several ways to bring
" over his present majesty's father, king James I.
" but in vain? Yet, at the same time, I
" flatter myself, it will be no hard task for
" Urban VIII. to make king Charles sensible,
" that he seeks neither interest nor convenience,
" but solely the good of his soul in the corres-
" pondence he would establish. All I can do
" is, to desire the conversion of that kingdom,
" where my power can do little, and where my
" sins, perhaps, are an obstacle to it. How-
" ever, willingly I would part with my life
" and substance in so glorious a cause."

The presents, which the cardinal mentions, were delivered to the queen by Panzani, and, considering the person to whom they were sent, a lady, we may imagine, as well pleased with curiosities as with things of value, they were well

Barberini sends presents to the queen.

well felected. They confifted chiefly of artificial flowers and fruits; a bottle of oil of Cedrino, a rarity not feen in England before; an extraordinarily fine relic-cafe, gilt, with one fide covered with a large chryftal of the mountains, and within it a bone of St. Martina, virgin and martyr, (whofe body was a little before found under the Capitol;) a fhort fummary of the faint's life, by way of exhortation to the queen; a book of *Roma Subterranea*, with an account of the churches difcovered and cleared from the rubbifh by Helena the emprefs, a Britifh lady, and an allufion to the Catholics abfconding in England, and now in hopes of appearing more publicly by the zeal and intereft of her majefty.

Panzani delivered thefe prefents with a compliment fuitable to the occafion; and in particular, he omitted not to fignify, that St. Martina would not fail to be a powerful interceffor for England's converfion, and fupport her majefty in her zealous endeavours that way.

The queen was extremely pleafed with thefe curiofities; but moft with the relic of St. Martina, whom fhe chofe for her future patronefs. The workmanfhip of the cafe was fo exquifite, that the king who had a good tafte, and was an admirer of fuch things, expreffed his

his furprife at the beauty of it. Hence alfo he took occafion to mention to father Philip, how defirous he was to purchafe the ftatue of Adonis, of which he had often heard, and which was now in the villa Ludovifia near Rome. Father Philip, at his majefty's requeft, wrote to the cardinal about it, telling him that no reafonable fum would be refufed for the purchafe. Barberini fpared no pains to gratify the king, but without fuccefs; and many letters paffed on the fubject. In his laft to Panzani the cardinal thus concludes: "I wifh I could effect "the matter fo, that the ftatue might be fent "to London, and that it might fhare a differ- "ent fate from what it had, when the emperor "Adrian placed it in the building wherein "our Saviour was born, that it might drive "the chriftians from that fignal place of "worfhip. I hope, I fay, it would not meet "with the fame reception in England. But "the truth is, the ftatue is not to be purchafed "by money. It belongs to the duchefs of "Fiano, who will not fuffer it to be feparated "from the reft of her ftatues and paintings, of "which fhe has a curious and a numerous "collection."

But to proceed to the bufinefs of the agency. —After frequent confultations, the king was pleafed to name Robert Douglas to be the agent on the queen's part. He was a perfon of great abilities,

Mr. Brett is appointed agent to Rome

abilities, and of singular candour; one in whom his majesty could confide, and himself no stranger to the court of Rome, where he had resided in the year 1633. But this gentleman dying soon after his appointment, they were at a loss for a successor. Father Philip proposed one Charles Waldegrave, a man of learning, integrity, and other great accomplishments; and who had received his education in the English college at Rome. Others mentioned Arthur Brett, a gentleman of good parts, brought up to arms abroad; but he was a stranger to the Italian language. In the opinion of many, this was a serious objection; and indeed, Mr. Brett himself alledged it, adducing other reasons why he was unequal to the undertaking. However, both the king and queen approved the choice; and his modesty in refusing it was not the least inducement to make them insist, that he should be the person. They told him, his deficiencies as to the language and other matters should be supplied by very able assistants, viz. by Mr. Conn, a Scotch clergyman of uncommon merit and abilities, well versed in all the ways of the Roman court, (and then at Rome,) as also by the cardinals Bagni, Spada, and Bichi, who had formerly been nuncios in France, and who would be disposed to shew him every attention on the queen's account, with whom they were personally acquainted.

Windebank,

Windebank, when he underftood that Brett was made choice of, could not conceal his concern from Panzani, telling him, he feared the king had made a falfe ftep, for the Italians would certainly reflect on the prudence of the managers in the nomination of a perfon fo remarkably unqualified. He named others, whom he thought more proper; and among thefe one Mr. White, a man of great capacity and well verfed in bufinefs. But father Philip oppofed this gentleman as being vifibly a creature of the Jefuits. The queen alfo would not hear of him, when fhe underftood that his wife was the late lord treafurer's daughter. *— The choice of Mr. Brett was equally difpleafing to fecretary Cottington, who apprehending that he had no great friendfhip for the Spaniards or Jefuits, concluded his agency would be prejudicial to that intereft. Some friends of the Jefuits muttered, as if the project would come to nothing, obferving that it was a public concern, and that they ought to have been confulted in it; that fuch a correfpondence was dangerous, being exprefsly againft the laws of the country. They exaggerated Mr. Brett's incapacity; and reprefented

Mr.

---

* Wefton earl of Portland. See his character Hift. of Rebel. vol. i. p. 47. &c.

Mr. Conn, who was to be his coadjutor, as a perfon wholly devoted to the Roman intereft. — Notwithftanding thefe difcourfes and furmifes, the queen was refolved to pufh the matter forward; which fhe did with unufual fervour, as well upon a view of the general good, as to convince the world that fhe was not flow in ferving the Englifh Catholics, as had of late been reprefented. The king, in this affair, was entirely under the direction of the queen; yet he enjoined the party to be cautious and fecret, for fhould fuch a correfpondence, he obferved, once get wind, it would be highly refented by the generality of the nation.

Converfation between Cottington and Panzani.

Things being agreed on, the two fecretaries laid afide their private views, and, apparently well pleafed with the choice of Brett, went heartily into the caufe. Panzani had frequent conferences with Cottington on the principal defign of the correfpondence. Happening to difcourfe on the re-union, Panzani told him, " it would not be amifs to level the way as " they went on; and as furgeons cut away all " the dead flefh before they can pretend to " heal a wound, fo the mifcarriages of Henry " VIII. when he firft made the breach, were " to be looked into, and his motives weighed." —" I beg of you, faid Cottington, never let " us mention the fcandals and calamities of
" thofe

"thofe times, of which all thinking men ftill
"retain a frefh idea. I only wifh that the
"king could be fully convinced, that the
"fee of Rome has a real affection for him.
"I do indeed," continues Cottington, "ob-
"ferve a great alteration in the enemies of
"the church of Rome. Formerly the word
"Rome could not be pronounced without
"horror and deteftation: but now we are
"grown more mannerly. On the other hand,
"I believe, the advice would not be unfea-
"fonable, that his holinefs fhould be reminded
"to give fpecial inftructions to his nuncios
"and agents abroad to be more complaifant
"to the Proteftant embaffadors in foreign
"courts."—Panzani replied, " That it would
"certainly be more edifying if old grudges
"and animofities were laid afide by all par-
"ties; adding that, if once the Englifh go-
"vernment would fhew itfelf good-humoured
"to the Roman Catholics, Rome would not
"be wanting in making a fuitable return to
"them and all other Proteftant powers. But
"why, faid he, fhould his holinefs's agents
"carefs Proteftant embaffadors, while the poor
"Englifh Catholics are haraffed, and punifhed
"even with death on the fcore of religion?"
— This difcourfe gave Panzani an opportunity of mentioning the infolence of informers, purfuivants, &c. who lived on the
calamities of the Catholics. Cottington promifed

mifed to ufe his endeavours to prevent the evil in future.

It was not long before notice was given to the court of Rome, that Mr. Brett was to be fent thither as agent. That court was not a little pleafed, that the Englifh had made the firft advances, and on their fide, immediately confulted to difcover a proper perfon to fend into England. In relation to thefe matters, Barberini wrote the following letter to Panzani, dated December 10, 1635.

<small>Barberini writes to the latter.</small>

"Our prayers are redoubled; and I have
"made a religious vifit to the feven churches
"to obtain by my poor prayers what, I have
"reafon to fear, my fins have otherwife made
"me unworthy of. However, *if I forget thee,*
"*let my right hand be forgotten: let my tongue cleave*
"*to the roof of my mouth, if I prefer not Britain*
"*above my chief joy.* — I cannot pafs over in
"filence the concern I feel, on account of
"that queftion of Mr. Cottington. Does his
"holinefs love the king, he faid? Love him!
"Yes, he loves him with a perfonal affection,
"equal to that he bears his nephew, not only
"as he is pope and a common father, but he
"loves him as he is Urban. This love is of an
"ancient date, and, as it were, hereditary,
"as his majefty's grandmother, queen Mary
"of Scotland, was once a witnefs. I daily
"fee

" fee manifeft tokens of the good inclinations
" of his holinefs towards his Britannic majefty:
" he expreffes not in words only, but with tears,
" how much he defires to renew the fame good
" underftanding which his predeceffors, for fo
" many ages, maintained with the Roman fee.
" I conftantly impart to him the contents of our
" letters; and he as often embraces his majefty
" at a diftance.—I very much approve the ob-
" fervation you made, that his holinefs's nun-
" cios do well to be referved, while other
" minifters give no tokens of good temper. I
" defire you will ftudy an opportunity to ac-
" quaint her majefty, what a fatisfaction and
" honour it is to me to be remembered on
" account of the trifles I fent her: return alfo
" to her the acknowledgments of his holinefs
" for becoming a guardian of the fpiritual blef-
" fings of the poor Catholics. St. Urban
" defired nothing more of St. Cecily than the
" converfion of Valerian her hufband. This
" is all the prefent pope expects from her Bri-
" tannic majefty. It is a comfort to me to be
" regarded by her, and no lefs to be the protec-
" tor of fo fair a kingdom. That country of
" late is much beloved in Rome: Men of
" diftinction and even the populace are rejoiced,
" when they hear of their welfare; and the
" thoughts of their converfion tranfport all forts
" of people."

About

Persons proposed for agents to England.

About this time, Barberini wrote to Mazarin* at the French court, to advise with him about a proper agent for England. In his answer, Mazarin mentioned two persons, whom he judged well qualified. The first was count Ambrose Carpegna, (or Cartagen) neither French nor Spaniard by faction, but entirely disinterested; a man of a sweet obliging temper, a diligent observer, quick in dispatches, could speak handsomely, and was very much in favour with his holiness and his family. The other was George Conn, a Scotch clergyman, of a singular character for piety and learning, in both which respects he had been, many years, celebrated in Rome: he, besides, knew men and business well, and was a particular favourite with the queen of England. One objection against him was, that he had been intimate with Monsignor Ciampoli.—Nor did Mazarin omit to propose himself, saying that he would, to make England a visit, expose himself to the most dangerous tempest at sea. Indeed, the queen had a singular respect for Mazarin; and father Philip took some pains to procure his nomination. But the cardinal thought it not proper, as appears from a letter to Mazarin dated February 23, 1636, wherein

---

* I have not remarked, that this was the Mazarin, who soon became minister of state in France.

wherein he applauds his zeal, but adds: "Would you have all the politicians of Europe leave their homes, and flock to London, to fish out what you had to do there? You would meet with a more dangerous storm at land, than you could experience at sea. No mischief would be hatched, of which Mazarin would not be accounted the author."

Besides the candidates just mentioned, there then resided at London one Gregory Spada, nephew to cardinal Barberini; and this gentleman, though his visit to England was from curiosity, was advised to put in for the agency. But to give a greater name to the business, it was thought proper that a person should be purposely sent and directly from Rome. Barberini on this made no further demur, but fixed on Carpegna.

It had been customary, when such negotiations were opened with Rome, for crowned heads to demand a cardinal's hat for some favourite: and Barberini apprehending that this would now be done on the part of the queen, gave a caution to Panzani how to proceed, in case the petition were made. This was: "That he should use his endeavours to wave all such matters, by signifying that the business they were engaged in being a general concern, the cases of particular persons, or their promotions

The cardinal's caution.

"tions were to be set aside for the present, lest, by occasioning disgust in other candidates, the grand affair of religion, which was the chief object of the agency, might be obstructed. He added that, in case such a petition were intended, the queen should be acquainted, that it was only usual for kings to be favoured with such grants, when they had performed some remarkable service for the church; so, in the present case, the obtaining liberty of conscience for the Catholics, &c. would be deemed a sufficient inducement. In the conclusion, he desires Panzani to be careful never to drop any thing, that might put the queen on making such a proposal."

The king's instructions to Mr. Brett.

Mr. Brett was now preparing for his journey to Rome, when the king, having some private instructions to give him, desired to communicate them to him in person. What his majesty charged him with was: The restitution of the Palatinate; a match between the king of Poland and one of the Palatine's daughters; and the form of an oath for the English Roman Catholics. If he proved successful in any of these points, the king engaged, that a Roman Catholic bishop should be permitted to reside in England.

The elector himself, at this time, arrived in London. Besides the restitution of his dominions

dominions which he earneſtly recommended to the king, he moved for the match juſt mentioned. The two ſecretaries held frequent conferences with Panzani on the ſubject; and they promiſed for the elector that, in caſe the match could be brought about, his highneſs was willing that liberty of conſcience ſhould be granted to the Roman Catholics through the whole palatinate. Panzani inſiſted, that the princeſs ſhould firſt declare herſelf a Roman Catholic; but this was not agreed to. Barberini thus writes to Panzani on the ſubject.

"Nature inclines us to have a ſingular "compaſſion for the children of the elector "Palatine, reduced, without their fault, to a "very deplorable ſtate. The nobleneſs of "their extraction moves me to do all I can in "their favour, and the more, becauſe their "family before its defection from the church, "was always tied by uncommon bonds to the "ſee of Rome. As to temporal happineſs, "they are in a deſperate condition; and they "are a great object of pity as to their ſpiritual "felicity, being, by the Calvinian hereſy, diſ"united from the center of unity. In the "preſent juncture it ought to be conſidered, "that the pope who preſides in the church, "not by inheritance, but by divine appoint"ment, ſhould not depart from the cuſtomary "methods of his predeceſſors, nor from what "the

Barberini's ſentiments reſpecting the family of the elector Palatine.

"the councils and fathers direct in such cases.
"Now it was never the practice, even at the
"inſtance of emperors and whole nations, to
"admit of a diviſion of the church of God.
"The diſcipline of the church will not allow
"of ſuch compoſitions: otherwiſe, (and I take
"a pride in ſaying it,) nothing would ſooner
"move me to diveſt myſelf of all worldly
"advantages, that I might purchaſe eaſe to
"that unfortunate family. As I love to be
"ſincere and grateful, ſo I am ready to make
"any return for the favours imparted to me
"by that illuſtrious houſe; though I ſee, at
"the ſame time, nothing that ſhould make
"them ſtand out, and refuſe to comply with
"what is expected from them. I will con-
"clude with aſſuring you, that the nuncio
"who reſides at the Imperial court never yet
"declared himſelf, on the ſubject of reſtoring
"the Palatinate. He only ſignified, that
"regard ought to be had to religion when it
"was reſtored; and that an abſolute and
"unconditional reſtitution would very much
"prejudice the Catholic intereſt. I cannot
"forbear putting you in mind, that liberty of
"conſcience is a new ſyſtem among the people
"of Germany, who uſually change their
"religion with their maſters. And the
"obſervation is ſtill more pertinent in regard
"of the Palatinate, who once were Lutherans,
"and have ſince become Calviniſts, a ſect not
                                    " much

" much admired in thofe parts, nor ever
" before embraced by any of the ftates of the
" empire."

It was not long before the king of Poland* fent an embaffador into England to fet on foot this treaty of marriage, in which he was governed by the meafures taken at Rome. By way of preliminary, he propofed at his firft audience, that the princefs fhould become a Roman Catholic. His Britannic majefty was fo much difpleafed at the propofal, that he told the embaffador, he looked on himfelf to be neither Turk, nor a Jew, but a Chriftian who lived in a commendable religion.—The embaffador was then introduced to the queen, and abbé du Perron was affigned his interpreter. Having opened fome private commiffions to her concerning the Englifh Catholics, he preffed her majefty to ufe her intereft, that the elector's daughter might become a member of the church of Rome. To this fhe willingly confented, telling him, at the fame time, that it was a point not to be infifted on, for it was her opinion it would not be granted. The king, foon after, learned from du Perron all the particulars of this conference, on which he very

Difficulties in the propofed match.

---

* Ladiflaus Sigifmund.

pertinently obferved, that the cafe was the fame with himfelf, who never demanded that the queen fhould become a Proteftant, when he treated about his match with the court of France.—And indeed, the generality of the Catholics blamed the embaffador for making that article a preliminary. Windebank alfo told Panzani in private, that he was well affured that, neither the pope, France, Spain, or even the Poles themfelves had any opinion of that match; fo that Mr. Brett was not likely to fucceed in that part of his commiffion.

<small>Mr. Brett's death and other obftacles to the agency.</small>

Providence, befides, fo ordered things, that the bufinefs of the reciprocal agency was very much retarded, and almoft brought to nothing. Arthur Brett had put to fea, and was on his journey towards Rome, when, a tempeft driving him back, he was feized with a fever, and died. This event kept the other agent, count Cartegna, at Rome: and, about the fame time, a great inundation happening at Ravenna, the pope deputed the bifhop of Camerino and count Cartegna to examine into that unfortunate accident, and to provide for the neceffities of the many thoufands who had fuffered by it.—New agents, therefore, were to be provided on both fides.

Mr.

Mr. Montague, as I before obferved, was advifed by the king, on his becoming a Roman Catholic, to abfent himfelf for a while; during which time he again vifited Rome, where his holinefs received him with extraordinary marks of affection. Barberini, in like manner, loaded him with civilities. His birth, qualifications, and the queen's letter of recommendation were advantageous circumftances. A noble apartment was allotted him in the chancellor's palace; and had not Mr. Montague's modefty prevented it, many other unufual civilities were defigned him. It was in this journey, that he publicly received the facrament of confirmation, the cardinal ftanding godfather at the ceremony. After fome time, he took occafion to open a private commiffion from the queen, which was recommended to the care of the cardinal. It was: To obtain a cardinal's hat for Mr. Conn. — Mr. Robert Douglas had formerly intimated the fame thing to the court of Rome, in the queen's name. Mr. Conn, by the ftrength of her majefty's recommendation, had already obtained a rich canonry in St. John's of Lateran. He was alfo in election for the fecretaryfhip of the fecret Briefs, on the demife of Monfignor Francefco Ervera; but Monfignor Julio Rofpiglofi ftept in before him. Befides, he was fecretary of the congregation of Rites, a domeftic of the cardinal of St. Onuphfrio and his principal favourite.

Mr Montague endeavours to obtain a cardinal's hat for Mr. Conn.

It was much noticed at Rome, that a perfon of Mr. Conn's modefty and virtue fhould lie under a fenfible difturbance, at being difappointed in the way of preferment. However he fank not in his character on that account. The world is willing to give allowances to confcious merit, as well as to indifference on fuch occafions. But to return to the affair of the cardinal's hat.

Barberini obferved to Mr. Montague, that it was a thing of great importance, and was not to be preffed too hard in the beginning: yet he teftified his entire refpect for the queen, the opinion he entertained of Mr. Conn's merit, and how difpofed he was to oblige them both in that, or any other way. Still he kept himfelf clear from any promife or engagement. And that Mr. Montague might prefs the fubject lefs, he infinuated that Mr. Conn would be a proper perfon for the epifcopal dignity, and to be fent with that character to England.— Mr. Montague judging of the tendency of this fuggeftion, obferved to his eminence, that he had recently received an exprefs from the queen, in which fhe infifted earneftly on Mr. Conn's promotion to the purple. — Barberini ftill ftrove to wave the difcourfe, adding only, that her majefty fhould have a fatisfactory anfwer; but that the thing was of fuch a nature, that it required a great deal of time

time and reflection to bring it to maturity. In the conclusion he signified, that Mr. Conn would also be a fit person to take count Carpegna's place in the agency of England.—Here Mr. Montague took the liberty to complain of Panzani's politics, saying, that he was sent into England purposely to obstruct Mr. Conn's promotion.—Barberini perceiving, that he was not thoroughly acquainted with Panzani's commission, endeavoured to set Mr Montague right, assuring him that he went over chiefly to inform himself of the differences between the clergy and the regulars, and to make up those breaches which were become almost scandalous; but, at the same time, he was incidentally to offer his services to the queen, in the pope and cardinal's name, as any occasion should offer. What he had done in Mr. Conn's affair, he said, was by virtue of a private commission, and in which he was no further concerned, than in making a bare enquiry how the queen stood affected in regard to that promotion.

Two days after, Mr. Montague made another visit to the cardinal, when he again insisted on the same petition. Barberini still observed the same caution, assuring him, that his holiness would not engage himself; but that nothing should be omitted to make the queen entire mistress of her desires. He added, that it was not cuſtomary with the Roman court to make any ſuch promiſes, not even at the requeſt of nephews; becauſe promotions to the purple were never made but on the niceſt ſcrutiny, whether it would be for the general benefit of the church, and whether it was ſuitable to eſtabliſhed rules. This method Urban invariably propoſed to himſelf. He joined a reflection formerly made, viz. That, in caſe his holineſs ſhould be difpoſed to promote Mr. Conn, it muſt not paſs upon the world as a compliment paid to the queen, it being never known, that queens, without ſome other prevailing inducement, were favoured in that manner. — Mr. Montague, finding he could gain no ground, was obliged to content himſelf with bare hopes, which even the cardinal would no further agree to, than on the confiderations mentioned. However, to put the queen in a way of accompliſhing her deſires, Barberini ſuggeſted, that a great ſtep towards it would be to expedite the agency: and ſhould Mr. Conn undertake that office in lieu of the count, and his behaviour in England give content to the holy ſee, it would be a means of arriving at a cardinal's hat. The protector concluded with a diſcourſe concerning the iſſue of all theſe projects, which he apprehended were not very promiſing, conſidering the king's behaviour to the Roman Catholics: and in particular he mentioned

his

his breaking into the articles of marriage between France and England; the sending away many of the queen's chaplains; the punishing of Catholics by pecuniary mulcts, contrary to promise; and suffering informers and purfuivants to range through the kingdom, and act almost at discretion. — Mr. Montague undertook to make an apology for the king, saying, that the French, on concluding a peace, were themselves willing to give up some of the articles relating to religion, and that other matters were in the way of being redressed.

Mr. Montague having now gone as far as he could in his commission, prepared to leave Rome full of hopes, and loaded with civilities. To the queen he brought a letter written by his holinesses's own hand, in answer to one she had sent to him by the same messenger. She placed a great value on it, often reading it over; and as often kissing it in token of the great respect she had for the see of Rome, but especially for him who then filled St. Peter's chair. The account Mr. Montague gave of his reception at Rome caused her a singular delight; and her joy was encreased when she daily heard, that all the English who went thither were treated in the same manner, respectively to their characters. — These extraordinary civilities to the British nation were a

Returns to the English court.

common

common subject of conversation at court. Both the king and the nobility were pleased with it. Among others, the bishop of Lincoln (whose nephew had been kindly entertained at Rome, and shared plentifully of Urban's favours) declared publicly, that cardinal Barberini had done more to reclaim the northern kingdoms by his civilities, than cardinal Bellarmin had ever done by his writings.

I cannot here omit an incident relating to the subject of these times. — One day, the queen, speaking of pope Urban to his majesty, said, that he was nuncio at the court of France at the time of her birth; and that, being ordered to wait on her mother, and congratulate with her on the occasion, by way of compliment, he said, he hoped the time would come, when that little princess would be a great queen. The queen-mother smartly replied: " And that will come to pass, when " you are a great pope."—King Charles made this observation: " It is manifest to all the " world, that both these things have proved " true. I always looked on our queen-" mother to be a great princess; but for " the future I must regard her as a pro-" phetess."

I will

I will dismiss this matter relating to Conn's promotion to the purple, having first observed, that it was no less the king's than the queen's desire; for his majesty had entertained a notion, that to have a cardinal his friend at the Roman court would be very much for his interest; and Mr. Conn was a person in whom he could confide. This it was that kept the queen's hopes alive, and encouraged her not to desist.

We are now to consider how Panzani proceeded in the principal article of his commission, viz. in reconciling the clergy and regulars. He took great pains to effect it; and after frequent meetings and consultations, an agreement was concluded between the parties, the Jesuits only refusing to come in, and join the rest. The following paper gives some idea in what manner they went on. *(The Clergy and Regulars are reconciled.)*

*The Instrument of Peace or Concord between the Secular Clergy and the Regulars.**

Because the common good of religion ought principally to be regarded by those who labour in the Lord's vineyard, and that good may be promoted with most ease

---

* Dodd, p. 132.

ease and success, when the labourers are united by one common principle; therefore, under the direction of the holy spirit, as we presume to hope, the secular clergy of England, on the one side, with the fathers Benedictins, Franciscans, Dominicans, and Carmelites, on the other, have resolved to settle a form of union amongst themselves adapted to this end, leaving their respective rights and privileges untouched. And that nothing may obstruct the progress of this desirable concern it is first resolved, that all former feuds and differences be now closed; and the parties mutually promise to bury their animosities, and to abstain from all recrimination. Wherefore, on this present day, the 17th day of November, an. 1635, being met in London. on behalf and in the name of the R. R. Bishop of Chalcedon and of the secular clergy, the underwritten N. N. N. and on behalf and in the name of the fath rs Benedictins, &c. the underwritten N. N. N. the same approved the following form of union, intended to endure till the Lord shall restore to these kingdoms the free practice of the Roman Catholic Religion.

The parties mutually promise, that they will unanimously attend to the common concerns of religion, and will aid one another, as often as it may be wanted; nor will they, as far as depends on themselves, suffer his holiness to be imposed on by false representations, or the honour and government of his majesty to be disturbed. To this end, it is, therefore, resolved, that, at least every quarter, and as often besides as may be occasion, deputies from both sides shall meet for the purpose of deliberation.

But

But as his holinefs has deputed hither the Rev. Gregory Panzani, it is our defire that he be requefted to meet our deputies, in order that our reconciliation be made more firm and folemn. And if the members of other orders be difpofed to join our union, we admit them to it.

The deputies then figned three copies of this inftrument, one to be delivered to the clergy, a fecond to the above regulars, and a third to Panzani, that he might make a report of it to Rome.

When the parties concerned were met to fign the articles of agreement, one father Roberts, a Jefuit, defired to be admitted. His bufinefs was to expoftulate with them, why Panzani was called to the affembly? He was anfwered, that Panzani was not prefent at their conferences, but was in a room near at hand, that he might be ready to confirm the agreement, and congratulate with them on the happy conclufion of their differences. He was affured, moreover, how agreeable it would be to them all, if he or any other, in the name of the Jefuits, would appear and fubfcribe as the other deputies did, adding, that there was a blank left in the writing for that purpofe. Father Roberts was far from being fatisfied, though they acquainted him with every particular. He even expofed the meeting, reprefenting it as a çonfpiracy againft their fociety. — Panzani having

The Jefuits only ftand out.

having notice that father Roberts was prefent, took fome pains to fet him right, affuring him, almoſt with tears in his eyes, that the only object of their meeting was peace and harmony; and he hoped the Jefuits would not ſtand off, but convince the world, by figning the articles of agreement, that they were ſtudious of peace, and had an equal regard with others for the good of the miſſion. The deputies alfo earneſtly begged for their compliance; but to no purpofe. Roberts would not depart a tittle from his refolution, though he feemed willing that the refult of the conference ſhould be communicated to his order.

Panzani, on the firſt meeting of the deputies, demurred whether he ſhould appear amongſt them, leſt his prefence might feem to favour the biſhop of Chalcedon's pretenfions, whofe cafe was not yet decided at Rome. But being affured that the biſhop's name was no otherwife mentioned, than as he was an eminent member of the clergy body, he hefitated no longer.—Soon after this, Panzani made it his bufinefs to find out Richard Blond, provincial of the Jefuits, whom he preffed very hard to join the other orders.* But he declined it, which

---

* Dodd, p. 134, *Ep. Greg. Panzani.*

which fo irritated the deputies, that they advifed Panzani to importune him no longer, for that it made him put too great a value on his concurrence.

The fecretaries, underftanding the agreement amongft the miffionaries was not likely to be univerfal, felt a fenfible trouble, as did all others who were favourers of the projects then on foot.

Blond, perceiving that his ftanding off difpleafed the generality of the Catholics, condefcended fo far as to fign a letter which gave an affurance of maintaining a friendly correfpondence with the other miffioners: but as to the articles of agreement, he faid, they were liable to feveral exceptions. The letter, by his order, was communicated to the deputies; and they, in return, fent him a copy of their agreement, and, at the fame time, defired, he would meet them, in order to remove the difficulties he apprehended.—Panzani, meanwhile, renewed his proteftations of impartiality, declaring that his only view was a lafting peace amongft them. He affured the Jefuits, they had nothing to fear from the bifhop of Chalcedon's being named with the reft; and that the other orders, equally jealous of their refpective privileges, made no account of it.—

Father Blond's conduct.

Father

Father Blond replied in a second letter* full of caution and reserve, viz. That his holiness having already by a Brief, beginning *Britannia*, dated May 9, 1631, given express orders, that all controversies between the clergy and regulars should be suppressed and silenced, it was more adviseable to stick to the letter of those orders, and to submit to them, than, by meetings and proposing articles of agreement, to raise grounds for new disputes. He, therefore, judged it inconvenient to enter upon any new projects, whence difficulties would certainly arise.

Gives offence.

This second letter of the provincial drew from some of the clergy a very sharp reply, in the nature of a manifesto. It represented the letter as a piece entirely made up of equivocation, artifice, and design.† — When the substance of this answer was communicated to Barberini, he charged Panzani to have it suppressed, apprehending it would occasion a reply

---

* Dodd, p. 135, *Ep. Ric. Blond.*

† See in Dodd, p. 153, another letter from Blond, more artful and evasive than the former, in which, speaking of the clergy, he says that " the *vain splendour of the hierarchy* had " drawn a veil before their minds;" and the *apostolic see* he terms the parent of all churches and the *source of the whole ecclesiastical order*. — It mattered not, that such expressions as these had often raised universal indignation, and been formally censured.

reply from the Jefuits, and fo renew the war. He, at the fame time, acquainted Panzani, that the court of Rome had neither declared itfelf for, or againft, the articles of agreement, becaufe the bifhop of Chalcedon's name was regiftered with thofe of the deputies, from which fome might conjecture, that his pretenfions were admitted at Rome, where as yet the cafe was undecided. But then he obferved, that father Blond's letter was fo full of caution and feeming artifice, that it afforded matter of fpeculation, and left room for the world to make their comments. He added, it was his opinion, that, if the Jefuits had not thought it convevient to have returned a candid anfwer to what was propofed, they ought, in a few words, to have declared, they would move in that affair as the Roman fee fhould direct, a method which, on all occafions, they feemed prepared to embrace.

This backwardnefs of the Jefuits to come into the agreement was not eafily digefted by the clergy, and the regulars who promoted it. And it was confidered as an aggravating circumftance, that the provincial would not treat in perfon with Panzani, but conftantly fent father Roberts. In one of their conferences, Roberts was commiffioned by his body to affure Panzani, that the Jefuits never had oppofed the bifhop of Chalcedon, and that all

the

the oppofition had been from the laity. This declaration was not unacceptable to Panzani, becaufe it difcovered a difpofition towards peace, and it gave him an opportunity of demonftrating to them, that the epifcopal character was not intended to prejudice their privileges, but to ftrengthen them, and protect them in the execution. Yet he omitted not ftill to prefs their conforming to the agreement, which Roberts as conftantly refufed, alledging the provincial's reafon, that it was fufficient to obferve the injunctions of his holinefs, which forbad them entering into any controverfies with the clergy.

The report of this agreement was now made public, both at home and abroad; and the Jefuits every where gave out that it was a defign againft their order. Panzani, by his diligence, difcovered that they were tampering with the religious of other orders to prevail on them to proteft againft it, and to withdraw their fignatures. This was alfo vifible by the extraordinary encomiums, they of late beftowed on father Prefton, the learned Benedictin, who began to exclaim againft the agreement, to which before he had confented. They had moreover made fecretary Cottington believe, that the whole was a contrivance of Panzani, and a prelude for fettling a bifhop amongft them. Panzani was at fome pains to fet Cottington right in this matter; which

which he did to his fatisfaction. He declared fincerely that he never moved one ftep in it, till the parties concerned had drawn up the articles; and that then it became his duty to exhort the Jefuits to come into the union, for, by that means, they might with more eafe put an end to all the differences between them and the clergy, relating to the bifhop, chapter, &c.

During thefe tranfactionsi, Barberini renewed his orders to Panzani for fuppreffing the clergy's manifefto, with which he charged him in a very preffing manner, exhorting him at the fame time, to find out fome way to create a good underftanding with the Jefuits.—This being fignified to the clergy; they met, and returned this anfwer in fubftance to Panzani: That they were forry the manifefto had ever been made public; but they thought the Jefuits were very unaccountable in their behaviour, having fpread it abroad every where, that the whole defign of the agreement was levelled againft their body: That, as for coming to a good underftanding with them, it was what they earneftly defired and fought for; but there were fo many obftacles on the Jefuits fide, that it appeared almoft impracticable: That they vifibly affected fuperiority; would not treat upon a level; and feemed difpofed to fruftrate every thing, unlefs it were a fcheme of their own: That their management fpoke indifferency as to reftoring religion in England,

The clergy fhew their defire of peace.

England, unlefs it were effected by their means; and in confequence of this, their common difcourfe was, that it could never be brought about but by force of arms.—Panzani writing to the cardinal obferves, that this temper of the Jefuits might, perhaps, be the reafon why father Smith, a perfon of note of their order, moved fo flowly in getting the order to the purfuivants fuperfeded; a thing he had undertaken, and was thought capable of effecting.

The clergy, to convince the world of their fincerity, deputed three of their body to treat with the Jefuits, viz. Mr. Blackloe, Mr. Mufket, and Mr. Lovel, whofe defign was to lay the foundation of a further correfpondence. " And
" now, fays Panzani to the cardinal, I expect
" to know the Jefuits refolution. I appear
" very ftirring on this occafion, that I may not
" be faid to have omitted any thing, though,
" indeed, I conceive fmall hopes of fuccefs.
" It is and fhall be my method fo to conduct
" myfelf with the Jefuits, that they may have no
" matter of complaint, or that I have ufed any
" violence to bring them to a compliance with
" the reft of the priefts. The greateft part of
" them are willing to come into the agreement;
" and I have acknowledged the favour as done
" to myfelf. But I cannot tell what to fay to
" the Provincial. His words tend that way,
" but his actions fpeak the contrary."

As

As for the rest of the regulars, they stuck firm to the agreement, publicly owning they had nothing to object against the clergy, for endeavouring to procure a bishop, it not appearing that there was any design to infringe their privileges. Their firmness, at last, worked on the provincial so much, that he consented to an interview with Panzani, and signified to him his willingness to come into the agreement. Panzani, to keep him tight to the point, drew up an an instrument which he desired him to sign; on which the provincial appealed to his letter, telling him it was a sufficient approbation of what was transacted among the deputies. Panzani then acquainted him, it was expected that he should sign the declaration contained in the following clause: *We did not impede the bishop of Chalcedon, nor hereafter will we be an impediment to any one, that he may not freely exercise that power which he shall have received from the apostolic see.* The provincial agreed that the clause should be inserted in his letter, and Panzani appeared satisfied: and that the union might be more lasting, he desired him to depute one of his body to confer with the clergy, whether they had any further demands? On this he demurred: he first would see in writing what their demands were. Thus they parted. The clergy's manifesto still remained on the provincial's stomach, and he threatened to have the author excommunicated, unless he made a public

Panzani and the Provincial meet.

public acknowledgment of the injury offered to his fociety. Panzani, at parting, told him he would take care it fhould be declared a fcandalous writing. The provincial was fatisfied.

Behaviour of the Roman court.

All this while, the court of Rome was filent on the fubject of the agreement, neither declaring for it, nor againft it, which occafioned the Jefuits to report every where, that it was ridiculed at Rome, and treated as an officious piece of management of no weight or confequence. On this father Price, a Benedictin monk, Francifcus a Sancta Clara, a Francifcan friar, in the name of the affociated regulars, and Dr. Leyburn, in the name of the clergy, complained loudly to Panzani, that fuch reports very much reflected on himfelf and all the parties concerned. They further faid, that it was now pretty plain, what power the Jefuits had at Rome, fince they were able to overthrow a defign of that nature, where nothing was intended but an entire fubmiffion to the court of Rome, in the general petition for a bifhop. To this they added, that Rome's not approving the agreement was a kind of tacit condemnation: that the Jefuits' reports were too much hearkened to: that many were induced to form a judgment of the agreement by the manifefto, which was only a private paper, and now recalled; but why, they afked, fhould it be a greater

greater crime to oppose the Jesuits by a manifesto, than to write against a bishop? Or was there not a great difference between a Jesuit and the episcopal order, as to their origin, institution, and respect due to them?

These and such like were the complaints to Panzani, and they pressed him earnestly to represent their case to his holiness by the means of the protector.—Panzani would make no promise, telling them they had their respective agents at Rome to represent matters: and as to the Jesuits, he twitted their associates, as if they wounded the Roman court through their sides; for by suggesting partial proceedings, they seemed to question, whether his holiness was a common father, equally favouring all parties; and he was confident, he said, the same justice was due to cardinal Barberini.—The deputies, unable to obtain a promise from Panzani that he would write, in their behalf, to the cardinal, were satisfied to rely on his prudence and management, which proved agreeable to their wishes, for soon after he wrote him the following letter.

" I have little to say, only that the Jesuits, " upon all occasions, ridicule the agreement. " It is father Philip's opinion, as well as of " many others, that the silence of Rome, on " that account, is declaring in favour of the " Jesuits,

Panzani expostulates with the cardinal, and mentions other matters.

"Jesuits. The judicious persons of this nation
"esteem the agreement to be an entire extinc-
"tion of all the great feuds between the clergy
"and Benedictins; and are of opinion it
"would be prudent in your court expressly to
"approve of what they have done. Father
"Philip also informs me, that the Jesuits,
"besides spreading abroad that his holiness will
"not confirm the agreement, have divulged
"the reasons of that caution, namely, because
"*they* are not mentioned as a party, and the
"bishop of Chalcedon is introduced; whereas,
"says he, it is not likely that his holiness de-
"signs to make the domestic interest of the Je-
"suits his only rule, and as to the bishop, he
"acted not in the agreement, by the strength
"of his character, but only as a clergyman of
"distinction, and a superior by way of interim.
"The clergy stand not upon their pretensions
"as to the bishop, nor is there any occasion to
"disgust them by rejecting a pacific treaty so
"much applauded by all intelligent persons,
"catholics as well as protestants, who are well
"affected to the catholic interest. However,
"I am ready to obey your eminence's orders.
"—There is another thing I cannot conceal
"from you. Mr. Bennet* is by many styled
"vicar-general.

---

* He was dean of the Chapter on the death of Mr. Colleton.

" vicar-general. I am confident such a title
" will not be allowed him at Rome, as the
" controversy stands between the bishop of
" Chalcedon and the regulars. On every side
" I see nothing but the seeds of discord. If I
" may take the liberty to speak my thoughts in
" reference to these matters—would it not be
" adviseable to mention a remedy formerly
" proposed, viz. to confirm the chapter's au-
" thority; for so they might chuse themselves
" a vicar, and the apostolic see afterwards con-
" firm the choice. By this means, districts
" might be appointed in the nature of parishes,
" and a regulation established for the good of
" the mission. The chapter claims now a
" power over the clergy; but the Jesuits make
" no account of it. Indeed, the other regu-
" lars, and particularly the Benedictins, treat
" with the chapter as if with a body in power,
" and seem to concur willingly towards ob-
" taining a bishop. Yet, after all, I am at a
" loss how to proceed. The clergy are con-
" tinually interrupting me with complaints,
" the substance whereof is, that the Jesuits are
" countenanced in all they say or write, and
" by their ample privileges run away with the
" credit of the mission; but that they, for
" their part, languish under all sorts of dif-
" couragement, and that their tongues, pens,
" ears, and eyes are all useless to them, when
" they desire to be heared at Rome. I endea-
" vour

"vour to sweeten every thing, and assure them
"of your eminence's impartial temper: but
"they still complain."

The cardinal replies.

In a letter to Panzani, dated July 31, 1636, the cardinal strives to give content on these subjects of complaint. He says, "That the
"associated clergy and regulars had no occa-
"sion to be so uneasy, or to consider their
"agreement as not allowed of at Rome, be-
"cause there was no express approbation of it;
"that they ought to attend to the maxim of
"the law, *qui tacet, consentiri videtur*; that, besides,
"it was not usual with the court of Rome to
"make such open declarations; that they had
"many persons to deal with of different hu-
"mours and inclinations, and must proceed
"with caution, not to give provocation; that
"it was prudent not to take notice, or appear
"disturbed at what the Jesuits say in favour of
"themselves, they being a party concerned;
"but as for that particular of the agreement
"being ridiculed at Rome, it was all fiction
"and without ground.—He then advises them
"to cease from all complaints, and not to use
"any stratagem or artifice to obtain their ends,
"which would only occasion new disturbances,
"and never prevail on the court of Rome.
"And of this kind he mentions the taking in
"the bishop of Chalcedon, as a superior *pro
"interim*. As to Mr. Bennet's being chosen
"dean

"dean of the chapter, and ftyled vicar-general,
"that affair, he obferves, fhould fleep, till an
"agent were fent to refide with the queen,
"who fhould have proper inftructions. Pan-
"zani is then cautioned to let nothing, in the
"mean time, drop from him, as if Mr. Bennet's
"character were confirmed."

I muft now refume the account of the reci- *Mr. Hamilton and Mr. Conn named agents.*
procal agency between his holinefs and the
queen of England. — On the death of Arthur
Brett, who was defigned for that employment,
their majefties confulted about fupplying his
place. There was about court one William
Hamilton, a zealous Catholic, brother to Lord
Abercorn, a young gentleman of about 25 years
of age, nobly defcended, and allied to the royal
family. His figure was fine; and in converfation he was agreeable and witty. This
perfon, by their majefties joint confent, was
appointed to go to Rome; and Panzani was
ordered to fignify the fame to the parties concerned, and, at the fame time, to fay, that
Mr. George Conn would be the other agent.

The latter choice was not very agreeable
to feveral of the Englifh, who would have been
better pleafed with an Italian agent. They
apprehended fomething might be carried on to
the prejudice of the Englifh nation, while two
Scotchmen were employed. And we may
reafonably

reasonably suppose, it did not go down with an English stomach to see their own countrymen postponed. But the king declared himself fully satisfied with the choice of Mr. Conn, for whom he had a personal kindness, on account of his general good character from all the English gentlemen who travelled to Rome, to whom he shewed himself a common friend upon every emergency. Again the king had retained a good impression of him, for some years past, from what happened in France; and it is well known, his majesty is altogether immoveable in his affection and aversion. Mr. Conn had been serviceable in expediting the English embassador's entry at Paris, before the pope's legate had his audience, which saved the crown of England a considerable sum of money, at the marriage ceremony with France. Indeed, Mr. Conn was a person excellently qualified for the office to which he was appointed. He was graceful in his person, of a fit age, affable in conversation, well acquainted with the methods of courts, and from his youth instructed in the Italian ways. Besides, to complete his character, he was of strict morals and unblemished reputation. The queen, in like manner, was well pleased with the choice; nor was the appointment disagreeable to Mr. Conn himself.

Things

Things being thus settled, Mr. Hamilton, before he left London, took care to inform himself of the state of the missionaries in England, that he might be prepared to answer all interrogatories at Rome. The Jesuits, observing him to be very prying and inquisitive, complained to the queen's confessor, that an agent was made choice of to misrepresent them; and it was no otherwise than what Mr. Brett had communicated to them as a secret, before he died, that things would be so with them. Father Philip assured them of the contrary, observing that such surmises reflected on their majesties, as well as on the memory of Mr. Brett.

The Jesuits particularly are dissatisfied with the agency.

They that were acquainted with this agency between Rome and England, judged it would not be very pleasing to several foreign princes, for, should they unite, it would be the means, they knew, of strengthening the interest of England. The court of Rome would naturally favour a nation once so dear to them, and now reconciled like the prodigal son. But Urban had other views. His chief concern was the nation's happiness as to religion, remitting interest and politics to the usual direction of Providence.

The resident of Spain was one of those timid speculators. He, one day, accosted Dr. Leyburn, one of the queen's chaplains, telling him, with a very suspicious countenance, that,

in a little time, we mould fee Signor Conn make his entry into London, in order to reconcile the nation to the Roman See.—The Jesuits were still more open in their reflections. As they apprehended the consequences of the agency, so they made it their business to discredit it, and acted so imprudently, that the measure became public, and occasioned great jealousies in the puritanical party. Also, by a refined kind of policy, they endeavoured to make several believe, that both Conn and Hamilton were creatures of their society, which they hesitated not to insinuate even to Panzani, thinking, by this means, to create a jealousy in the king and queen, and so prevent the agency. Thus does Panzani write to the cardinal June 17, 1636: " But providence rules all things; and,
" as your eminence observes, we must be pre-
" pared against such attacks. If the affair of
" the union should not succeed, I am content
" to grow grey in the drudgery towards accom-
" plishing it. I will not make use of many
" words, but it appears to me that a mutual
" agency is the natural, and the only way, to
" promote it. It only remains that God touch
" with his omnipotent and merciful hand, the
" hearts of the king and of his principal mini-
" sters. I have not failed to acquaint the queen,
" that there is a rumour already abroad, that
" Mr. Conn comes over to reconcile the king.
" She immediately imparted it to his majesty,
" when

"when he obferved, that he was concerned at the malicious report; but fhewed himfelf content that Mr. Conn fhould come over."

Notwithftanding the caution which was ufed to keep thefe matters private, feveral perfons, unconcerned, made ftrong conjectures, and often difcourfed upon the faifiblenefs of an union; nor did they want plaufible arguments to induce a belief that fuch a thing might be effected. The perfons employed, therefore, often enjoined fecrecy to one another, and were particularly cautious to keep all they could from the Jefuits. Windebank was moft apprehenfive of being difcovered; wherefore, he admonifhed as well Panzani as the cardinal never to mention his name.

Among thofe that moft fufpected thefe proceedings was Mountague, bifhop of Chichefter, a perfon of remarkable learning and moderation.* This gentleman's curiofity led him fo

The bifhop of Chichefter and Panzani confer.

---

* He had been impeached in the laft reign before the Houfe of Commons, for a work entitled *Appello Cæfarem*, wherein he had endeavoured to reconcile the two churches, and to alienate, it was faid, the minds of the king and his fubjects from the eftablifhed religion of the country. But the king had been able to contrive that the impeachment fhould not be carried to the upper houfe. Mountague was feverely attacked by many of the puritanical party, and as warmly defended by the friends to epifcopacy and the regal fupremacy.

far, as to defire a private interview with Panzani. When they met, he immediately fell upon the project of an union, as if he had already been acquainted with the whole affair. He fignified a great defire, that the breach between the two churches might be made up, and apprehended no danger from publifhing the fcheme, as things now ftood. He faid, he had frequently made it the fubject of his moft ferious thoughts, and had diligently confidered all the requifites of an union, adding, that he was fatisfied both the archbifhops, with the bifhop of London and feveral others of the epifcopal order, befides a great number of the learned inferior clergy, were prepared to fall in with the church of Rome as to a fupremacy *purely fpiritual*; and that there was no other method of ending controverfies than by having recourfe to fome centre of ecclefiaftical unity. That, for his own part, he knew no tenet of the church of Rome to which he was not willing to fubfcribe, unlefs it were the article of *Tranfubftantiation*, which word, he had reafon to think, was invented by pope Innocent III after the council of Lateran was rifen. He owned, he had fome fcruples concerning communion in one kind; but as for particular points, he thought the beft method would be to chufe moderate men deputies on both fides, to draw up the differences in as fmall a compafs as they could, and confer about them. Such a congrefs, he thought, might be moft conveniently held in France, not only

only becaufe the French and Englifh came nearest to one another both in doctrine and difcipline, but becaufe of the ftrict alliance and affinity between the two crowns, and the apt fituation of the place. — Panzani modeftly replied, that he did not know but his holinefs might approve of the fcheme he had laid, but he could fay no more to it till the motion were made, either by the king, or by fome of the chief of the miniftry in his name. Bifhop Montague was pleafed with Panzani's referved- nefs and caution, and told him at parting, that he would take the firft opportunity to difcourfe the primate on the fubject; but infinuated that he was a cautious man, who would make no advances unlefs he were well protected.

This conference between bifhop Montague and Panzani being tranfmitted to Rome, the Italians were extremely pleafed with it; and it was a great fubject of joy to underftand that feveral of the Proteftant bifhops and clergy were ready to join with the univerfal church in the article of a fpiritual fupremacy, and to hearken to an accommodation as to particular matters. — Panzani, in return, was ordered to acquaint the bifhop, what a value they had for him at Rome, and how much his learning and pacific difpofitions were applauded, with an exhortation that he would continue the good work he had begun, and never ceafe till he had brought

The agent is directed to compliment the bifhop.

brought that distracted nation back, and directed them into the paths of their ancestors. As for looking into particular controversies, or specifying the terms of communion, it was too soon to speak to those matters. At present, it would be most adviseable to dwell upon generals; and especially the Protestant bishops and clergy ought to examine the motives which first occasioned the breach with Rome, which being found human and unwarrantable, it would be their duty to come forward and sue for a reconciliation. Afterwards, particular points might be debated with some hopes of an accommodation, when there was a court of judicature established to pronounce upon them. They might assure themselves, the bishop of Rome would make no unreasonable demands, but content himself with the essentials of his primacy, and such privileges as were annexed to it *jure divino*.

And receives other instructions.

Panzani is then directed by the cardinal to enquire into the characters of the Protestant bishops; for as they were to be employed in the projected scheme of union, it was requisite to be fully informed what sort of men they were, and how qualified as to learning, morals, religion, politics, &c. that those who were to treat with them, might know how to come at them by proper and suitable addresses. But he had a strict charge to be very cautious and secret

secret in the enquiry. Above all things, Panzani was advised never to favour the discussion of particular points, the issue of such conferences being always fruitless. Besides, it was never the custom of the Catholic church to admit of such kind of disputes, till the fundamental point of a supreme judge were first settled, for then other matters would come in of course. And as there were many positive laws, or practices out of the limits of the *jus divinum*, which were disagreeable to the English nation, as it was in the power of the church to alter them, so they should meet with all the tenderness imaginable, and such mitigations as the cause would bear upon a fair representation. In a word, authority and doctrinal points were the two capital objects; and the first was to be determined before the other could be debated.

Having received these instructions from Rome, Panzani took the first opportunity to wait on bishop Montague. He omitted not to acquaint him how much he was admired in Italy on account of the many and excellent qualifications he was master of.—The bishop, who was not a little vain, relished the compliment, and returned it, as far as was convenient, upon his admirers. He repeated his former discourse concerning the union, adding that he was continually employed in disposing mens minds for it, both by words and writing, as often as he

Has another conference with Montague.

met with an opportunity. He then again mentioned the pope's supremacy, whose feet, he said, he was willing to kiss, and acknowledge himself to be one of his children. He added, that the archbishop of Canterbury was entirely of his sentiment, but with a great allay of fear and caution.* Then he renewed the proposal of appointing deputies on both sides.

Panzani replyed, that he had orders not to touch upon particulars, nor give encouragement that there should be any relaxation on the Catholic side, as to the *credenda* or fundamentals of religion, observing, that the union designed was not only to be politic and ceremonial, but real and in *unitate fidei*, without any mixture of creeds.—The bishop assured him, that he aimed at a total union.

The truth is, Panzani was apprehensive the bishop still entertained some opinions inconsistent with the fundamentals of the Roman Catholic religion.

Montague

---

* Various are the opinions entertained of this unfortunate prelate, of whom, I believe, it is most true to say with the noble author of the *History of the Rebellion*, that " his enemies, for want " of another name, called him *Papist*, which no body believed " him to be, and the contrary to which he had manifested in his " disputations and writings." " But under this senseless appel-" lation, he observes, they created him many troubles and " vexations." p. 89, 93.—That the hat of a cardinal was ever offered to him by Rome, I do not credit, though it has been confidently related. Athen. Oxon. vol. 2: p. 57.

Montague then having occafion to mention his character and priefthood faid, he looked upon them as unqueftionable.—Panzani judging this to be too intricate a point, and knowing what exceptions fome learned men had made againft it, would not deliver his opinion, but paffed to another matter, which was to put the bifhop in mind, how neceffary it would be that the Proteftants fhould make the motives of their defection from the church of Rome the fubject of their firft enquiry.—Thus they broke off the conference, with a mutual defire of having another interview.

From the whole, it was pretty plain that there was a great inclination in many of the eminent proteftant clergy to re-unite themfelves to the fee of Rome; but they kept themfelves to themfelves, never imparting their minds to one another, much lefs to the king, for they imagined the fpiritual fupremacy was a prerogative he would not eafily part with. It was, indeed, obferved by fome of the miniftry, that when his majefty had occafion to mention pope Urban, or cardinal Barberini, he difcovered an extraordinary affection for them; but his praifes running moftly upon their perfonal qualifications, and generous behaviour to the Englifh nation, they could form no judgment from the circumftance, only that it might be a remote difpofition towards an union. Of the

the sentiments the great men of those times had of the matter, there was one instance. Dr. George Leyburn assured Panzani, *in verbo sacerdotis*, that the archbishop of Canterbury encouraged the duchess of Buckingham to remain contented, for, in a little time, she would see England re-united to the see of Rome.

Dissatisfaction of Windebank.

The discourse of this re-union at last became so public abroad, especially in Italy, that Windebank taxed Panzani with violating the rules of secrecy; but he justified himself, and gave him his word, that neither he nor the cardinal had departed the least from the assurances they had given in that respect; but he would not answer as much for several others who were willing to publish all they knew, that the scheme might prove ineffectual. He said that secretary Cook and others of the puritanical party daily instilled their suspicions into the people; nor was it in any man's power to bridle their tongues, who utter all they know, or even imagine, as they find it suitable to their interest, or agreeable to their humour or passion.—Windebank then inveighed bitterly against the Jesuits, that they, knowing how inclinable the court was to carry on a correspondence with Rome, should, at so critical a juncture, renew the ungrateful controversy about the oath of allegiance, exclaiming every where against it, and threatening to publish books

books on the subject. Wherefore, he defired Panzani to remind them of their duty; and fhould they not defift, he knew of a way how to make them more prudent and public-fpirited.—Panzani alledged feveral things in their excufe; but this would not pacify Windebank. "They are," he faid, "a reftlefs and feditious "fet of people, to whom no man can give con- "tent, unlefs he will tamely fubmit, and fuffer "himfelf to be trampled under their feet."— On this Panzani advifed the provincial of the Jefuits to iffue out his order to all his fubjects, not to engage in the controverfy about the oath of allegiance, either in word or writing, without exprefs licence from the fee of Rome, for that a contrary management would certainly irritate the king, and occafion a frefh quarrel with his holinefs. He gave the fame advice to the fuperiors of the other religious orders.

In relation to thefe matters, Barberini gave his thoughts in a letter to Panzani, dated May 8, 1636, which he concludes thus: "I beg "you will make excufes where they are ne- "ceffary; for I find there are fome who have "not a juft regard to religion; who, either out "of fome domeftic views, perfonal averfion to "his holinefs, or little affection to my family, do "take fome pains that things may not fucceed. "And, indeed, nothing could redound more "to the credit of my family, fince it would be

"more agreeable to me, that such an union
"should be effected while I am at the head of
"affairs, than if the Barberinis, upon any other
"account, became masters of the whole king-
"dom. I am very well pleased at the manner
"of your treating with the embassadors of
"foreign courts."

Third conference with the bishop of Chichester.

It was not long before there was another interview between Panzani and the bishop of Chichester. Among other discourses, Montague said something relating to the correction of the calendar, owning that the Roman computation was much more exact; and he believed, the Protestants would easily be induced to adopt it. Then they began to mention persecution, especially what the Roman Catholics suffered in England. The bishop said, at that time they were not disturbed, though the pursuivants and other officers could not as yet be discharged, till the order for that purpose had gone through some formalities at court.—Panzani being curious to know the characters of the chief of the Protestant clergy; Montague told him, there were only three bishops that could be counted violently bent against the church of Rome, viz. Durham, Salisbury, and Exeter*; the rest, he said, were very moderate.—But Panzani received

---

* Morton, Davenant, and Hall.

ceived a particular character of each bishop from another hand. It gave an account of their age, family, way of life, qualifications natural and acquired, moral and political, and, as far as could be gueſſed, how they ſtood affected as to the preſent management of affairs at court. This account was carefully tranſmitted to Barberini.

During the above conference, the biſhop happened once more to mention his orders, which, he ſaid, he derived from St. Auguſtin, the apoſtle of England, though he was ſenſible, the writers of the church of Rome made little account of Proteſtant ordinations.—Panzani managed as before, telling him, it was a tedious, intricate controverſy, the particulars whereof he was a ſtranger to.—The biſhop then obſerved, that the king had been often heard to ſay, that there was neither policy, chriſtianity, nor good manners in not keeping a correſpondence with Rome, by ſending and receiving embaſſadors, as was practiſed by other courts; and that, if his majeſty ſhould think fit to ſettle ſuch a correſpondence, he would himſelf make intereſt for that honourable charge.—" Then, replied
" Panzani, the world would immediately con-
" clude, that you were going over to the
" church of Rome."—" And what harm would
" there be in that?" ſaid the biſhop.—Panzani once more falling on the union, expreſſed
himſelf

himself in a very desponding manner, considering the many difficulties with which they had to struggle. "Well, said the bishop, had you "been acquainted with this nation ten years "ago, you might have observed such an alte- "ration in the language and inclinations of "the people, that it would not only put you "in hopes of an union, but you would con- "clude it was near at hand." Then he solemnly declared, that both he and many of his brethren were prepared to conform themselves to the method and discipline of the Gallican church, where the civil rights were well guarded; "and as for the aversion we discover in our "sermons and printed books, they are things "of form, chiefly to humour the populace, and "not to be much regarded."

Among those of the episcopal order who seemed to desire an union, none appeared more zealous than Dr. Goodman, of Gloucester,* who every day said the priest's office, and observed several other duties as practised in the church

---

* He afterwards gave great offence by refusing to sign certain canons of doctrine and discipline, drawn up in a synod held in 1639, under archbishop Laud; and was committed to the Gate-house prison. His scruples, however, were seriously conscientious; wherefore he retired from public life, and in that retiretment died a member of the church of Rome, in 1655. Dodd, vol. 3, p. 258. Fuller, Hist. of Church, p. 170.

church of Rome. — Among the laity, none thirsted more for this union than the earl of Arundel, who propofed liberty of confcience as the firft ftep towards it, and that no demand, on the other hand, fhould be made of the church lands.—At the fame time, feveral thinking perfons fpeculated not much amifs, that the union would be retarded by the regulars, who, by their claim to ancient privileges and exemptions, would darken the caufe as with a cloud, and go near to ruin it. And the Jefuits were chiefly apprehended in this refpect. The clergy, to prevent being impofed on by falfe brethren, caufed an oath to be privately adminiftered to all new miffionaries of their body, whereby they were to difown themfelves to be Jefuits in mafquerade.

The great affair of the Purfuivants, meanwhile, was at a ftand, and nothing done towards fuppreffing them, though the Jefuit Smith had all along promifed he would take care of that matter; but he always found fome pretence or other to hinder Panzani from applying to the miniftry for that purpofe. This gave him a jealoufy, that the affair was not rightly managed, and occafioned him to say that, if, from the beginning he had fuffered himfelf to have been directed in his agency by the Jefuits, he queftioned whether he fhould ever have come to an interview with Windebank,

The Purfuivants are difmiffed.

bank, Cottington, Montague, or even with the queen herself. And what further convinced him of their imprudence and unfair dealing was: if the pursuivants, at any time, committed any insolence, they immediately cried out there was a persecution, and sent notice of it to all parts abroad. This seems to have been their reason, why they refused to give Panzani a list of their members, or any satisfactory account of their affairs, as other regulars willingly did, pretending that such a scrutiny would render them public and raise a persecution. But it was not long before a stop was put to the pursuivants proceedings.—Panzani waited on both the secretaries upon that affair; and, by the queen's consent, it was communicated to the king, who being made sensible of the insolence of the pursuivants, and that they treated the Catholics in a barbarous and arbitrary manner, they were all cashiered, and, for the future, Catholics were not to be molested or imprisoned, without express orders from above directed to the justices of peace. This new order was a great satisfaction to the queen, and being known at Rome, was received with great joy.

<small>Barberini, in acknowledgment, sends other presents to the queen.</small>

Cardinal Barberini, in acknowledgment of the favour, prepared a far richer present for her Britannic majesty than he had formerly sent. It consisted of several excellent pieces
of

of painting of the best hands of the present and last century, being the works of Albani, Corregio, Veronese, Stella, Vinci, Andrew of Sarto, Julio Romano, Pietro de Cortona, and other artists of the first repute. The news of these presents soon reached London, and the king, being a good judge and a great admirer of such performances, was impatient till they arrived. They came whilst the queen was lying in; and Panzani, who was commissioned to deliver them, took care that they should be immediately taken to her apartment. She ordered them to be brought to her bedchamber, which was crowded with ladies of the first quality. The king, mean time, hearing of their arrival, hastened, with several of the nobility, to the queen's palace. The boxes were opened in the presence of their majesties, and the pieces viewed one by one with singular pleasure. They represented various stories; but the queen, finding that none of them had any relation to devotion, seemed a little displeased. However, when Mr. Conn came over, the cardinal satisfied her curiosity that way; when he also presented the two secretaries with several valuable pictures, in acknowledgment of the favours shewn to Panzani, and for their late service concerning the pursuivants. Yet he cautioned Panzani not to divulge him to be the author of these presents.

Mr.

Hamilton goes to Rome, and has an audience of his holiness.

Mr. Hamilton was now arrived at Rome, suppressing the title of agent or resident to avoid some ceremonious controversies, in which the residents of Poland and the queen-mother of France were involved. The one pretended, he was resident of a king actually possessing the crown, while the other only administered as regent. Hamilton, at his first audience, made an elegant speech in his mistress's name, tendering her obedience to his holiness in proper and engaging terms. He declared her intention of keeping one of her servants to reside at Rome, that the state of the Catholics in England might be well understood there, and to settle a good correspondence among the missionaries. He touched something concerning a bishop for the English, and concluded with a modest representation of the elector Palatine's case, which, he hoped, his holiness would consider, so that it might purchase ease to that distressed family, and contribute to the general good of religion.—Urban, point by point, replied to Hamilton's harangue, with a great deal of good nature and sweetness of temper; but as to the case of the elector, it was involved, he said, in a great many intricacies, and that the Roman see was seldom applied to in composing such differences; but that nothing should be wanting as far as he was concerned.

This

This general assurance not being well understood, Hamilton requested a further explanation from the cardinal. His eminence advised him to acquaint the queen with all the particulars of his reception, especially with the answer of his holiness as to the Palatinate, assuring him he should hereafter have a more specific account of the pope's inclinations, in regard of that affair.—Soon after, Barberini and Hamilton discoursed this point over between themselves. Hamilton asked what would be done for the Palatine family, in case they came over to the church of Rome?—The cardinal replied, that all his substance and credit should be sacrificed for their good: that it had always been a family very obsequious to the see of Rome, till prince Louis unfortunately made a breach.— Hamilton mentioned several obstacles that might hinder their conversion. — These the cardinal endeavoured to remove, alledging that they were Calvinists by sect, a sort of people very odious to the king of England; and as he would not be willing to assist them unless they renounced that persuasion, so a step or two further would bring them back to the mother church. He added, that the Calvinistic system was generally abhorred by the princes of Germany, as being disrespectful to crowned heads: that both the electors of Bavaria and Cologne laid the Palatine's sufferings to heart, and their becoming Roman Catholics would

And of the cardinal.

endear

endear them further to them, which, together with the intereft of the court of Rome, might prove a means of their re-eftablifhment. Then turning his difcourfe to England, the cardinal faid, he did not wonder at the prefent good difpofitions of the inhabitants, fince they had been formerly fo entirely devoted to the Roman fee, and it was almoft impoffible to deftroy that ancient amity fo far, but that now and then tokens of it would difcover themfelves, as branches grow out from the original ftock. — The fame anfwer he made in regard of Urban's perfonal affection to the king of England, which, he faid, had been of a long ftanding. He had fhewn his zeal in expediting the difpenfation upon the match between their prefent majefties: he had a long time been protector of the Scottifh nation, and always bufied himfelf in promoting the happinefs of his majefty's dominions: and, to go back to the prefent king's father, had not the unfortunate gunpowder plot broken out a little before he was fent nuncio into France, he had private orders to treat with king James, by the mutual confent of his holinefs then fitting and that prince: finally, though that execrable plot alienated king James from the Roman Catholic intereft, yet Urban's endeavours, while he was nuncio, were extremely well taken by his majefty.

Thefe

PANZANI.

These were the overtures of Hamilton's agency.—Mr. Conn, mean time, was pursuing his journey to England; while the Spaniards and some others were full of jealousy upon the issue.

Mr. Conn being arrived at Paris was immediately introduced to the king, the queen, and cardinal Richelieu, by the mediation of the pope's nuncio Baglonetti. They were all extremely well pleased to find a correspondence set on foot, which was likely to produce much good to the Catholic cause. They extolled the zeal of Urban and of his prime minister, cardinal Barberini, offering to contribute their part in so laudable an undertaking. — The English embassador then residing at Paris gave his master an account of Mr. Conn's reception: he praised his behaviour, and distinguished him by the name of the pope's minister. *(Conn comes to England.)*

Soon after the arrival of Mr. Conn at London, Panzani was recalled; but before his departure, he took leave of the queen, who failed not to remind him of the hopes she had, that Mr. Conn would be promoted to the dignity of cardinal. Panzani assured her, that his holiness was well disposed to oblige her in that way, and that the cardinal would make it his business to keep alive that good inclination in him: but, as had been more than once signified, *(Panzani takes leave of their majesties.)*

nified, that it was not the custom of the Roman court to enter into any engagements of that kind, and that great caution was to be used in Mr. Conn's case, left other queens should expect the same favour.—To this her majesty replied; that she was far from expecting any special privilege, or to be the greatest of queens; but, on the contrary, being the most undeserving of her rank, and the more inconsiderable for not having a Catholic husband, still she hoped, that unfortunate circumstance entitled her to some extraordinary assistance, and that Mr. Conn's promotion, on several accounts, would be a great advantage to her.— Panzani repeated the same assurances over again, on the part of his holiness and the cardinal; but to advance the matter, he insinuated that Mr. Conn ought first to do some signal service for the church, under her majesty's influence and protection, with whom, however, the cardinal did not pretend to capitulate or make conditions.—The queen was satisfied. Then Panzani taking leave of her, she presented him with a diamond ring of great value, and charged him with such compliments as were due to Urban and cardinal Barberini.

Panzani, afterwards, paid his last respects to the king, returning him thanks for his royal protection and great clemency to his Catholic subjects. His majesty seemed very much pleased pleafed with Panzani's complaifance, and, after fome difcourfe, demanded of the queen who was prefent, whether fhe had put him in mind of what related to Mr. Conn's promotion. She replied, that fhe had done what was requifite in that affair. "Then," faid the king, "I have no occafion to prefs it further. I leave it to her."—Laftly, Panzani took his leave of the chief minifters, and of feveral of the nobility from whom he had received great civilities: nor did he omit to pay his refpects to fome of the ladies of diftinction about court, who, though proteftants, recommended themfelves to his holinefs, and defired his bleffing.— It was the end of the year 1636.

On his return to Rome, Panzani was kindly received by his holinefs and the cardinal, and, as a reward of his labour and fidelity, was made a canon of the rich church of St. Laurence in Damafo. He was alfo honoured with a civil judicature in the city of Rome; and afterwards, being made bifhop of Mileto, he governed his diocefe with that zeal and conftancy which were always confpicuous in his conduct.

REMARKS

Subjoined to the MS Copy of the Memoirs,

By Mr. DODD.

It remains that I caution the reader as to the use and credit of this relation of Panzani's agency. The thing being entirely new, never before published in print, and the MS not in above one or two hands, no remarks have hitherto been made upon it. I venture, therefore, to deliver my own thoughts.

If the author was not Panzani himself; he certainly was some other who had his memoirs and private notes in keeping. The original is in Italian, from which it was translated by an eminent prelate of singular candour and scrupulosity, as appears by his exactness in adhering to every obscure expression of the author. I have, sometimes, taken the liberty to open the style, without at all altering the sense, or omitting any passage in the relation. The substance of the account is verified from an infinite number

number of books which have treated upon the same subject; but the credit of many particulars depends upon the author's authority, and the intrinsic tokens of veracity.—The reader may be led away into a belief, that there was a formed design between Urban VIII. and king Charles, to unite the two churches; but where lies the intrinsic proof of such an intention? What was done in that regard, was amongst some of the ministry; and in this both parties appear to have been too sanguine and credulous. It is a common misapprehension among foreign Roman Catholics, to imagine that England is immediately returning to the church of Rome, if either the King, or any of his chief ministers, says or acts any thing in their favour. Some gentle treatment they frequently experienced in king Charles's reign, his own pacific temper, and the affection he had for the queen, inclining him to indulge that party. It may by some be thought that his majesty went too far against the laws of the realm, in conferring with the pope's minister; but as the agency was not directed to him, others may view it as a private concern of the queen s, for which he was not answerable.

As to the encouragement given by the secretaries, and others of the nobility and clergy, towards carrying on a correspondence with Rome, and by that means effecting an union, it appears to me to have been their real design, though at a great distance, being strangers to the king's inclinations that way, and much more to the humour of the nation's representatives, if once the point came to be debated. That several leading persons both in church and state, at that time, were well affected towards the church of Rome, is plain. The two secretaries, Windebank and Cottington, both became Catholics, as also Dr. Goodman, bishop of Gloucester. Montague, bishop of Chichester, had made the nation very jealous of him for a long time; and it cannot be thought that the primate would ever have been tempted with a cardinal's hat, unless his previous carriage had induced the court of Rome to make him the offer.

Now I am sensible, I shall be taxed with imprudence for publishing this piece of history, and that chiefly on two accounts. First, because it exposes too much the intrigues of the court of Rome against the church of England; and again, because it reflects upon the regulars, particularly the Jesuits, in relation to the controversies they had with the bishop of Chalcedon and the clergy.

All I have to say is this:—My intentions are to inform and instruct mankind; which never can be done without offence, where parties are

are concerned. If no man purfues his *right* without fomething of paffion and human frailty, there muft always of neceffity be a great deal of foul play, when pretenfions are *unjuft*. Either, therefore, the world is not to be inftructed by fuch pieces of hiftory, or, when they are publifhed, juftice muft be done to every one. As for the exceptions mentioned: The whole affair of the Englifh miffion may be called an intrigue againft the eftablifhed church, if we regard the end and purpofes of it; and of this we may be informed without Panzani's Memoirs. Indeed, the account contains feveral particulars, reflecting upon the politics of the Jefuits, as alfo fome unfair practices; but the reader is left to his liberty as to the author's credit and partiality. The Jefuits may, perhaps, be furnifhed with records to juftify themfelves, which they may produce, by which they will not only oblige themfelves, but all others who are not defirous of being deceived.

SUPPLEMENT.

SUPPLEMENT.

From the close of the agency of Panzani an. 1636, to the appointment of apostolic vicars in the reign of James II.

WHILE the events, which the *Memoirs* of Panzani have recorded, amused the observation of the court, roused the suspicions of the disaffected, and engaged the solicitude of the Catholics, the general state of politics became daily more alarming, and a cloud, charged with ominous forebodings, involved the cabinet, the senate, the city, the army, and the distant provinces. That the storm must soon explode, was obvious to every observer; and where its violence would principally fall could be hidden to few. And in these circumstances it was, (however extraordinary it may appear) that the royal family could talk of a union of churches; that some of their ministers, duped in the same project,

State of the nation and the catholics.

project, could occupy themselves with a scheme of mutual agency from and with the Roman court; and that other plans, equally wild and insufficient, could be agitated. The diadem, the mitre, the coronet were seen visibly to tremble on the brows of their respective possessors, the cry of the growth of popery and of the indulgence, with which its ministers were treated, was echoed from mouth to mouth; and this, reader, shall be the period, when men can seriously attempt to bring back the influence of the tiara, and the forms of a hierachy that, in days of a more brilliant monarchy, had been exploded as too splendid and too fondly attached to privilege!

The bishop of Chalcedon, meanwhile, lived in France, protected by cardinal Richelieu, who had bestowed on him the abbey of Charroux, and whence he exercised his jurisdiction over the English Catholics by vicars-general, and other ecclesiastical officers.* Tired out with incessant

---

* I subjoin the *Relation of the Regulars* which, in recapitulating some events, will bring their views and their peculiar prejudices more distinctly before the reader: " In these times " of trouble, it says, Smith, the new bishop of Chalcedon, a " man of an ardent mind and addicted to the principles of the " Sorbonne and the Gallican bishops, attempted many things " to the prejudice of the Catholics and the injury of the holy " see. Arrogating to himself the appellation of *Ordinary* of " England

fant oppofition, and hopeful that the meafure might tend to reftore peace, he had generoufly offered to refign his ftation in the church. The court

---

" England and Scotland, he behaved rather as a *patriarch* than a *bifhop*, confirming the dean and chapter, extending his jurifdiction, erecting an external tribunal, and calling in queftion the confeffions which Catholics made to the regulars, he pronounced them to be void, becaufe their powers of hearing confeffions had not been approved by his predeceffor or himfelf. — When Urban was informed of thefe pernicious commotions, he directed his nuncio in France, on the 16th of February, 1627, to fignify to the bifhop, That he was no *Ordinary*, having been appointed not the bifhop of England, but of Chalcedon in Afia, and that the powers he poffeffed were reftricted by the apoftolic fee, and were revocable at will, under the clauſe in the Brief *we delegate*: That the miffionaries who are fent into England by that fee, are not bound to receive any approbation from him, as their deftination, their capacity, and their perfons are known to thofe who fend them."—This refolution of his holinefs was repeated in the following year. But who would have thought it? The very meafures that fhould have fufficed to reprefs in the bifhop that luft *(libidinem)* of *ordinary* jurifdiction, were the caufe that, tacitly appealing, as it were, from the chair of St. Peter, and relying on the protection of the moft chriftian king which he feemed too much to abufe, he recurred to the divine right and the facred canons, in order to fhew the neceffity of bifhops, and of an ecclefiaftical hierarchy for each particular church.

" For he publifhed Letters and Books; as did, likewife, Dr. Kellifon and other French divines, the intent and object of all which were to prove, " That the inftitution and government of the archpriefts, and confequently the government of the fee apoftolic was fo far anarchical; that it departed from the *jus divinum*, and was abhorrent from the
" perpetual

court of Rome replied, "That he might pro
"ceed in the usual discharge of his office, till
"the pontiff's declaration should be signified
"to

"perpetual practice of the church: that it was incumbent on
"the Roman pontiff to provide a bishop for each particular
"church, furnished with ordinary jurisdiction: that he was
"not empowered to govern by delegates not only whole churches,
"but not even parishes: that an ecclesiastical hierarchy was
"essential to each particular church: that the episcopal juris
"diction emanated immediately from God; or that the single
"sacrament of confirmation was so obligatory on the faithful,
"that a bishop was necessary for its administration: that it
"was rash to say, that the power of such administration might
"be delegated by his holiness to a simple priest, &c."—And
"as if these things did not suffice, to such madness did the
"party run, that, losing sight of the apostolic authority, they
"had recourse to other judges, namely, to the meeting of the
"Gallican clergy, to the Sorbonne, and to the archbishop of
"Paris, with all whom, by the favour of his patron, the car
"dinal Richelieu, the bishop soon so far prevailed, that the
"works of the regulars, (for they, in defence of the apostolic
"power, had written against the books of Dr. Smith and his
"followers) were devoted to every curse, and stigmatised with
"such dark and bitter censures, as could hardly be cast, it
"seemed, on Luther himself or Calvin."

"What dissentions and schisms then grew between the
"regulars, who deserved so well of the holy see by their stre
"nuous defence of its authority, and the bishop with his abet
"tors who assailed it with direful insults, as if, for so many
"years, by not supplying England with bishops, the *jus divi
"num* had been unknown, or had been violated, may be plain
"ly collected from the works published on both sides."

"To the cure of these evils, Urban and his cardinals judged
"it proper to apply an efficacious remedy. This was a *Brief*,
"prepared

" to him."* This declaration was never signified; and the business of the English Catholics went on, as it ever had done, with disorder and discontent,

---

" prepared for the 9th of May, 1631, copies of which were
" delivered to the superiors of the regulars, lest the bishop, as
" he had before acted in regard to other apostolic decrees,
" should bury this also in silence and obscurity.†

" Of this Brief, which begins with the word *Britannia*, the
" principal contents are: It expresses, in the first place, great
" complaints and reprehension of the excesses that had hap-
" pened: then, in regard to the principal cause of the disputes,
" it declares, " that the confessions, which have hitherto been
" heard by the regular priests, were valid, and so shall be here-
" after. For since they did hear them hitherto, and so shall
" do hereafter, by apostolical authority; ordinary leave, or
" approbation, neither was, nor is hereafter needful unto them.
" Moreover, let them use and enjoy their privileges and facul-
" ties in the self-same manner, as they did before these con-
" troversies."—The Brief then restricts the further hearing of
" the cause to the see apostolic; it suppresses all books that have
" been written, or shall be written on the subject; it exhorts
" all to mutual peace and charity; and it reminds the bishop
" that, recollecting in what country and troublous tempests he
" lived, he would strive to be a quencher of disagreement, and
" stirrer up of love and charity."

" This

* Abstract of Transactions, p. 42.

† See this Brief in Dodd, vol. iii. p. 158, as translated by the Benedictin monks; but he had before, p. 17, said, that it was, at the time, deemed spurious or surreptitious by many, and that it was never canonically promulgated, or delivered by proper officers into the bishop's hands. The mode of introduction, as given above, would itself excite suspicion of its authenticity.

discontent, the regulars still pleading their exemptions and privileges, and occupying the ears of his holiness with complaints and with the tender of their services.

These

"This *Brief* being afterwards published, it was thought that the bishop would have submitted to the judgment of the holy see, and would no longer have disturbed the glorious labours of the regular missionaries. But it proved far otherwise. For being desirous to decline, or if he could, even to impede the execution of a Brief that crushed the very seeds of his diocesan pretensions *(prosternens femina legis diocesanæ)* he had recourse to the most subtile inventions. This drew a new decree from the pope, in 1634, in confirmation of the Brief *Britannia*."

"But the bishop still persevered in his ways; and delaying irreligiously to execute the Brief, he again attacked the pontiff, asserting, with manifest injustice, that he was not fully acquainted with the true state of things. All these refractory attempts, however, failing of success, and when he could no longer, without blushing, meet the eyes of the English Catholics, and, what was more than all, when, by reason of the king's proclamations, he could be no longer safely sheltered, he withdrew into France.* No sooner was he arrived at Paris, than, to the great surprise of all men, he took a resolution of writing a letter to his holiness, in which he resigned his office and his jurisdiction over the English church.—Than this resignation nothing could be more welcome to the pope and cardinals; for tired with the troubles he had caused, they had long wished for the event. Wherefore, they instantly accepted his resignation, which they viewed as a certain remedy for all the evils. And, truly, he that will compare the

"tranquillity

---

* There is great inaccuracy in this statement, for the bishop had quitted England five years before, in 1629.

Thefe exemptions and privileges I have mentioned, will have been found by him, who, with fome attention, has read the annals of general hiftory, to have proved an endlefs fource of difcord. They were granted to religious orders by the pontiff, either, at their firft foundation, in compliance with the requefts of real, or in reward of exalted virtue, or were afterwards obtained under various pretences. On the fide of the *grantee*, the object was to be releafed from the common rules of difcipline, in the order of fervice and the jurifdiction of ecclefiaftical fuperiors;

Exemptions of the Regulars.

" tranquility which enfued among the Englifh catholics with
" the troubles they had experienced, muft be compelled to
" afcribe this refignation of the bifhop to the peculiar provi-
" dence of heaven."

" And now all difcord fhould have ceafed. But the bifhop,
" actuated by the fame levity with which he had made his re-
" fignation, foon repented of the ftep, beginning to concert
" means whereby he might procure his remiffion into England.
" Wonderful it is, with what effect he laboured to obtain the
" interceffion of the Englifh queen, and the more vehement
" fervices of the French monarch and of cardinal Richelieu,
" to be addreffed to the pontiff and to his nephew Barberini.
" He alfo fent his agent, Peter Fitton, to Rome. On this a
" particular congregation was held, in which, after repeated
" difcuffions, the holy office decided, " that neither the bifhop
" of Chalcedon fhould be fent back into England, nor other
" bifhops be fubftituted in his place."—A man lefs daring
" would here have clofed his career of ambition: the bifhop of
" Chalcedon only did not lofe courage, and by his agent perfe-
" vered in his applications. Perfons were therefore fent,

among

riors; while on the side of the *grantor*, the concession proceeded on the plainest maxims of policy. " I grant unto you," was the Roman bishop understood to say, " the privileges and ex-
" emptions for which you plead; but, in return,
" you must be faithful to me and uphold the
" prerogatives of my chair." And history tells us that they seldom violated the condition of the grant. Hence was an army raised, attached by domestic interest, to the Roman court; and they guarded the chair of Peter with a trusty vigilance.

" among whom was the cardinal Roffetti, to collect the most
" accurate information, and he became a witness, how vehe-
" mently the king of England (though his queen earnestly fa-
" voured the clergy) and the ministers abhorred the establish-
" ment of episcopacy among the Catholics; what troubles to
" themselves and the Catholics they thence apprehended; what
" a melancholy renewal of strifes and scandals would thence
" ensue; and how little that mode of government was adapted
" to the times and the general state of things. That cardinal
" therefore received orders that, having, by gentle means, if it
" could be affected, suppressed the dean and chapter, he should
" re-establish an archpriest for the government of the secular
" clergy."

It is remarkable that not a word should here be said of Panzani, who had been in England during the precise series of time through which this relation goes. But the reader will have discovered, what was *his* opinion of the regulars and their cause, which may account perhaps for the omission. And the Roffetti who is here introduced as a cardinal seems rather to have been a count Roffetti, whom I find busied in the concerns of the Catholics about the year 1640.

vigilance. But the bishops, whom a primitive institution had named the regular guardians of their flocks, beheld with pain these exemptions, which, while they curtailed their canonical jurisdiction, must sow the seeds of strife, and obviously divide those whom the spirit of the christian institute and of their own prelacy meant to make of one mind and of one heart. And the direful effects they foresaw, followed, and continued to disturb the peaceful administration of ecclesiastical polity. But let me observe, as the limits of the episcopal jurisdiction were thus restricted, the prerogative of Rome grew and spread its branches. They became the subjects of Peter, whom exemptions released from all ordinary controul.

The reader is not unacquainted with the *exemption* pleaded by the regulars, in their controversy with the bishop of Chalcedon. It had been wisely ordained, that no ministers of religion should exercise their functions, without the approbation of their canonical governors, the bishops, in their respective dioceses, after an examination taken of their characters and endowments; and the council of Trent, agreeably to the same spirit, had enacted that no regulars should hear the confessions of the laity or of the secular clergy (which function is deemed a part of the sacred ministry) without the said

appro-

approbation.* The bishop, finding that this regulation, in the time of his predecessor, had been unattended to, and aware of its importance to the just discharge of the parochial duties, with a zeal for the establishment of ecclesiastical discipline, which betrayed, however, his ignorance of the genuine spirit of monachism, proposed to the superiors of the regulars a due attention to this wise arrangement. At first some submitted; but murmurs were soon heared, and to them succeeded a stern and obstinate resistance. They charged the prelate with an assumption of power that belonged not, they said, to a *delegated* agent: they spoke of the supreme bishop of the universal church, from whom their commission to the Catholics of England was immediately derived. The regulars, they said, were only amenable to his tribunal, and owed no submission to an inferior prelacy, the essence of whose jurisdiction, they presumed to believe, flowed from that exalted source: The decrees of the council of Trent, they maintained, (and herein perhaps, they reasoned well) had no binding force in the kingdom, of England, where it had never been solemnly received.

Such were the beginnings of this wretched controversy, the progress and various acts of which

---

* Sess. 23. c. 15.

which have been sufficiently detailed. And the torch of discord flamed, and the hearts of Christians were divided, because the disciples of a Dominic, a Benedict, and an Ignatius, themselves styled the humblest of the race of man, would not condescend to receive from a prelate, whose just controul the Catholic flock acknowledged, permission, after an examination of their characters and endowments, to hear the confessions of a few lay sinners!* I blush for human nature that the bickerings of children can thus degrade.

The bishop maintained his rights; was driven into exile; and still maintained his rights: while the regulars, in possession of every avenue to the ear of the pontiff, successfully persevered in their resistance, as their own *relation* which I have quoted amply proves.

It will hardly, I think, be asked why the court of Rome took sides with the regulars, rather than with its agent whom it had delegated

Rome favourable to them.

---

* The bishop, on this occasion, wrote an *Address* to the lay Catholics, in which he explains the motives of his conduct, distinctly stating, *what* it was he demanded of the regulars; with what *authority* he demanded it; upon what *cause* or occasion; and in what *manner*. The *Address* is written with great moderation, perspicuity, and pastoral solicitude.

to govern in its name? For it will be recollected, that that agent in his writings, and the abettors of his caufe, had maintained, (what they deemed to be) the divine and independent rights of epifcopacy; that a hierarchy was neceffary to every church; and that the holy fee in its late arrangements, had departed from the venerable maxims of antiquity and the common practice of modern times. He had even ftyled himfelf the *ordinary* of England and Scotland, which was faying, that he held his powers from an inftitution, to which the tiara and the mitre muft equally bend.—The regulars, on the other hand, had combated thefe doctrines, which they denominated *direful infults* to the authority of Rome: Rome, therefore, muft patronife their labours, and vindicate their claim to privileges, when it was become manifeft how much thofe privileges had attached them to its neareft interefts, the fupremacy and univerfal fovereignty of its bifhop.

Thefe affertions may appear fevere; but the facts of hiftory prove their truth, and this truth is no where more clearly proved than in the feries of events which the reader has already witneffed, and which will continue to hold up the fame impreffion to his mind.

The

SUPPLEMENT.

The mode of government which Rome still maintains in this kingdom, and from which, in no kingdom, it ever departed but when driven to it by hard necessity, draws very near to that feudal system of polity, to which the nations of Europe were once subject. It contained one sovereign or suzeraine monarch, in whose hands was lodged the *supremum dominium*, and this he apportioned out to a descending series of vassals, who, all holding of him *in capite*, returned him *service* for the *benefice* they received, in honours, jurisdiction, or lands. And to this *service* they were bound by gratitude which an oath of *fealty* also strengthened.— The application of the system to the *sovereign* power of the pontiff, and to a chain of descending vassalage in archbishops, bishops, and the inferior orders in the ministry, is direct and palpable. And here also there is an oath of *fealty*.*

Feudal nature of church government.

But as the feudal system, which in itself was a system of slavery, gradually ceased to oppress the civil state of man; so also has it been in the ecclesiastical order of things. Churches, with their ministers, learnt what their own rights were, and vindicated to themselves their

---

* See the *oath* taken by bishops at their consecration.

exercife, how loud foever were the reclamations, and ftrenuous the refiftance of their once fuzeraine lord. The government of the Englifh Catholic church has remained *feudal*, in part owing to the tame fpirit of its clergy; but more to the clamours of that band of retainers, whofe privileges, and immunities, and exemptions I have mentioned.

The Chapter. The dean and chapter alfo, which the firft bifhop had erected, and which Dr. Smith had confirmed, and which he afterwards fanctioned by a more exprefs declaration,* was attacked by the regulars. They infifted that, as neither of the bifhops were *ordinaries*, the inftitution of a chapter was an illegal act, and that the authority which it affumed was null. It is true, the erection of chapters, as a permanent council to the bifhop, and, *fede vacante*, to exercife jurifdiction, is coeval with the earlieft ages of the church. But as the power of forming fuch councils only belonged, as it is agreed, to ordinary bifhops, and the two of whom we are fpeaking were not fuch, as, I think, has been fufficiently evinced, it cannot be denied that, on this fcore, the regulars reafoned forcibly, compelling the clergy, contrary to the tenour of

---

* Dodd, vol. 3, p. 151, 2, 3.

of the Briefs, to maintain that their bishops were really invested with ordinary powers. The court of Rome, I know, though repeatedly addressed by that very chapter, and fully informed, through a succession of years, of its existence and many acts, did not suppress it, or treat those acts as invalid and abusive: but as they never, by any decree, confirmed it, it should rather, perhaps, be inferred that they ridiculed its existence, and despised its weak display of jurisdiction. Or may it not be said that, aware that the nominal dignity amused the clergy, they permitted the enjoyment of it, that so they might be less urgent in their applications for a bishop? The regulars, however, would in, no form, acknowledge the jurisdiction of the chapter.*

While

---

* Continuing the *Relation*, which I suspended at the last note, the regulars thus proceed: "The clergy now apprehended the suppression of their chapter; wherefore they "dispatched Dr. Holden to Rome,† suspecting that their agent Fitton,

† Dr. Holden was the author of many works, among which that entitled *Analysis Fidei*, has principally given celebrity to his name. It is written with great precision, elucidating what the pride of theologians had obscured, and separating the tenets of faith from the superstructure of the schools. I wish it were more read, and better understood by the ministers of our religion. Some have complained, that the style is too elaborate, that a metaphysical refinement oppresses the subject, and that, from a desire to be analytical, the author is too diffuse, involving in many phrases what a single expression would have more happily enounced. We

want

Sufferings of many Catholics.

While the Catholics (whom the great disturbances which now agitated the nation could not withhold from domestic controversy) were thus engaged, many of their clergy suffered under the severest execution of the statutes. The parliament, whose power became daily more predominant, complained of the growth of popery, which they now confounded with an attachment to royalty, and urged the king to rigour. His natural gentleness of character was in their eyes a degrading weakness; and every act of mercy to that proscribed people was

---

Fitton, was too gentle a negociator. The efforts of Holden were solely bent to procure a confirmation of the chapter, as all hopes were vanished of re-establishing the episcopal dignity. But *latebat anguis in herba:* for as the abettors of the bishop of Chalcedon had taught, that, "when the bishop of any particular "see died, the jurisdiction, *jure divino,* devolved on the dean "and chapter; and that this chapter enjoyed full power to elect "a successor to the see; so that, should the pontiff refuse, or "neglect to appoint a successor, or to confirm his nomination, "the neighbouring prelates could, and were bound, by a canon "of the council of Nice, to consecrate the elected bishop:" Hence, the matter being well considered in a special congregation, the petition of Holden was rejected. He left Rome, therefore, with his companion, the other agent of the clergy; and the remaining years of the pontificate of Urban, which accorded ill with their ambition, were permitted to close in peace."

want, perhaps, an *Epitome* of this work arranged by a masterly hand. It might then be more universally read; and it would silence the quibbles of some and the pedantry of others, who disturb the faith of the multitude. —Dr. Holden resided in the university of Paris, venerated for his learning and virtue, where he died about the year 1665. Dodd, vol. 3, p. 297.

was a violation of the majefty of the laws. In 1641 feven priefts had been condemned, whom the king reprieved. Both houfes of parliament joined in a petition, that his majefty would take off the reprieve, and order the feven to be executed. Their prieftly character was their crime, as enacted by the 27th of Elizabeth. To this petition the king replied from York:—
"Concerning the condemned priefts, it is true, they were reprieved by our warrant, being informed that they were, by fome reftraint, difabled to take the benefit of our proclamation; fince that we have iffued out another, for the due execution of the laws againft papifts, and have moft folemnly promifed, upon the word of a king, never to pardon any prieft without your confent, who fhall be found guilty by law; defiring to banifh thefe, having herewith fent warrants to that purpofe, if, upon fecond thoughts, you do not difapprove thereof. But if you think the execution of thefe perfons fo very neceffary to the great and pious work of reformation, we refer it wholly to you, declaring hereby, that, upon fuch our refolution fignified to the minifters of juftice, the warrant for their reprieve is determined, and the law to have its courfe."*—The unexpected meffage

---

* *Impartial Collections*, by Nelfon, vol. ii. p. 732.

fage difconcerted parliament, who did not wifh that the odium of perfecution fhould lie againft themfelves; and the priefts were permitted to linger out their lives in Newgate.

Two years before, a Mr. Goodman alfo had been condemned, whom the king was willing to reprieve. The lords and commons on this held a conference, to whom his majefty fent a meffage: " That having informed himfelf of
" the names and natures of the crimes of the
" perfons convicted at the laft feffions, and
" there finding that John Goodman was con-
" demned for being in orders of a prieft *merely*,
" and was acquitted of every other charge:
" his majefty being tender in matters of blood
" in cafes of this nature, in which queen Eliza-
" beth and king James have been *often* merciful;
" but to fecure his people, that this man
" fhould do no more hurt, he is willing that
" he be imprifoned or banifhed, as their lord-
" fhips fhall advife.—And he will take fuch fit
" courfe for the expulfion of other priefts and
" Jefuits, as he fhall be counfelled by their
" lordfhips, &c."

But the two houfes concurred in a remon-ftrance to the throne, that Goodman might be executed, and the laws enforced againft all other priefts and Jefuits: wherefore they waited on the king, to whom he thus delivered him-felf:

felf: " I take in good part your care of the
" true religion eftablifhed in this kingdom,
" from which I will never depart.—It is againſt
" my mind that popery or fuperftition fhould
" any way encreaſe; and I will reſtrain the
" fame by cauſing the laws to be put in exe-
" cution. I am reſolved to provide againſt the
" Jeſuits and prieſts, by ſetting forth a procla-
" mation with all ſpeed, commanding them to
" quit the kingdom within one month.—Con-
" cerning John Goodman the prieſt; I will
" let you know the reaſon why I reprieved
" him. That, as I am informed, neither queen
" Elizabeth, nor my father did ever avow that
" any prieſt, in their time, was executed
" merely for religion, which to me ſeems to
" be this particular caſe. Yet ſeeing that I
" am preffed by both houfes to give way to his
" execution; becauſe I will avoid the incon-
" veniency of giving ſo great a difcontent to
" my people, as I conceive this mercy may
" produce; therefore I remit this particular
" cauſe to both houſes."*

The next day his majeſty communicated to
the houſe of lords the following petition ſent to
him by Mr. Goodman:

To

---

* *Impart. Collect.* vol. i. p. 738.

To the king's most excellent majesty,
The humble petition of John Goodman, *condemned,*
humbly sheweth,

"That whereas your majesty's petitioner hath been informed of a great discontent in many of your majesty's subjects, at the gracious mercy your majesty was freely pleased to shew unto your petitioner, by suspending the execution of the sentence of death pronounced against him for being a Roman priest; these are humbly to beseech your majesty, rather to remit your petitioner to their mercy, than to let him live the subject of so great discontent in your people against your majesty.

"This is, most sacred majesty the petition of him that should esteem his blood well shed, to cement the breach between your majesty and your subjects upon this occasion."*

The magnanimity, which this petition breathed, greatly moved the king, and seemed to soften the parliament into some sentiments
of

---

* *Impart. Collect.* vol. i. p. 738.

SUPPLEMENT.

of humanity: for Mr, Goodman was not executed, and after five years confinement, I find he died on the *felons fide* of Newgate!

I have adduced thefe inftances, to which more might be added, to fhew how ftern was now become the fpirit of the nation, when the genius of republicanifm, falfely imagined favourable to the feelings of humanity and its amiable virtues, had, with an iron grafp, taken hold of the minds of many. Their refentment, I know, was excited, becaufe the queen, who was a Catholic, was fuppofed to bear a great fway in the councils of the king; and becaufe the principal part of thofe of her perfuafion were obvioufly attached to him. To punifh or to weaken this attachment, which, in fome regards, perhaps, was not fufficiently enlightened, and to thwart her majefty's preponderance, Parliament judged it expedient to overwhelm by feverity that body of men, with the influence of whofe principles and conduct they were not unacquainted.

But the reader will obferve how much the ftate of things was altered. In the two preceding reigns, as I feduloufly noticed, the Catholics fuffered and their priefts were executed, either becaufe they refufed the oath of allegiance, under James; or becaufe, under Elizabeth, they had feemed to have confpired with
the

the enemies of their country in some hostile measure. "I am informed (the king has just been heard to say) that neither queen Elizabeth, nor my father, did ever avow that any priest, in their time, was executed merely for religion." But in the reign of Charles, of the twenty priests that suffered death, and of many others who died in prison, I do not find one against whom any other crime was alleged, than to have received orders abroad, and have returned into the realm, which by the 27th Elizabeth had been declared *high treason*. In 1642, a Mr. Roe, as he stood in the cart at Tyburn, thus addressed the sheriff: "Pray, Sir, if I will conform to your religion, and go to church, will you secure me my life?"—"That I will," said the sheriff, "upon my word; my life for yours if you will but do that."—"See then," observed Mr. Roe, turning to the people, "what the crime is for which I am to die; and whether my religion be not my only treason."*

Indeed, as not the cause of *allegiance*, but the weakening of *royalty*, now engaged the thoughts of parliament, and no hostile views or co-operation with external enemies could be objected to the Catholics, it is plain why their religion,
taken

---

* *Memoirs of miss. priests*, vol. ii. p. 200.

SUPPLEMENT.

taken with the relations I before mentioned, would be deemed a crime that called for severe chastisement.

And, while their ministers were imprisoned or suffered death, the lay-community, under the same imperious arm, were exposed to great distress. In the year 1643, parliament made and published several rigorous acts and ordinances, which they afterwards more strongly enforced, against *Delinquents*, as they called them, and *Papists*; whereby all, whether Catholics or others, that had already, or should hereafter, assist the king against the parliament, were to have their whole estates seized and sequestered into the hands of committees, named to that purpose; and all Catholics, (that is, all such as harboured any popish priest, or were convicted of recusancy, or that assisted at mass, or whose children were brought up in the popish religion) were to forfeit two-thirds of their whole estates, real and personal, to be disposed of for the uses of parliament, unless they took an oath, which any magistrates could tender to them, abjuring the pope, transubstantiation, purgatory, &c.*

These

---

* *MSS Collections* by Knaresborough in the same Memoirs, p. 322.

Thefe acts were executed with extreme feverity on the whole body of Catholics, as the victories of the parliamentary forces, and the decline of the royal caufe empowered the fequeftrators to proceed. Few families efcaped their rapacious violence; while the Purfuivants, with their wonted audacity, entered their houfes, clearing away the furniture and what elfe invited their infatiable love of plunder. Difmay, and forrow, and perplexity fank the Catholics low; for the fenfibilities of charity feemed to be fufpended, and the tear of human kindnefs did not flow for their diftrefs. Such, I have faid, was the ftern nature of republicanifm, brooding over its plans of felfifh independence, and meafuring with a contracted fpan, what portion of property, of liberty, of enjoyment, it was expedient, each member of the community fhould be permitted to fhare.*
The loweft orders fuffered in the general fequeftration: even they " tripartited the day-
" labourers

---

* Not that I am an enemy to the republican form of government, which in theory, I think, bears a decided pre-eminence. But it is not to the brilliancy of theory only that the legiflator muft look, when he is framing a conftitution for *man*, and the thoufand relations in which he ftands, of times, habits, and external influences, prefs for obfervation. And it may be, that the republican form is only adapted to coalefce with an infant community, where it may grow with its growing greatnefs, modify its progrefs, and check the dangerous luft of wealth and
power

SUPPLEMENT.

"labourers goods, and very houfhold ftuff, and have taken away two cows where the whole ftock was but three."*

Thus, in gloomy rotation, paffed the remaining years of Charles, which the Catholics ennobled by their loyalty, and a dignified refignation to their fate. Their loyalty, as they conceived it, was founded on patriotifm, and their refignation was the fruit of virtue. In the fchool of adverfity they had been long trained. Lord Caftlemain has left us a lift of the names of thofe Catholics, who loft their eftates or their lives in the royal caufe.†—The king was executed on the 30th of January, 1649.

The bifhop of Chalcedon, whom the calamity of exile had withdrawn from a fcene of greater calamity at home, continued in France; for neither had the regulars fufpended their oppofition, nor would the court of Rome relent. Devoted to retirement and ftudy, he occafionally

Death of the bifhop of Chalcedon.

---

power. With nations of long exiftence it feems not to comport, wherein the ftamina of life have been ufed, and there is not fufficient virtue left to invigorate the new order of things. Befides, the evils of *Revolutions* are uncalculatable.

* *Chriftian Moderator* by Auftin, p. 9, &c. as quoted in the above *Memoirs*.

† See *Catholic Apology*.

ally enjoyed the fociety of the learned; and from the various works he publifhed, as particular occurrences called up his attention, we find, that a paftoral folicitude for his flock was his neareft care. Cardinal Richelieu remained his friend; but when he died in 1642, and Mazarin became minifter of ftate, from what motives I know not, but from what influence I can guefs, the new favourite withdrew his protection, and even deprived the exiled bifhop of his abbey. Thus reduced in his circumftances, he was no longer able to relieve, by a generous attention to their wants, the crowds of Englifh that followed the fortunes of their prince into France; and in this inability, he retired to an apartment near the convent of fome Englifh nuns, upon the Foffes St. Victor in Paris.*
This convent, a few years before, he had himfelf contributed to found; and here he lived till 1655, when he died aged 88. The nuns, in pious gratitude to his memory, laid a ftone upon his grave that records the leading incidents of his life, the prominent lines of his character, and their own filial affection.††

The

---

* Dodd, vol. 3, p. 19, 78.

† Ibid, p. 171.

‡ The *Relation of the Regulars* having, in its ufual way, ftated an unfuccefsful application for the confirmation of the *chapter*,

in

SUPPLEMENT.

The character of Dr. Smith, as it ever is with men whom fortune draws from the crowd, has been variously portrayed. The regulars viewed him as an arrogant pretender to power and the enemy of their institute; the court of Rome as an ungrateful agent, who aspired to the dignity and the independent rights of a christian bishop: but to the clergy he was the champion of the prelacy, and a martyr to the just claims of the British church. I have read his works with attention, in which I discover much that merits praise, little that merits censure. And his life, I believe, was edifying and pastoral.

---

in the beginning of the pontificate of Innocent X. which the queen enforced, thus proceeds: "But afterwards, the friends to epis-
"copacy and the chapter did not desist. The matter, there-
"fore, under Innocent, was brought to a more accurate dis-
"cussion, and the following reasons for refusing a bishop to the
"British church were adduced: That the whole business hav-
"ing been repeatedly brought under examination by Paul V,
"and the opinions of the apostolic nuncioes and the English
"Catholics taken, it had been rejected; that the new form of a
"hierarchy which was demanded, and the confirmation of the
"chapter, though strongly enforced, had not been approved by
"the holy see, because such a hierarchy was odious to the here-
"tics, was dangerous to the Catholics, and, at this time, was
"impracticable. Besides, were it conceded, there was reason
"to think, that the clergy, who so often attempted things con-
"trary to the laws of discipline, would arrogate to themselves
"a power, *ex lege divina*, of electing their own bishops, and
"should the apostolic see refuse confirmation, of procuring
"their

pastoral. In attacking the immunities of the regulars, he manifested more zeal than prudence; and when the foe was roused, ridicule not reasoning should have been his weapon. In his contest with Rome I would thus have addressed him: "Prelate, you have assumed
"the title and the powers of an *ordinary*, neither
"of which the *Brief* of your appointment war-
"rants, and under that *Brief* you were conse-
"crated to your see.—But the good of my
"church, you say, and the venerable practice
"of ages disclaim all precarious jurisdiction,
"and call for an establishment which the ca-
"pricious will of no man shall subvert or
"hereafter

"their consecration from France. The danger also was, that
"the English Catholics themselves would remonstrate against
"such a hierarchy, in their own defence, as they had done un-
"der Urban. In fine, that no advantage in the present state
"of things, could be derived from it, either for the reforma-
"tion of the clergy, or the keeping the Catholics in their duty,
"as no external court could be maintained, with the various
"usages appertaining to it."

"At last," it goes on, "these vexations ceased, with which
"the holy see had been often troubled by those, whom a wan-
"ton itch of episcopacy urged forward. Necessity, however,
"and not inclination did it; for, on the death of Charles, the
"English government was subverted, and in the general wreck
"the whole body of the nation was involved."

The statement is untrue; for the *vexations*, as they are termed, that is, *applications* continued to be made to the Roman see for bishops, as the series of events will shew.

"hereafter modify.—Then fummon the cler-
"gy to your aid: tell them, if they be igno-
"rant of it, what has ever been and is the
"ufage of the Chriftian church; what have
"ever been and are the rights of epifcopacy
"and the priefthood; what has ever been and
"is the claim of a believing laity. Define the
"prerogative of the Roman bifhop; fpecify
"the effential jurifdiction of his chair; and to
"that effential jurifdiction, which bounds the
"center of orthodox unity, attach their belief,
"their veneration, their Chriftian fealty.
"Thus inftructed your flock will rally round
"you; and fecure in their fupport you may
"convey to Rome their united fuffrages, which
"fhall tell his holinefs that you are *chofen* by
"your people (as were the prelates of ancient
"days) to be their paftor; that you implore
"his benediction; that you acknowledge him
"for your head; and that, as the difcipline of
"modern days requires, you intreat his *confir-
"mation* or *inftitution*,* and the fulfilment of fuch
"forms as may be deemed expedient."

On

---

* This office of *Confirmation* or *Inftitution*, though, in times long paffed, exercifed by patriarchs, and metropolitans, and often by the bifhops of provinces, now exclufively refides in the pontiff of Rome. That it originally belonged to his fee, and was thence *delegated* to others, is thought by fome; while others teach, that it has been permitted by the epifcopal body gradually to *devolve* on their common head. He who has contemplated

The Chapter assumes jurisdiction.

On the death of the bishop, the same episcopal jurisdiction which they had before exercised, again devolved on the chapter, that is, they again assumed to themselves its exercise. But this council, by a resolution of the general assembly of the clergy, held in 1653, had now acquired a more direct and permanent establishment. The resolution was: "Should our "bishop

---

templated, through the ages of ignorance, the absorbing vortex of the Roman see, will know to which side of the question he should incline.—The *election* of bishops has been more various. It was once in the clergy and laity, then in the provincial bishops, in the cathedral chapters, and, as the feudal system obtained, in the hands of princes and their sovereigns.—The whole *exercise*, therefore, whether of *Institution* or *Election*, must be resolved into discipline. What has changed could not have been *divinely* appointed. Indeed, his present holiness, tenacious, as he justly may be, of his present prerogative, against the invading politics of France, has himself unequivocally spoken: "But this power," says he, "of *conferring* jurisdiction, by a "*new discipline (ex nova disciplina)* now received for many ages, "and confirmed by general councils and the concordates of "kings, can by no means appertain to metropolitans, because, "brought back to that see whence it had gone out, it alone re- "sides with the chair of Peter."*—And provided the important chain of *episcopal succession* be preserved unbroken, it matters little, by whose hand the descending links be added; nor is it necessary I should say, that as he only can confer *order* who has been himself ordained, so can he only confer *jurisdiction*, who is himself canonically possessed of jurisdiction. The *election* of superiors, undoubtedly, should ever belong to the clergy, who are most interested in their appointment, and whose cause is the cause of their flocks.

* Pius VI. *Episcopis Galliæ, &c. April 13, 1791.*

"bishop die before any change of government come upon us by the comming in of one or more bishops, or otherwise, our determination is, that all the clergy stand in a modest defence of the dean and chapter, and yield due obedience to them."* And the same *Resolution*, by a similar authority, was again confirmed in 1657:† we must, in future, therefore, view this chapter (if not as a canonical meeting in its first institution) as the representative body of the Catholic clergy and their delegated organ.

Though much, at the time, was written on the subject, I shall barely mention the controversy to which the opinions of Thomas White, *alias* Blacklœ, gave rise. He was a minister of our church, and a man of uncommon learning; but his sentiments were often paradoxical, and he took a wanton pleasure in departing from the

Mr. White, *alias* Blacklœ.

---

* *Encyclical Letter by the Dean and Chapter*, an. 1660, p. 25.— I have by me the minutes of this general assembly, composed of deputies from all the districts of England and Wales, and which continued sitting from the 11th to the 18th of July. The object was to settle, by a general arrangement, the concerns of the clergy, lest, at the bishop's death, which was expected, all order might be overturned. They, therefore, came to distinct resolutions on ten points that were laid before them. The deputies were 15 in number, with Mr. Harrington the bishop's vicar general. † Ibid.

the received idiom of the fchools. Having taught much in our foreign feminaries, he had acquired many friends, the admirers of his virtues, rather than the followers of his opinions. Thefe opinions excited a general notice, and the ignorant, and the malevolent, and the bigoted taking the alarm, reprefented the author as a dangerous innovator, and more than unftable in his faith. The whole body was divided; but moderate men and men of learning would not facrifice to the cries of ignorance the reputation of a perfon, whofe extreme errors were the mere extravagancies of genius. Dr. Holden came forward in his defence: "You know," fays he to a friend, "the greateft part of his adverfaries (I mean "thofe whofe profeffion is to judge of fuch "things; for the laity, *in matters of doctrine belonging to religion*, ought to be hearers and learners, "not teachers or judges) are brought up in "your private feminaries; and thence eafily "conceive, whatever they hear, either oppo- "fite to, or unmentioned in their mafter's "dictates, to be erroneous. Whereas, if they "knew the latitude of our moft learned men's "fingular, and fometimes new-invented or re- "newed opinions, daily maintained, and pro- "blematically difputed, in our public fchools, "without the leaft fufpicion of their integrity "in Catholic belief, they would not (if no "way blinded with paffion) fo flightly fhoot
"their

SUPPLEMENT.

" their cenfuring bolts at random, efpecially againft a brother, and fuch a brother."* This he wrote from Paris in 1657, where, as I before obferved, he always refided. But the tongues of fuch adverfaries could not be bridled, and the leading men amongft the clergy, the heads, particularly, of the chapter, were ftigmatifed as the abettors of error under the appellation of *Blackloifts*. Mr. White finally fubmitted his writings to the judgment of the holy fee.†

I cannot omit a curious inftance of arbitraty jurifdiction, exhibited at this time, by the Roman congregation *de Propaganda fide*, who iffued a *decree* whereby, every apoftolic miffionary that, in future fhould publifh any work, without the exprefs licence of the congregation, was deprived of his functions, and *ipfo facto* excommunicated; this fentence to be referved to his holinefs; and the licence, when obtained, to be prefixed to the work, under the fame penalty.‡

The chapter, which I had juft left, by their agent, gave an account to his holinefs of the bifhop's

Proceedings of the chapter.

---

* Dodd, vol. iii. p. 354.
† See *Records of Mr. White*, Dodd, p. 350.
‡ *Decretum*, Ibid, p. 388.

bishop's deceafe, and requefted to know his pleafure concerning the future government of the Catholic church in England. He replied: "I will not difapprove of your chapter; but will let you alone with your government."* This was Alexander VII. who had lately fucceeded to Innocent.

In the fame year, 1655, the chapter difpatched Mr. Plantin, a new agent, to Rome, to fupplicate for a fucceffor to bifhop Smith. His holinefs, in compliance with their requifition, promifed, they fhould have a bifhop within feven months." "And how," obferved the agent, "fhall our church be governed in the interim?"—"Have you not a dean and chapter?" replied Alexander.†

Thefe anfwers of the pontiff were clearly an implied approbation of the chapter's jurifdiction.

Having occafion to write to Rome in the following year, the chapter, though the feven months were expired and no fucceffor appointed, addreffed a letter of thanks to his holinefs for his paternal care in promifing them a fuperior

---

* *Tranfactions*, p. 56.   † Ibid. p. 57.

rior with *ordinary* powers.* He had made no such promife; but it was wife to fignify the extent of their own wifhes.

In 1657, the chapter in a general affembly nominated fix perfons as proper for a bifhop, and conftituted Mr. Pendrick their agent to Rome; to whom, fome months after, with a perfeverance that became them, they gave orders forthwith to wait upon his holinefs, and fupplicate him in their names to make good his promife. Letters likewife, to the fame effect, were fent to the protector Barberini. The inftructions to the agent were; 1ft, to defire a bifhop *cum poteftate ordinarii*; 2dly, that they dare not accept of any *extraordinary* authority, which would be againft the laws of their Catholic anceftors, and the will of the ftate; 3dly, that the bifhop be chofen out of the fix named by the chapter; 4thly, if any other *perfon*, or *authority*, contrary or inconfiftent with this, be endeavoured to be impofed, that he *refolutely oppofe it*; and, in the name of the chapter, proteft againft it, 1ft, becaufe the *ancient* laws of England admit of no *extraordinary power* of the pope; 2dly, becaufe there is a fevere penalty, called a *Præmunire*, againft thofe that fhall receive any fuch; 3dly, that, in the reign of Henry VIII. the clergy,

---

* *Tranfactions*, p. 57.

by reason of this, were compelled to renounce the pope's authority; 4thly. that all the laity will fall under the same *præmunire*; and therefore, 5thly, that the chapter think themselves bound in conscience to acquaint the laity of the danger to which they will be exposed, by accepting such an authority; lastly, that the state is already too jealous of any intrenchment from the power of the court of Rome: The chapter, therefore, dares not receive any superior but an *ordinary bishop.**

These manly sentiments, thus forcibly expressed, tell us what then was the conviction of the clergy, and how true they were to the firm conduct of their ancestors. In what softer shades of colouring the resolutions were conveyed to his holiness, we do not learn; but we learn, that no change was made, and that the promise to be fulfilled in seven months remained unexecuted. In 1659, Dr. Gage was appointed agent.

State of the Catholics under Cromwell.

The reader will connect this series of small events with the great occurrences of the times, when the wise fabric of our ancestors was dissolved, when a commonwealth was established, and

---

* *Transactions*, p. 58, 59. *Encyclical Epist.* p. 35.

and when Cromwell, with a mighty arm and a mind of deep intelligence, had affumed the reins of government. The Catholic party was now confounded with thofe who were enemies to the new order of things; and loyalty not religion became their crime. To conciliate the affections of all was the obvious policy of the protector; and had not the fpirit of loyalty been of that ftern complection, which no threats or allurements could bend, fuccefs, probably, would have crowned his wifhes. Indeed, I have little doubt, had providence indulged him with a longer fpan of life, that the whole nation would tranquilly have fubmitted to a controul, the wifdom and ftrength of which Europe viewed with envy; and that to this day, perhaps, the commonwealth had ftood, firm, happy, awful, magnificient, as was that of ancient Rome.

Of the two priefts who fuffered death, at this time, under the fatal ftatute of the 27th of Elizabeth, in 1651 and 1654, Mr. Southworth the laft, in a fpeech he delivered at Tyburn thus obferved: " I am innocent of any fin againft
" man, the commonwealth, and the prefent go-
" vernment. How juftly then I die, let them
" look to it who have condemned me. It is
" fufficient for me, it is God's will. I plead
" not for myfelf: I came hither to fuffer; but
" for the poor perfecuted Catholics I leave be-
" hind me. Heretofore, liberty of confcience
" was

"was pretended as the cause of the war; and it was held, as a reasonable proposition, that all the natives enjoy it, who behave themselves as obedient and true subjects. This being so, why should their consciences, acting and governing themselves according to the faith received from their ancestors, involve them, more than all the rest, in an universal guilt, which conscioufness is the very religion that clears others, and makes them innocent? It hath pleased God to take the sword out of the hand of the king, and put it into the protector's. Let him remember, that he is to administer justice indifferently, and without exception of persons, with God, whom he ought to resemble. If any Catholic work against the government now established, let him suffer: but why should those that are guiltless (unless conscience be a guilt) be made partakers in a promiscuous punishment, with the greatest malefactors."*

In the expression of sentiments thus just and dignified, and which became the minister of religion who submits, without clamour, to the ruling powers of the state, Mr. Southworth met his fate. He was the first and last that suffered in the protectorate of Cromwell.

By

---

* Dodd, vol. 3, p. 361.

By the brilliant scenes of festivity and folly that, with the *Restoration*, soon broke upon the nation, the Catholics with their ministers were not so dazzled as to lose sight of their favourite object; and the clergy again renewed their application to Rome. I have said, that Dr. Gage was now their agent there: him, therefore, they instructed to present the same supplication for an *ordinary*, and to protest against the introduction of *every other* jurisdiction, as Mr. Pendrick had lately done.*

The chapter continues to apply for an ordinary.

He was soon able to inform his employers, that Alexander, mindful of his early promise, was inclined to favour them; but that the cardinals, under the influence of a party which had ever stood in the way of their designs, were averse from the measure. He seems not, however, in the first stage of the business, to have acquainted the chapter that the *bishop*, whom the pontiff was inclined to send, was to bear the title of *Vicarius Apostolicus*. The appellation was new; but in its obvious import, it conveyed more distinctly that idea of *dependence*, which, jealous of all its prerogatives, the court of Rome was resolved not to surrender. Dr. Gage, wearied out and assailed on all sides, was at one time

almost

---

* *Transact.* p. 60.

almoſt prevailed on to accede to the propoſal, when the watchful vigilance of the chapter, apprifed of the defign, averted its completion.*

While the agent was in Rome, a fcheme was agitated among the clergy which fhewed their refolution and exhaufted patience, and which, it would have been well, they had executed. The fcheme was, fhould the *firſt ſee* refuſe to give us biſhops, to apply to the neareſt metropolitan, as the council of Sardica, they ſaid, had enacted. And the archbifhop of Rouen, it is aſſerted, had really been confulted, and had given his confent. Such an encroachment on the pontifical prerogative, however much the difcipline of ancient days might authoriſe the meaſure, was not to be borne; and the court of Rome, we are told, when appriſed of the defign, firſt careſſed, and cajoled Dr. Gage with additional promiſes and with kind but evafive expreſſions, whilſt, by the means of potent friends, they prevailed on the archbifhop to defiſt from the dangerous enterpriſe.†

The agent, in his various letters, now confeſſes, how much the policy of that artful court
had

---

* Tranſact. p. 61, 62. Dr. Leyburn's *Encyclical Anſwer*, p. 79.

† Tranſact. p. 61, 62.

had impofed on his honeft credulity; and it was not to be managed, he faw, by the methods he had firft purfued, fubmiffive fawnings, humble addreffes, acknowledgments of fignal favours, no pretenfions of right or equity : " It " is my opinion," he fays, " that, if it were in " their power, they would abolifh all autho- " rity but what depended immediately upon " themfelves; and this they will do, when " there is not a power able to refift them."— But the chapter, fearful of his too eafy con- defcenfion, recalled him from his poft; whence before his return, he gave them this affurance: " In the *interim*, make no doubt of the chapter's " authority ; for it is moft evident, that this " court admits it." * — This was in the year 1661.

A general affembly was this year held; but, under an apprehenfion that fome umbrage might be given to government, lord Aubigny, fon of the duke of Lenox and afterwards almo- ner to queen Catherine, was requefted to ac- quaint his majefty, that the defign of their meeting was merely to fettle fome private concerns, and to procure a bifhop for their fuperior ; but that he might be affured, they would

---

* Tranfact. p. 61, 62.

would chuse such a man for the office as should be well principled, and his loyal and faithful subject. The king consented to their meeting, and sent this gracious answer: "That he "commanded them not to meddle with, or "accept of, any *extraordinary* authority from "Rome: That, as for the laws made since the "reformation against Catholics, he would "protect them from them; but could not do "it in respect of the ancient laws, provided in "Catholic times, against such authority." The assembly, on this, met, and passed a decree, *Never to accept of any such authority.* *

Satisfied with the firmness of this decree, the chapter, for some years, seemed little solicitous in the prosecution of their favourite plan; but hearing in 1665, that the scheme of a *vicar apostolic* was revived, they ordered a *letter* to be written to his holiness signifying, that they could not receive *such* a superior; and praying him not to impose it, because the example of the *archpriest* alarmed them; because the Catholics are now placed under a settled authority, and unanimously agreed in it; because there have been many contracts between the chapter and its officers, over all England, which, should they not stand to the chapter, would fall to the ground,

to

---

* Transact. p. 64, 65.

to the great scandal and injury of Catholics; because the state has ordered them not to accept of a *vicar apostolic*.—The same instructions as had been before given, were repeated to their agent, to insist on an *absolute ordinary*, and resolutely oppose all other *titles* or *authorities*, as directly forbidden by the state, and against the constant sense of his brethren; and to add, that the laity reclaimed against it; protesting that they durst not submit to any such jurisdiction.*

Still nothing succeeded: their resistance only, it should seem, prevented the appointment of a Roman delegate, whose approach, under every denomination, the clergy so much dreaded. Alexander VII. was dead, and his successor Clement IX. was in the chair of St. Peter. The chapter ordered Mr. Holt, their agent, to present their gratulations to his holiness, to move for a bishop, and to signify, that the honourable Philip Howard, if invested with the powers of the late bishop of Chalcedon, would be agreeable to them. This Philip Howard, grandson of Thomas earl of Arundell, was, at this time, a Dominican friar; was afterwards, in 1675, promoted to the purple, and became protector, in the language of Rome, of the English nation.—The chapter

---

* *Transact.* p. 67. 68.

then again resolved that, under no pretence or palliation, the word *Vicarius Apostolicus* be admitted, on the grounds they had before urged, as directly contrary to the king's command, offensive to the state, provided against by the ancient laws of the realm, and extremely dangerous to Catholics. They resolved, should Philip Howard be their bishop, that his jurisdiction must be *ordinary*; that it is the right of the old English *chapters* to chuse their *bishops*; and that they will not yield this right to the pretensions of the Roman court.*—This was in the year 1670.

Mr. Holt, in return, informed the assembly, that, having had an audience, his holiness had assured him, " that he had great consolation in " the English clergy;" that his nephew told him, " his holiness was infinitely satisfied with " the English clergy;" and that Signor Baldeschi, secretary to the *Propaganda*, acquainted him, " that the Jesuits reported, the clergy de- " sired not a bishop."—After this, he says, a congregation was held, wherein it was agreed to give us a bishop; that Philip Howard was judged a fit person; but what his authority should be, was not determined.†

And

---

* *Transact*. p. 69, 70. † Ibid.

And here the matter rested. Fifteen years Reflections. had elapsed since the death of Dr. Smith, which the clergy, as has been seen, consumed in reiterated but useless applications to the Roman court. They receded not from the resolutions they had passed, which as occasion served, they even confirmed in other meetings; but they ceased to prosecute an endless measure. I traced, with pain, the series of their applications, that the reader might, in one view, contemplate the policy of the court they courted, its insincere promises, its evasive shifts, and, above all, its immutable resolution never to co-operate in the establishment of an authority that, in a single act, should be independent of its own paramount will. For this, as we have seen, was the archpriesthood instituted; for this, was a saving clause, which annihilated the very essence of the supposed grant, inserted in the briefs of the two succeeding bishops; for this, was the present supplication of the clergy resisted, and a superior offered, whose very name of *vicar apostolic* should define his dependent and delegated powers. Strange it may seem, that men who could reason as the clergy reasoned, to whom all the artifices of Rome were familiar, and whose fixed determination it seemed to be not to submit to imposition, should not have chosen for themselves an obvious path, and have pursued it. The remark has been already made, and the cause of that conduct analysed.

The chapter had now long exercised *episcopal* jurisdiction over the whole English Catholic church; and as Rome was perfectly acquainted with the circumstance, which it neither disapproved or controuled, the inference was direct, that it possessed every requisite form to render its character canonically complete.* What defect there might have been in its first institution, was now compensated by the approbation of Rome tacitly given to its acts, and, what in my estimation was far more valuable, by the consent of the clergy testified in their approbation of, and submission to, its jurisdiction. The regulars, it is true, with their usual hostility resisted; but, since what period has their consent been deemed necessary to the formation of a government, the first acts of which, perhaps, must inevitably clash with their privileges and exemptions?

<small>Some transactions of the reign of Charles II.</small>

As I would not break the series I had commenced, it is necessary to revert to certain transactions in which the Catholics were concerned, and thus bring up the narrative to its proper period.

Nothing was at first done for them: yet their pretensions were great, and they seemed
to

---

* *Transact.* passim.

to look for a proportionable indulgence. "It was the king's defire," fays Clarendon, "which he never diffembled, to give them "eafe from all the fanguinary laws." Without importunity or complaint, had they patiently waited that event, they might, poffibly, have foon recovered the common privileges of fubjects. "For," adds my noble author, "that "gracious difpofition in the king to his Catho- "lic fubjects, did not then appear ingrateful. "to any." But the vanity and prefumption of fome were great: they feized every opportunity of extolling their own loyalty; and they fpoke of their fufferings in the royal caufe as deferving of more than common notice. It is true, as I have already obferved, they had done much. His lordfhip even owns, that fome of thofe, who fuffered moft for his father, did fend fupplies to the king when he was abroad; "though, fays he, they were hardly able to "provide neceffaries for themfelves."

An addrefs being made to the houfe of peers, the year after the Reftoration, for fome relaxation of the laws againft them, a committee of that houfe was appointed to examine and to report all thofe penal ftatutes, which reached to the taking away the life of any Catholic for his religion; "there not appearing one lord "in the houfe, who feemed to be unwilling that "thofe laws fhould be repealed." After the committee

committee was appointed, the Catholic lords and their friends, for fome days, diligently attended it, and made their obfervations on feveral acts of parliament in which they defired eafe. " But, on a fudden, this committee was " difcontinued, and never after revived; the " Roman Catholics never afterwards being foli- " citous for it."

The truth is, they very foon quarrelled amongft themfelves. The lords and men of eftates, little anxious about the abolition of laws which concerned principally the lives of priefts, defired rather a repeal of thofe, whereby their own property, as recufants, was affected. The churchmen, on the other hand, were not much folicitous about the removal of laws, by which they might gain the glory of martyrdom, whilft they continued under other reftraints more grievous far than death.—A committee was then chofen from among themfelves of the fuperiors of the regulars and of the fecular clergy. They met at Arundell houfe, along with fome of the principal lords and gentlemen. Here alfo difputes foon began; and they difagreed about the form of an oath or fubfcription, which, it was intended, fhould be made or taken by all Catholics. A propofition had likewife been made, that none but fecular priefts fhould be tolerated in England, who fhould be under a a bifhop and a fettled form of government; and
that

that all the regulars, in particular all Jesuits, should be, under the severest penalties, forbidden the kingdom. The same plan, as appears from Panzani, had been agitated in the former reign. The committee, as was natural to expect, was dissolved, and met no more.*

From this time, owing principally to that rooted dislike which the nation had long entertained, their transient goodwill to the Catholics, generated by loyalty, passed away, and they became, as before, common objects of aversion. The marked propension, that the king felt and ever expressed for them, was regarded with an eye of peculiar jealousy. In his declaration for liberty of conscience to the dissenters, in 1662, he says: " It is divulged " through the kingdom, that we are highly in- " dulgent to papists, not only in exempting " them from the penalties of the law, but even " to such a degree of countenance and encou- " ragement, as may endanger the protestant " religion.

---

* This statement, founded on Lord Clarendon's narration, is taken from the *State and Behaviour of English Catholics*, p. 46, a work I published some years ago. In reviewing many things contained in that book, I have the satisfaction to find, they were given with great accuracy: but there are some *reflections* which do not now please me, and which, as they gave offence, I am sorry were ever admitted. It is well, that experience should correct the too hasty effusions of younger years.

"religion.—It is true that, as we shall always,
"according to our justice, retain, so we think
"it may become us, to avow to the world the
"due sense we have, of the *greatest part* of our
"Catholic subjects of this kingdom, having de-
"served well of our royal father, of blessed
"memory, and from us, and *even from the pro-
"testant religion itself*, in adhering to us with their
"lives and fortunes, for the maintenance of
"our crown in the religion established, against
"those who under the *name of zealous protestants*,
"employed both fire and sword to overthrow
"them both. We shall, with as much free-
"dom, profess unto the world, that it is not
"our intention to exclude our Roman Ca-
"tholic subjects, who have so demeaned them-
"selves, from all share in the benefit of such
"an act, as, in pursuance of our promises,
"*(to the Dissenters)*, the wisdom of our parlia-
"ment shall think fit to offer unto us, for the
"ease of tender consciences. It might appear
"no less than injustice, that those who de-
"served well, and continue to do so, should
"be denied some part of that mercy, which we
"have obliged ourselves to afford to ten times
"the number of such, who have not done so.
"Besides, such are the capital laws in force
"against them, as that, though justified in
"their rigour by the times wherein they were
"made, we profess it would be grievous to us
"to consent to the execution of them, by put-
"ting any of our subjects to death for their
"opinion

"opinion in matters of religion only. But at the fame time, as we declare our little liking of thefe fanguinary laws, and our gracious intentions to fuch of our Roman Catholic fubjects as fhall live peaceably, modeftly, and without fcandal, we would have them all know, that if, for doing what their duty and loyalty obliged them to do, or from our acknowledgment of their well-deferving, they fhall have the prefumption to hope for a toleration of their profeffion, or a taking away either thofe marks of diftinction, or of our difpleafure, which, in a well-governed kingdom, ought always to be fet upon diffenters from the religion of the ftate, or to obtain the leaft remiffion in the ftrictnefs of thofe laws, which either are, or fhall be made to hinder the fpreading of their doctrine, to the prejudice of the true proteftant religion; or that upon our expreffing (according to Chriftian charity) our diflike of bloodfhed for religion only, priefts fhall take the boldnefs to appear, and avow themfelves, to the offence and fcandal of good proteftants, and of the laws in force againft them; they fhall quickly find, we know as well to be fevere, when wifdom requires it, as indulgent, when charity and fenfe of merit challenge it from us."*

---

* Dodd, vol. 3, p. 390.

These sentiments of the king are just and manly, considering the times in which they were delivered; but they did not satisfy the sullen humour of many: wherefore, in the following year, speaking to his parliament, he repeated the same declaration, in words equally consistent and humane. "But let me explain "myself," he says, "left some mistake me, as "I hear they did in my *declaration*. I am far "from meaning by this a toleration, or quali-"fying the papists thereby, to hold any offices "or places in the government. Nay further, "I desire some laws may be made to hinder "the growth and progress of their doctrines."*—Emboldened by the last clause, which a desire rather to conciliate, than any conviction of its propriety, seemed to have drawn from Charles, both houses joined in a petition, that his majesty, by proclamation, would command all Jesuits and priests, to depart the kingdom by a day, under pain of the severest penalties of the law.† To this the king consented.

Yet, as had been the fate of many similar proclamations in the preceding reigns, means were used to evade its execution, and few, if any, Jesuits or priests were banished. The circumstance that, at this time, excited peculiar jealousy was the presence of two Catholic queens,

---

* Dodd, vol. iii. p. 391. † Ibid. p. 187.

queens, with their feparate courts, Catherine of Portugal whom the king had lately married, and the queen-mother. She was come over on a vifit to her fon; and the aufpicious occafion drew around her, and round the court of Catherine, many priefts and others of the Catholic communion.

The next year, 1664, a defign was formed, which originated with the king himfelf, of bringing a bill into parliament, ferioufly meant to ferve the Catholics, by putting them on that footing of eafe and fecurity, that their conduct, as good fubjects, he thought, merited. Meafures of afcertaining their numbers had been previoufly taken, that men the moft hoftile to the Catholics might know, there was litte to be feared from fo inconfiderable a body. He wifhed alfo that a diftinction fhould be made betwixt thofe, who, being of ancient extraction, had perfevered in the religion of their fathers, and thofe who became profelytes to the Roman church. In the new bill it was intended to provide againft fuch changes in religion. The king had likewife refolved to diminifh the number of priefts, and to reduce them into fuch order, that he might himfelf know all their names, and their feveral places of refidence. " This meafure," obferves lord Clarendon, " muft have produced fuch a fecurity to " thofe who ftayed, and to thofe with " whom they ftayed, as would have fet
" them

"them free from any apprehension of any pe-
"nalties imposed by preceding parliaments."
—But this design, which comprehended many
other particulars, from the perverse opposition
of some weak heads of the party, vanished as
soon as it was known. Moderate men, who
then desired nothing but the exercise of their
religion in great secrecy, and a suspension of
the laws, were cruelly disappointed, and in
their conferences with the king often complained " of the folly and vanity of some of
" their friends, and more particularly of the
" presumption of the Jesuits." All further
thoughts of the bill were dropt; nor was there
ever after mention of it.—The passage is taken
from lord Clarendon.

It is unnecessary for me to trace the ill-
will of the nation to the body of Catholics, as
it visibly encreased through a series of events,
—the fire of London, in 1666, which was ma-
levolently imputed to them; the machinations of the *cabal* ministry, in 1670, and the
following years; the imprudence of the duke
of York in the too open declaration of his religious sentiments; the money treaties between
Louis XIV. and the English king, which betrayed the dearest interests of the nation, and
in the first of which the commissioners, chosen
to transact the shameful business, were of the
Catholic persuasion.

These

Thefe, and other events of an irritating tendency brought forward the *Teft Act* in 1673, which, though eventually it involved the Proteftant diffenters, was primarily intended, as the words plainly fignify, *to prevent dangers which may happen from Popifh recufants.** It is, therefore, enacted that all perfons who accepted any office of truft or emolument in the realm, fhall, befides taking the oaths of allegiance and fupremacy, receive the facrament according to the ordinance of the eftablifhed church, and, at the fame time, make the *declaration* againft tranfubftantiation.

Nor did this act, which configned the Catholics to infignificance and obfcurity, as yet allay the difquietudes of the public mind. Even the clouds daily thickened round their heads: The moft trivial occurrences were mifconftrued: defigning men whifpered fufpicions which themfelves had engendered: the weak and timorous were alarmed: the nation was on tiptoe, looking round for fome dreadful explofion.—And at this crifis it was, in 1678, that Titus Oates produced his *plot*, the work of his own malevolent contrivance, or the ftratagem of a deeper villain.

I will not recount the atrocities of this fad period, when, for the fpace of more than two

long

---

* 25 Car. II. cap. 2.

long years, the mind of the English people was infatuated; when both houses of parliament, with a credulity unheard of, drank down the baneful illusion; and when the Catholics, charged with the blackest designs, and innocent of all, were delivered up to the most cruel persecution. The *plot*, of which they were accused, was to assassinate the king, to overturn the government, and to extirpate the Protestant religion. Of the numbers that thronged the prisons, six Jesuits were hanged, and as many laymen, protesting with the last breath their innocence; and the scene closed with the execution of the venerable viscount Stafford.—Still other victims, I must add, were sacrificed to the ill-humour of the nation; for, in 1679, eight priests more suffered for their character, that is, for having taken orders in the Roman church, and remaining in the realm contrary to the statute of the 27th of Elizabeth. Some died in prison, and others experienced his majesty's mercy. Finally, Mr. Thwing was hanged at York, and Dr. Plunket, the titular archbishop of Armagh, at Tyburn, in 1681, both accused of conspiring against the state, and both innocent.*

The national phrenzy had now spent its wildest rage; and humanity and reason resumed their

---

* *Memoirs of Miss. Priests.* Also Dodd. passim.

their fway. It fhould be remarked, perhaps, that the king, from the beginning, was almoft the only perfon who treated the plot, as afcribed to Catholics, with a becoming contempt: but he could not ftem the popular fury, nor avert from the fufferers its direful effects. Who were the movers of this atrocious fcheme, has not been clearly afcertained; but fufpicions have fallen on many, and on none, with more femblance of truth than on Anthony Afhley Cooper, earl of Shaftefbury, whofe object in it was, not to perfecute the Catholics, but to *exclude* the duke of York, who had embraced their religion, from the throne of his anceftors. The reader will recollect with what pertinacity the queftion of the *exclufion* was agitated in more than one feffion of parliament.

To fome of the priefts that fuffered, had been tendered the oaths of *fupremacy* and *allegiance*; and this reminds me to obferve, that, about this time, the controverfy regarding the lawfulnefs of thofe oaths had been revived among the Catholics. Many of the laity, prompted by the advice of fome of the clergy, had taken, it feems, the oath of fupremacy.* This roufed anew the fpirit of oppofition; the court

The controverfy on the oaths revived.

---

* *Letter of Barberini*, Dodd, vol. 3. p. 383.

court of Rome was alarmed; and the moſt rĕ-ſpectable part of the clergy, by a public inſtrument, declared their diſapprobation of the oath, becauſe, they ſaid, "it obviouſly renounced "the plenary juriſdiction conferred by Chriſt "on Peter, and through him, on his ſucceſ-"ſors, of feeding and of governing the uni-"verſal church."*—But the *oath of allegiance*, againſt which no ſuch argument could be oppoſed, was not ſo eaſily ſurrendered either by the laity or clergy.† Wherefore, cardinal Howard, lately made protector of the Britiſh nation, thus wrote: "The declaration ſent me "laſt year ſerves to free you from the impu-"tation, in as much as concerns the *oath of ſu-*"*premacy*; but I have nothing to alledge in "your behalf, for not making appear your "obedience to this holy ſee, in ſubmitting to "what hath been declared by it againſt the "*oath of allegiance*; which nevertheleſs is expec-"ted from you." He then more than intimates, "that it will not be in his power, with-"out their concurrence, to hinder the ill im-"preſſions that may be cauſed in the minds of "his holineſs and others, on whom they (the "clergy) muſt neceſſarily depend, for obtain-"ing what they judge moſt important (the "appointment

---

* *Letter of Barberini*, Dodd, vol. 3. p. 384.
† Ibid. p. 385, 386.

" appointment of bishops) for a right go-
" vernment amongst themselves, and the flock
" committed to them."*

Thus, like his predecessors, was the English cardinal true to the maxims of the Roman court: and he could say to his countrymen, that, if they dared to declare their allegiance to their king in words, which that court had censured as hostile to its favourite prerogative, they must expect no favour thence, though that favour regarded the *canonical* government of themselves and of the flock committed to them!—If I repeat reflections, it is the inveteracy of unvarying conduct that compels me to it.

Many writings were published in vindication of both oaths; and on that of *allegiance*, the faculty of Sorbonne being consulted, returned an opinion favourable to those who maintained its lawfulness.†—But this *opinion* produced no acquiescence in the adverse party: They insisted, that the Bulls of Paul V. which forbad the oath to be taken, " because it contained
" many things openly contrary to faith and
" salvation," must ever remain in force;—
that the clause in the oath wherein lies the

---

* *Letter of cardinal Howard*, p. 385.
† *Opinion of certain Paris doctors*, Dodd, p. 388.

whole difficulty, and which abjures as *impious* and *heretical* the position, " That princes, ex-communicated or deprived by the pope, may be *deposed or murdered* by their subjects," cannot be understood *conjunctim*, as the French doctors had pronounced, but must be taken *divisim*;—that the application of the words *impious* and *heretical*, in a *formal* sense, to the word *murdered*, and, in a *material* sense, to the word *deposed*, was futile;—that, as many popes and many distinguished divines have so taught, and do so teach, it is not a certain truth, *that princes in certain cases, may not be deposed by the Roman bishops*;—that, as the oath may be deemed a public profession of faith, it should be taken according to the plain and common understanding of the words, as in the close of the oath itself is sufficiently indicated;—that the distinction of *material* and *formal* sense, introduced by the doctors, and applied to their respective words, is above the reach of the vulgar, and not admitted, perhaps, by the magistrates who may tender the oath;— that the most venerable and learned of the Sorbonne had not approved the oath, even with the annexed interpretation, and that the forty-eight, who had given their names, were men of less distinction, and many of them but lately raised to the doctorial degree.*

So

---

* Dodd, p. 387.

SUPPLEMENT.

So eafy is it to involve the plaineft things in obfcurity; and thus perplex the minds of the well-meaning and the illiterate.—The favourers of the oath replied; and difcuffion rofe on difcuffion.

Among the priefts who were brought to the bar, (one of whom was condemned, but afterwards pardoned) two, it appears, had taken both the oaths, Charles Serne* and Andrew Bromwich.† The latter in a fpeech he had prepared to deliver at the place of execution, thus fpeaks: " I am not to be executed for re-
" fufing any allegiance to my gracious fove-
" reign. I have profeffed that fully, by the
" *oaths* before his majefty's juftice of the peace;
" and am fatisfied in my confcience, that, un-
" der God, belongs only to his facred majefty
" Charles II. the fupreme coactive jurifdiction,
" fovereignty, and rule over the perfons of all
" his fubjects, within any his dominions, of
" what eftate, or condition foever they be. I
" have profeffed, that neither the pope, nor
" any foreign perfon, hath right to exer-
" cife any external power, or coercion by civil
" and corporal punifhments, without his ma-
" jefty's authority, upon his fubjects within his

---

* Dodd, p. 304. † Ibid. p. 293.

" dominions.

"dominions. I do not mean, that the king
"can exercife any power of the keys, or any
"act of jurifdiction purely fpiritual, or in-
"ternal; as to preach, minifter the facra-
"ments, confecrate to holy orders, abfolve,
"define, or excommunicate: becaufe all
"thefe things, being merely or purely fpiri-
"tual, belong to thofe, whom the holy ghoft
"hath placed to rule the church of God. I
"have profeffed, that neither the pope, di-
"rectly nor indirectly, hath power to depofe
"the king for any caufe whatfoever, or ab-
"folve any of his fubjects from their natural
"allegiance, or give licence to murder princes;
"whereby I have given to Cefar what is due
"to Cefar; and do not know, that I have
"taken any thing from God, which belongs to
"God. I am not to be executed for the plot:
"I was never accufed of it."*

With what an admirable precifion are the difficulties, which hang about the oath of fupremacy, thus removed, and its claufes reconciled to Catholic belief. But neither before that period, nor fince, have there been many found, whofe minds were as enlarged, and whofe difcrimination was as accurate, as were the mind and difcrimination of
Andrew

---

* *Speech of Andrew Bromwich*, Dodd, p. 359.

Andrew Bromwich; and therefore, has his example been loſt upon us. He was reprieved, as I have ſaid, and afterwards pardoned, and lived to ſee ſome years of the preſent century, reſpected in his neighbourhood, revered, and loved. I am happy alſo to add, that I inhabit the dwelling that once was his; breathe the air which he breathed; and ſtrive, not, I hope, quite ſuccesſlesſly, to imbibe his ſpirit, and, in a feeble tranſcript, to copy his virtues. The whole of that excellent ſpeech, part of which I have extracted, ſhews that, if he reaſoned on a point of controverſy, with the accuracy of a philoſopher, he, at the ſame time, entertained every gentle and generous ſentiment of a Chriſtian, and was prepared to die with a martyr's fortitude, had he been called, as he expected, to the awful trial, by the ſtern juſtice of his country.*

---

* "A worthy and virtuous brother of ours, Mr. Daniel
"Fiſher, ſeeing, in the plot time, ſome Catholics out of fear
"take the oath of *ſupremacy*, and, upon long ſtudying the par-
"ticulars, being fully perſuaded that it might be taken, writ a
"Treatiſe to ſhew that that *oath* neither *did* nor *could* mean to
"attribute any power *purely ſpiritual* to the *prince*, or take it away
"from the pope; but only meant *external* and *coercive* juriſ-
"diction in *external courts*, in the ſame ſenſe as we call *Doctors*
"*Commons*, the *ſpiritual court*; all which *ſpiritual power*, it is ma-
"nifeſt, the king of Spain claims and exerciſes in Sicily. This
"diſſatiſfied ſome of our old-faſhioned zealous brethren.—The
"queſtion was much agitated at that time. Sir John Winter

End of Charles's Reign

The commotions that the plot had raifed, having fubfided, the Catholics began to look to better days, though, by the *teft act*, they were now debarred from all participation in the government of the country; though, by the ftatute of the 30th of Charles, their peers and wealthy commoners were excluded from both houfes of parliament, unlefs they fubfcribed a *Declaration* fubverfive of their Catholic belief; though the general body, laity and clergy, from the late charges of treafon and fedition, had received an additional ftigma on their name which the lapfe of many years, and conduct the moft irreproachable, fhould hardly efface. But the king, from this time, governed with more firmnefs; the thinking part of the nation feemed to blufh at their late credulity and extravagance; the parliament, no longer poffeffed of popular favour, fpent their ftrength in vain efforts; and the duke of York, the immediate heir to the crown, whom a powerful faction had haraffed with unceafing acrimony, openly profeffed

---

"had publifhed a Treatife to prove it lawful, fo had Mr. Hutchinfon; fo had Mr. Creffy. Dr. Godden oppofed it by a paper he fent us out of France." *The Appeal*, p. 4. by John Sergeant, a man of uncommon erudition among the clergy, who died in 1707. Dodd, vol. ii. p. 472. Creffy's *Reflections on the Oaths* were printed in 1661: the works of the other two I have not feen; but I have by me fome MSS. anonymous Tracts written at that time, as alfo, I believe, Dr. Godden's *Paper* juft mentioned.

professed his religion, which, it was now obvious, he would carry with him to the throne. This, with regard to Catholics, was the altered state of things, wherein the short-sighted, the ignorant, the bigoted of that communion would see ample cause for exultation, and the wise and temperate would read, perhaps, the symptoms, and know the signs, of misfortunes and of accumulating evils. On the 6th of February, 1685, the king died; and because, in his last hours, he professed himself a Catholic, it is probable that, at all times, in his few serious moments, he had been strongly inclined to the principles of that religion. Indeed, there is no doubt of it; and two papers he left behind him, written with his own hand, prove that, he had weighed the subject with some deliberation.*

James ascended the throne; and all the gloom which, for years, had seemed ominously to threaten, was, as by a magician's wand, at once dissipated. The Tories were clamorously triumphant; the Whigs in sullen silence hung their heads; the Presbyterians looked for toleration; the Catholics for something more than ease; while the church, passive and unresisting, was

Reign of James II.

---

* See them in Dodd, vol. iii. p. 98.

was difpofed to go along with every wifh of her fupreme head, provided her own afcendancy were maintained inviolate.—As they are connected with my fubject, I muft ftate fome of the events of this reign, as much as may be, in the order of their fucceffion.

Aware of the good opinion many entertained of his virtue and fincerity, the new king was refolved to confirm that opinion; wherefore, on the day of his brother's death, he thus fpoke to the privy-council: " I have been re-
" ported to be a man of arbitrary power; but
" that is not the only ftory has been made of
" me; and I fhall make it my endeavour to
" preferve this government both in church and
" ftate, as it is now by law eftablifhed. I
" know the principles of the church of Eng-
" land are for monarchy, and the members of
" it have fhewed themfelves good and loyal
" fubjects, therefore I fhall always take care to
" defend and fupport it. I know too, that the
" laws of England, are fufficient to make the
" king as great a monarch as I can wifh; and
" as I fhall never depart from the juft rights
" and prerogative of the crown, fo I fhall
" never invade any man's property. I have
" often heretofore ventured my life in defence
" of this nation; and I fhall go as far as any
" man in preferving it in all its juft rights and
" liberties."

"liberties."*—With what sincerity this was spoken, the procefs of events will shew; but it was received with applause, and the nation re-echoed it.

He made no changes in the council, none in the chief places of truft; but then it muft be remarked that, in the laft years of his brother's reign, his influence had directed all general meafures.—On the third day, after his acceffion, he went publicly to mafs.—Charles's funeral was then folemnized; the vacant offices filled with Proteftants; addreffes received from the counties, cities, and boroughs; and, his coronation and that of the queen being celebrated on the 23d of April, which was followed by the trial of Titus Oates and others, the new Parliament affembled on the 19th of May. To them, among other things, the king repeated the declaration he had made to his privy-council, which was anfwered by a vote of thanks, and the fettling on him an annual revenue of more than two millions fterling.†—The Catholic lords, who had been imprifoned for the plot, were difcharged from the tower, and, in a flow of general fatisfaction, the tide of affairs proceeded, when news came that the earl of Argyle was

---

* Rapin, vol. 2, p. 741. † Ibid. p. 746.

was in arms in Scotland, and prefently after, that the Duke of Monmouth, with about eighty followers, had landed in the weft of England. The reader knows how thefe rebellions ended; and he has heard of the cruelties exercifed by Jefferies and Kirk on the followers of the unfortunate Monmouth; cruelties which have ftained the hiftory of the firft year of James, but which, I think, have been too wantonly imputed to the orders of a monarch, whofe difpofitions, furely, were beneficent and humane.

At this moment of fuccefs and general favour, when the king looking round him, faw no obftacle that could impede the accomplifhment of his moft fanguine wifh, he feems to have conceived the project, the thought of which, probably, he had long indulged, of bringing back the nation to the Roman Catholic faith, or, at leaft, of preparing them for it. How little did the ftate of things warrant the feafibility of the project! He knew the temper of the people moft hoftile to that religion, and he had upon his recollection the words which his parliament by the mouth of their fpeaker had lately uttered: " We bring not to your majefty any bill " for the prefervation or fecurity of our reli- " gion, which is dearer to us than our lives, " and we reft fatisfied in your own repeated " declarations."

"declarations."* But his priests or his advisers had darkened, in a cloud of zeal, the natural penetration of his mind. It is related, that the Spanish embassador Ronquillo, at his first audience, said to the king: "I see several "priests about your majesty, who will be im- "portune to have the established religion al- "tered; but hearken not to their advice, for if "you do, you will have reason to repent of it "when it may be too late."—"And does not "your king," observed James angrily, "ad- "vise with his confessors."—"He does," re- plied Ronquillo; "and therefore our affairs go "on so ill."†

The great attempt was now to be made; and he would enforce it, it seemed, by mea- sures which imprudence alone dictated, and which the laws of the country proscribed. On the 9th of November he again met his parlia- ment, to whom, having observed how inade- quate the standing forces of the kingdom were to maintain the peace and quiet of his subjects and the security of government, as the late events had proved, he acquainted them that he had more than double the army, to support which he now asked for supplies. "Nor can "I doubt," he said, "but what I have begun,
"so

---

* Rapin, p. 747.   † Ibid. p. 751.

"so much for the honour and defence of the government, will be continued by you with all the chearfulnefs and readinefs, that is requifite for a work of fo great importance."—
He then proceeded: "Let no man take exception, that there are fome officers in the army not qualified, according to the late *tefts*, for their employments. The gentlemen, I muft tell you, are moft of them well known to me; and having formerly ferved me on feveral occafions, and always approved the loyalty of their principles by their practice, I think them fit now to be employed under me; and, will deal plainly with, that, after having had the benefit of their fervices in fuch time of need and danger, I will neither expofe them to difgrace, nor myfelf to the want of them, if there fhould be another rebellion to make them neceffary to me. I am afraid fome men may be fo wicked, to hope and expect, that a difference may happen between you and me on this occafion. But I will not apprehend that fuch a misfortune can befall us, as a divifion, or but a coldnefs between us."*

This misfortune, which he deprecated, was inevitable. The Tories, of which the parliament

---

* Rapin, p. 752.

ment was almoſt wholly compoſed, were blindly attached to the prerogative, and they would have patroniſed its extenſion even by a ſtanding army, ſo long as they ſaw that the encreaſing influence of the crown would be exerted in the ſupport of their own paſſive principles, and to counteract the deſigns of the Whigs. But when they beheld that the preſent meaſures obviouſly tended to the overthrow of a religion, which, they had declared, was dearer to them than their lives, and to the emancipation, if not to the aggrandiſement, of a party, for whom they had ever felt an unaccountable averſion, notwithſtanding the ſimilarity of their mutual political tenets, they began to open their eyes, and to perceive that there was room for jealouſies and fears, and that the aſſertion often made by the Whigs was too well grounded, namely, "that the intereſts of a Roman Ca- "tholic king were not reconcileable with thoſe "of a Proteſtant kingdom." Great debates enſued in both houſes, which, however, were followed by a vote of thanks to his majeſty, and by a ſupply to be granted of ſeven hundred thouſand pounds for the maintenance of the army. This had been augmented from ſeven to fifteen thouſand men.[*]

The

---

[*] Rapin, p. 753.

The affair of the Catholic officers was not so easily passed over; for here they saw a *dispensing* power exercised, which, if not checked, must utterly frustrate the legislative capacity of parliament, invalidate all law, break down the sacred tenure of liberty and property, and subvert the constitution. It mattered not, that other kings had claimed and used that power, as a part of their prerogative: it was time that the reign of despotism should close. The commons, therefore, addressed the king, expressing their satisfaction in the suppression of the late rebellion, " which threatened," they say, " the over-
" throw of this government in church and state,
" to the extirpation of our religion as by law
" established, which is most dear to us, and
" which your majesty hath been pleased to
" give us *repeated assurances* you will always de-
" fend and maintain; which, with all grateful
" hearts, we shall ever acknowledge." They then continue. " And as to that part of your
" majesty's speech relating to the officers in the
" army, not qualified for their employments,
" as the law directs, we do humbly represent
" to you, that these officers cannot by law be
" capable of their employments; and that the
" incapacities they bring upon themselves that
" way,

---

* Rapin, p. 753.

" way, can no way be taken off but by an act
" of parliament: therefore, out of that great re-
" verence and duty we owe unto your majesty,
" we are preparing a bill to pass both houses,
" to indemnify them from the penalties they
" have now incurred: And because the conti-
" nuing them in their employments, may be
" taken to be a dispensing with that law, with-
" out an act of parliament, the consequences of
" which are of the greatest concern to the rights
" of your majesty's subjects, and to all the laws
" made for the security of their religion, we do
" most humbly beseech your majesty, that you
" would be pleased to give such directions there-
" in, that no apprehensions or jealousies may
" remain in the hearts of your majesty's most
" loyal subjects.*

To this address the king returned an ambiguous reply, expressive of some anger and of
much surprise: " I did not expect," said he,
" such an address from the house of commons."
Nor were the commons much satisfied with their
own patriotism, which tended too directly, they
saw, to the subversion of that *nonresisting* principle
they so cordially cherished. To make some
amends, then, for the offence they had given,
they proceeded to ways and means for raising
the

---

* Rapin, p. 753.

the supply; and besides the indemnity bill they had mentioned, they resolved to offer another to the king, to qualify such officers to serve in the army as he should think proper.

But these flattering appearances vanished. James understood that great opposition was meditated against the proposals just offered, and that the endeavours of his friends would fail: wherefore, on the 20th of November he prorogued the Parliament, tho', by the prorogation, he lost the supply of seven hundred thousand pounds, and finally dissolved it, purposing to govern by a council that should be more pliant, and more subservient to his wishes. Of this parliament, Burnet has said, but not with truth, " that in all England it would not have been " easy to have found five hundred men so weak, " so poor, so devoted to the court."*

Particulars of the appointment of the first vicar apostolic.

While the great concerns of state thus proceeded, the internal business of the Catholic body had undergone some change, and Rome had established over them her favorite theory of dependence and controul. The reader knows, how vigorously the secular clergy had opposed every arrangement, but that of an ordinary superintending prelacy, for which they had perseverantly

---

* *Hist. of his own Times*, p. 668.

feverantly petitioned; and that the Roman court had as inceffantly rejected their prayer. When cardinal Howard was named protector, they had preferred the fame fupplication to him, enclofing the names of fuch perfons as they deemed moft proper for the office. Thirty years had paffed fince the death of the bifhop of Chalcedon, and the clergy could indulge no hope, that Rome would be more propitious to their wifhes, unlefs, perhaps, the improving ftate of things at home, or the manifeftation of the royal will, fhould plead more powerfully for them. The chapter, therefore, maintained its jurifdiction, refolute to accede to no mode of difcipline, that fhould not place them on the fame footing with other chriftian churches. In cardinal Howard, they doubted not, the firmeft confidence might be placed, not aware that he had, for fome years, breathed the air of Rome, and worn its purple.

About the fpring of the year 1685, news was brought to the chapter that Mr. John Leyburn, fecretary and auditor to their protector, and nine years before, prefident of Douay college, was appointed bifhop, with the appellation and authority of *vicar apoftolic*, over the kingdom of England. Ignorant of the fecret influence that had completed the meafure, but confcious that the impofition was affected, *infcio et invito toto clero*, the chapter, in confternation, met, when it was refolved that their dean, Dr. Perrot, fhould wait on on his majesty, and by remonstrances, if possible, avert the blow. The king received him graciously, and listening to his discourse on the *convenience* of *ordinary* jurisdiction, and the *inconvenience* of any other authority, to which the dean added the *suitableness* of the former to the kingdom and its circumstances, and the *unsuitableness* of the latter, his majesty replied: " I will admit " of no prelate from Rome, but with *ordinary* " powers; nor shall Mr. Leyburn be received " with the character of *vicar apostolic* : but I beg " you will send me in a *memorial* stating more " distinctly the difference between an *ordinary* " and a *vicar apostolic*."* Drs. Godden and Giffard accompanied the dean to this interview with the king.

In obedience to his majesty's commands, the chapter prepared a *memorial*, which was presented July 23, 1685. It stated,

" That, by a bishop who is an *ordinary*, is " meant one who hath power of his *own*, or in " *himself*, to govern the flock over which he is " set; and whilst he acts accordingly, he is not " responsible to any, or revocable at pleasure.

" On

---

* *Transactions relating to the secular clergy*, p. 74, 75.

SUPPLEMENT.

" On the contrary, a *vicar* is one, who hath no power of his *own*, or in *himself*; but only the *use*, or *exercise* of the power of the perfon who *fubſtitutes* him; fo that what he doth, he doth not by his own power, but by the power of the perfon whom he reprefents: to whom, therefore, at all times he is accountable, as ufing purely *his* power, by whom that power, and himfelf too, are revocable at pleafure.—Whence it follows, that a *vicar* need not be a *bifhop* at all, but in certain cafes; and, although he be confecrated, and fo have the title and character of a bifhop, yet acting only *in* and *by* the power of *another*, according to the order and inſtructions given by *him*, he is not properly a *bifhop* of the flock to which he is fent, but *officer* or *delegate* of the perfon who fends him."

This difference being ſtated, they humbly crave leave to reprefent to his princely confideration:

" 1ſt. That, if an *apoſtolic vicar* be admitted, then his majeſty's Catholic fubjects will be governed, in *eccleſiaſtical* matters, after a different manner from all other Catholics in moſt parts of Chriſtendom, even in *Italy* itſelf; which will be apt to breed in them jealouſies of being involved in the fame inconveniencies,

" conveniencies, as they were by the power
" given to the *archprieſt*.

" 2dly. That this power not being the vi-
" car's *own*, but *his* in whoſe name he acts, it
" may be taken from him at pleaſure, *etiam ſine
" cauſa*, and the Catholics left without any ſu-
" perior, either *ordinary* or *extraordinary* to go-
" vern them.

" 3dly. That the *vicar* being obliged to act,
" not by the known laws and rules of the *church*,
" but by *ſpecial orders* and *injunctions* from his
" delegant; the government will be *arbitrary* and
" *uncertain*; which muſt be of a pernicious
" conſequence as well in *eccleſiaſtical* as *civil*
" affairs.

" 4thly. That divers *laws* enacted by his
" *Catholic* anceſtors, in providing againſt the
" inconveniencies of *foreign pretences* of the court
" of Rome, viz. Ed. I. Ed. II. Ed. III. Rich. II.
" ſtand ſtill in force; and an *ordinary biſhop* will
" be obliged to eſpouſe his majeſty's and king-
" dom's intereſt, in the due execution of the
" ſaid *laws*, which a *vicar* cannot be expected to
" do; but, if enjoined, act contrary to them.

" 5thly. That the very name of a *vicar
" apoſtolic* will raiſe in his majeſty's Proteſtant
" ſubjects

" subjects an apprehension of the kingdom's
" being subjected to the *immediate jurisdiction* of
" a *foreign court*; against the *pretensions* of which
" court, either *ecclesiastical* or *civil*, all his *Catholic*
" *ancestors* thought themselves obliged to stand
" upon their *guard*.

" To avoid these *inconveniencies*, it is humbly,
" therefore, offered to his princely considera-
" tion to provide, that the *bishop* to be sent for,
" be declared true and proper *ordinary* of the
" Catholics in England, with command to go-
" vern them as other *ordinaries* do."*

The determination of his majesty expressed to Dr. Perrot, seems to have been additionally confirmed by this memorial; for he ordered a letter to be written to Paris, to inform himself of the truth of Mr. Leyburn's appointment, and to forbid his arrival in England with the title of *vicar apostolic*.† But favorites, with other views, in possession of the ear, and probably, of the conscience of James, suggested the propriety of co-operating with the wishes of Rome; and the reader need not be told, how open a Stuart was to secret influence, and how, with the wind of opinion, his mind could vary. Be

---

* *Transact.* p. 90, 1, 2.   † Ibid. p. 75.

this as it may: bishop Leyburn, who had been consecrated at Rome, with the title of *Episcopus Adrumetenus*, and, by commission, *Vicarius Apostolicus* in England, arrived in this kingdom towards the end of the year, and had an apartment prepared for him at St. James's, with a pension, from the exchequer, of 1000 pounds *per annum*.*

"Thus (says the author, writing in the name of the chapter, whom I quote below) we were compelled by obedience to his *majesty* to a non-opposition; for what could be done or proposed with reason as likely to have any probable effect, against the determination of the *pope* and *king*? So that a *tacit acquiescence* was our only refuge.†"

Yet certain persons, commissioned by the chapter, waited on the vicar, to know from him the name, and nature of his jurisdiction as to the secular *clergy*, as also how he would conduct himself in regard to the chapter?—To the first he answered, that his title was *vicar apostolic*, and his power *extraordinary*: to the second, that he had no commission either to allow, or to deny the chapter, but that he would carry himself *abstractedly* towards it: and, as to his proceedings

---

* Dodd, p. 466.   † Transact. p. 75, 6.

ceedings with the clergy, he would exercise *common* authority except on extraordinary occasions.*

In this manner, (the secret history of which is undiscoverable, but which comports well with the views and policy of the Roman court) in direct opposition to the wishes of the clergy, and in derision of all their efforts, was a Roman delegate forced upon them. The circumstance of the king's desertion, probably, compelled them to submit; for had he remained firm, or even neutral, in the transaction, I am inclined to believe, judging from the characters of the men, that they would not have received Mr. Leyburn in the capacity he came, so degrading to their honest pride, and subversive of the plan, which they, and their predecessors, through the progress of many years, had indefatigably abetted. They *acquiesced*, when to resist would be fruitless, perhaps, even detrimental to their interest with the king; and their *acquiescence*, for I can deem it nothing more, has descended to us. In them or in us, there could be no *approbation* of a measure, against which their last *memorial*, and all the acts of their predecessors, so loudly remonstrated, and which

we,

Reflections on that appointment.

* *Transact.* p. 76.

we, under the conviction that reason and the order of Christian discipline were on their side, cannot cease to condemn.

In himself and in his endowments, Mr. Leyburn was conspicuously valuable; and he had dedicated those endowments to the service of the public.* But no worth of character can compensate for his acceptance of a *delegation*, he knew to be so odious to his brethren; and great, truly, must have been the confidence, the effrontery rather, that could have emboldened him to present himself in the capacity of their superior amongst men, who had not called for his services, nor approved his nomination; on the contrary, who had resolutely deprecated his appointment, and resisted it. Did he think, the Catholics of England so depended on the will of the pontiff, or were so completely a part of his stock, that, without their consent, he could dispose of them, or give them away, as he may his sheep that roam for food over the putrid plains of Campagna, or on the parched sides of the Appennines? The clue that leads through the difficulty is palpable. Power is pleasing to man, whatever be his professions of humility, through whatever channel that power may

---

* Dodd, p. 466.

may come: Mr. Leyburn was nephew to Dr. George of the same name, whose whole life had been hostile to the jurisdiction of the chapter and to many of its members: Mr. Leyburn had passed nine years in Rome, within the air of the court, in the family of a cardinal.—Wonder not, reader, if, under these impressions, he was induced to sacrifice the interests of his body, the honour of Catholics, the venerable form of ecclesiastical discipline, to motives of ambition, of family resentment, of a fascinating persuasion, of a zeal for that prerogative, which he had, doubtless, learned immeasurably to value.

How he was received by the Jesuits and other regulars, I have not found: but, probably, as his appointment was distressful to the clergy whom, as has been related, they did not cordially love, and to the chapter particularly, whose jurisdiction they professed to vilify, we may be allowed to think, that it was to them a cause of some triumph. To say that they advised, or urged, the decision of Rome, I am not authorised; for history is silent, and their own *relation* furnishes no documents.

The opposition which Parliament had made to the power of dispensation exercised by the king, did not abate his resolution, or make him cast one serious reflection on the cause of the

<small>Further proceedings of the king.</small>

the evils that overwhelmed his father. Collision warmed his zeal. He had difpenfed with the laws; and he was determined that authority fhould fanction the meafure; for we can hardly believe that twelve judges could have been found of the king's opinion, if fome extraordinary influence had not been ufed to feduce their judgments. Men were employed to fhew, *that a power in the king to difpenfe with law, was law*; and the judges, one excepted, in the cafe of Sir Edward Hales, an unqualified Catholic gentleman, gave the fame decifion in four diftinct propofitions.*

Nothing, but the popular prejudice, now ftood in the way of the Catholics, and they began publicly to open chapels, and to eftablifh fchools.—Five Catholic noblemen were admitted into the privy-council.—The clergy were forbidden to preach on points of controverfy, that animofities among the people might ceafe; but the inhibition not being complied with, a court of *ecclefiaftical commiffion* was erected, that dreadful engine which can bring the thoughts and confciences of men to its bar. The members of it were all Proteftants; but Jefferies the lord chancellor, and fecretary Sunderland, were two of thofe members. It had been firft, I believe,

---

* Dodd, p. 416. Rapin, p. 755.

believe, eftablifhed by Henry VIII. and was afterwards ufed as the legal organ of the royal fupremacy.—James himfelf attempted to make profelytes, and he fucceeded in the earl of Sunderland: on Rochefter and others he made little impreffion. Colonel Kirk, it is faid, was alfo fpoken to, when he replied; " He was pre-" engaged; for he had promifed the king of " Morocco, that, if he changed his religion, he " would turn Mahometan."* The earl of Caftlemain was fent embaffador extraordinary to Rome.†

In fuch meafures as thefe was fpent the fecond year of James's reign, 1686, which only enthufiafts

---

* Rapin, p. 756. Burnet, p. 683, 684.

† The object of this embaffy, which took place at the beginning of the year, is not diftinctly known: but it appears, principally, to have been to prepare the way for a *declaration of fubmiffion*, in the king and the realm, to the apoftolic fee.—I have before me, in Italian, a pompous detail of the embaffy, beginning with his excellence's departure from Greenwich, in February 1686, and clofing with the magnificent audience of his holinefs, after a refidence in Rome, dignified by every atteftation of refpect, of fifteen months. It was written by one of his lordfhip's attendants, who, captivated with the pageantry of fhews and entertainments, has hardly recorded a fact that merits remembrance; and from whom no document can be collected that may lead the hiftorian into the real defign or motive of that imprudent tranfaction. That lord Caftlemain was not cordially received by his holinefs, and what was fome part of his commiffion, will be feen in their place.

enthusiasts could applaud, and which the moderate and the wife among the Catholics, without the spirit of divination, saw must shortly issue in some fatal catastrophe.

But, in the succeeding year, the same course was held.—Desirous of strengthening his measures by the goodwill of the Non-conformists, the king now published a *declaration* for liberty of conscience, " making no doubt, he says, of the " concurrence of both houses of Parliament, when " he shall think it convenient for them to meet." The *declaration* states, that his subjects of the church of England shall be maintained in the free exercise of their religion, and in the full enjoyment of their possessions; that it is his royal will, all penal laws, enacted on the score of religion, be immediately suspended; that, in no meetings held for religious service, any thing be preached or taught, which may tend to alienate the hearts of the people from him, or his government; that, to the end he may not be deprived of the services of any of his subjects, he again declares that the several oaths, tests, and declarations shall be taken or subscribed by no persons, who are or shall be employed in any office, or trust, civil or military, under him or his government.*

Though

---

* Dodd, p. 418.

Though the royal intention, in this arbitrary act, could be concealed from no one; yet did the Proteſtant diſſenters, whom a ſeries of rigour had long oppreſſed, declare their approbation; and addreſſes of thanks were preſented from their various ſocieties. The church, in ſullen reſignation, ſubmitted; for they had too ſtrongly promulgated the doctrines of non-reſiſtance, to depart ſo ſoon from them; nor could they juſtly blame, however much it might provoke their laughter, that exceſs of loyalty manifeſted, on the occaſion, by the Diſſenters, of which themſelves had given ſuch glaring inſtances. " So " true is it," it has been obſerved, " that the " two parties neither did then, nor yet do, fol-" low, on all occaſions, *their own principles*, with " relation to the royal power, which they ex-" tend or contract, as the king is more or leſs " favourable to them."

The Catholics received the indulgence, as it was meant, and turned it to advantage in opening other chapels, and ſpreading, by books and ſermons, the principles of their faith. And as the perſuaſive charm of royal favour now patroniſed that faith, it will not appear ſurpriſing, if, in the eyes of many, it ſhould have loſt much of its former features. The king, at the ſame time, provided himſelf with Catholic chaplains, men of learning and probity, whoſe ſermons were made public; while others were encouraged, by
every

every effort, to attempt to reconcile the differences of the two religions, and to justify that of Rome. Many valuable works, it must be allowed, were published; but which were powerfully opposed by several eminent writers of the English church. Great was the waste of words, if, from these controversies, the cause of christian truth received no benefit.

His majesty's *visitatorial* and *dispensing* power, were next extended to the universities, wherein as yet his religion had no commanding interest; and the histories of the times record two signal attempts made by him, to set aside established statutes, and to force his creatures into the colleges, first of Cambridge and then of Oxford. The resistance of the fellows, though, in part, successless, to the royal mandates and the injunctions of the ecclesiastical commissioners, deserved much praise; for so bent was the king on the measure of appointing a man of his own choice to the presidentship of Magdalen, that he went himself to Oxford, threatening the refractory members, "that they should feel the weight of "his hand," if they refused compliance. They did refuse, and were expelled.*

Unable to conquer the firmness of the members of the lower house, on whom, for many months, every art of seduction it appears, had been

---

* Rapin, p. 759. Dodd, p. 424, 425.

been exhausted, James indignantly dissolved them on the second of July, after repeated prorogations as I before noticed. And now he was resolved either to have a new Parliament entirely at his devotion, or to govern, as he had done, by his own sovereign controul. *Quo warrantoes* were issued against several corporations, that such new charters might be granted, as would make him master of their elections: Emissaries were sent into the counties and towns, with instructions to gain the people, by arguments, promises, menaces: Lord-lieutenants and magistrates were displaced: the king himself made a progress through several counties, stopping in the cities and great towns, to caress by smiles, or by frowns to intimidate, as it might seem expedient. But coldness, if not aversion, every where met him; and he might have seen that the measures of his power were universally odious, as he was soon made sensible that such a parliament, as would second his designs, could not be raised from the people. The aid he principally wanted from a parliament was, their sanction to his own acts in the measures he had taken for liberty of conscience and the suspension of the laws, which shews that, he entertained some doubts of the legality of those measures and of the power he had exercised.

A new scene now struck the eyes of the public.—Lord Castlemain, I have said, had been sent embassador to the court of Rome, where his reception

The Pope's nuncio is received at Windsor.

reception, splendidly magnificent, had attested to Europe the pontiff's grateful sentiments. Not to be outdone in piety and princely munificence, the king, therefore, resolved to return the compliment; and, as he had long entertained near his person a secret nuncio from his holiness, now to admit this nuncio to the honour of a public audience at Windsor. The day appointed was the third of July. Ferdinando Dadde (that was the nuncio's name) archbishop of Amasia, among the infidels, habited in his robes, and preceded by a cross-bearer, took his place in the procession, when a train of priests, and monks, and friars, in the dresses of their respective orders, with the sound of musical instruments, began to move. The duke of Grafton, on the refusal of the duke of Somerset to attend, walked by the side of the nuncio; and thus they reached the castle, where the king was ready to receive them.* The multitude, with amazement, viewed this unusual spectacle, at which the prophane smiled, and wise men shook their heads.

Father Petre.

Still more to publish his defiance of national prejudices, James, a few months afterwards, swore into the privy-council the Jesuit, father Edward Petre. He had before made him clerk of the closet; and that he might enjoy a frequent

---

* Rapin, p. 760. Burnet, p. 716.

frequent and eafy accefs to his converfation, apartments were affigned him within the precinets of the palace. This man, it is faid, was the oracle to whom James reforted with implicit faith, and whom he regarded as his political and religious preceptor. Yet Petre was a man of flender abilities, and a fcanty proportion of learning; and his fpirit, enthufiaftic and headlong, rufhed upon its objects without difcernment, heedlefs of the obftacles that intervened. He was ignorant of every rule of prudence, and of the moft common arts of managing the tempers of men. To his afcendency over the mind of the king, and of his confort, were afcribed the opennefs, the precipitancy, the violence of thofe plans, that I have mentioned, plans which the prudent adherents to his own religion condemned, and which finally proved deftructive to the purpofes they were meant to ferve, and to the interefts of the royal family.* But, on this occafion, even the queen difapproved of the elevation of Petre; and by many it has been confidered as a mafter ftroke of Sunderland, to bring down ruin on the king's affairs. Sunderland, when we fpeak of James's advifers, fhould keep the place that is his due. Unprincipled, and flexible, and of the moft dexterous accommodation of manners, he alfo had
acquired

---

* *Hiftory of Political Tranfactions,* &c. p. 156, by Dr. Somerville.

acquired the confidence of his master; had become, as I have said, a convert to his religion; honoured priests and friars; joined in their consultations; and often prompted, as is justly suspected, the most violent attacks upon the religion and laws of the country. The Jesuit, therefore, and the minister, with views of a different aspect, one to exalt, the other to overthrow, proceeded, hand in hand, to the accomplishment of the great work of Providence, *the reign of liberty*.

The earl of Castlemain, when he went to Rome, had been instructed to petition his holiness, then Innocent XI. in favour of father Petre; and this he had done by presenting a *memorial*. The manner of doing it, or something in the memorial, gave offence to Innocent, which he ordered his nuncio at London to intimate to the king, and, at the same time, to acquaint him that he could not comply with the prayer of the petition. This was to raise father Petre to the mitre.—His majesty, hurt by this news, wrote a *letter* to the pope, dated from Windsor, June 16, 1687, and countersigned by the earl of *Sunderland*, president of the council. In it he assures Innocent, that his embassador had no orders to propose any thing that could give occasion of offence, and he begs pardon for any error into which he might, unintentionally,

intentionally, have fallen, by his endeavours to establish a mutual correspondence between the courts. " To preserve this," he says, " as " my efforts have never yet been wanting, so " never shall they." He expresses much concern, that the promotion of father Petre to the episcopal dignity should be attended with such unexpected difficulties: " For him (whose ad- " mirable endowments and whose exalted merits " are known to me) I asked that favour the " more willingly, because I was aware, with " what ardour he had ever served the cause of " the church, and of my throne, and that the " dignity, I had petitioned for him, would " still give more efficacy to those services." He, therefore, repeats his request. But should his holiness, moved by some special reasons, persist in his refusal, he will not, he trusts, reject another request that he shall then make, which will be, that he will be pleased to favour the said Edward Petre with the *hat* of a cardinal, as there have been many instances of persons of his society being raised to that dignity. " So " many dangers, so many troubles," he concludes, " have I undergone in support of the " Catholic religion; and so immoveably fixed " is the purpose of my mind, by every means, " to promote its encrease and glory, that I am

" induced

"induced to aſk this favour, and I am per-
"ſuaded, it will not be refuſed to me."*

It is not known for what ſee father Petre was deſigned; but had the pope complied with his requeſt, as that of York was vacant, it has been plauſibly conjectured, it was James's intention to have promoted him to that elevated ſtation.

Innocent ſoon replied to the king's letter. In his reply he firſt ſpeaks of his own extraordinary regard for him, of the many things James had done, and ſtill continued to do, *(immortali cum nominis tui laude)* for the welfare of religion and the tranquillity of the church, ſo that no event could give him ſo much pain as the ſmalleſt diminution of their mutual love. He then takes notice, as he had before done to the nuncio, of the vehemence of Lord Caſtlemain's memorial, from which he utterly exculpates his majeſty, and he pardons the earl's tranſports. But as for promoting Edward Petre to either of the dignities, ſo earneſtly requeſted, his holineſs feels regret it has been ſo urged, becauſe he cannot, *tuta conſcientia*, comply. "And
"as we are convinced," he goes on, "that
"your majeſty, in all your thoughts and ac-
"tions,

---

* *Letter of king James*, Dodd, p. 533.

SUPPLEMENT.

" tions, alone purfues the glory of God and his
" church, for which you have magnanimoufly
" expofed to danger your kingdom and your-
" felf, we cannot think you will any further
" infift on a matter, which, if granted, would
" reflect on your majefty's fame." For further
fatisfaction on this head he refers him to the
Nuncio.—The letter is dated from Rome, the
16th of Auguft.*

James was not fo eafily to be moved from
his purpofe; wherefore he again addreffed the
pontiff.—He expreffes his joy at the good opinion entertained by his holinefs, of his devot-
ednefs to the apoftolic fee, and his firm refolution, by every effort, to extend the bounda-
ries of the Catholic faith : " of all which," he
fays, " I will daily ftrive, by new proofs, to
" give a more complete evidence to the world."
He, reluctantly, on the ftrong expreffions of his
holinefs, drops his firft petition in favour of
father Petre; but renews more earneftly his
fupplication for the purple, and concludes, in
many words, with extolling the *infignia merita* of
the man, which, when duly weighed, he flat-
ters himfelf, will remove every obftacle to his
promotion.†—This letter is dated from Wind-

---

* *Letter of Pope Innocent*, Dodd, p. 511.
† *King James's Anfwer*, Dodd, p. 512.

for, September 24, and counterfigned *Sunderland*.

The pontiff again anfwered, on the 22d of November, that as he defired nothing fo much, as fignal occafions of gratifying his majefty, whofe merits he ever had in view, and which merits exceeded all his powers of compenfation; fo it was peculiarly painful to him, when impediments intervened that irrefiftibly obftructed all compliance with his wifhes. Such were the impediments, he fays, that ftood in the way of Edward Petre, and of which the king may be informed from the nuncio. "And fo highly," he adds, " do we think of your majefty's piety,
" as to be fatisfied that you will be convinced,
" my refolution, on this point, is directed to
" the greater glory of God."*

Still James perfevered.—He had been informed, he fays, that it had been ftated to his holinefs, that father Petre was ambitious, and that he had himfelf urged, by inceffant entreaties, this application for the purple. He refutes this charge, as a groundlefs mifreprefentation. " The reverend father," he adds, " has reli-
" gion alone in view; and I am fure, that his
" promotion will contribute much to its pro-
" pagation and enlargement. He feels no
" cupidity

---

* Innocent's Reply, Dodd, p. 512.

SUPPLEMENT.

"cupidity for the facred purple; nor do I be-
"lieve there is a man lefs influenced by ambi-
"tion: therefore it was, that I fo earneftly en-
"treated your holinefs, to grant me the requeft
"I made." Having removed all objections,
and again ftated his motives, he expreffes an
ardent hope that the way may be now cleared to
the completion of his wifhes: " I have repeatedly," he concludes, " afked the favour, and
" ftill prefume to expect that, out of your holi-
" nefs's paternal love towards me and my king-
" dom, it will not be refufed me."*—The *letter*
is dated from Whitehall, 22d of December, and
counterfigned *Sunderland*.

The determination of Innocent was fixed;
in a laft *letter*, therefore, dated February 14, of
the enfuing year 1688, he acquaints the king,
that he is moft willing to clear father Petre from
the charge of *ambition*, on his majefty's affurance,
and that he entertains an high opinion of his
virtue and his deferts; but that there had been,
and ftill were, fuch difficulties in the way of his
promotion, that to comply with his majefty's
wifhes was impoffible. Thefe difficulties, he obferves, he had more than once explained to the
king, through his own minifters at Rome, and
by the nuncio in London. He concludes: " And
" viewing

---

* *Letter of King James*, Dodd, p. 513.

"viewing thofe religious fentiments, of which your majefty has given, and ftill continues to give, fuch fignal proofs, I have reafon to truft that my refolution thus deliberately taken will be well received by you. And may heaven, with our apoftolical benediction, grant an extenfion of the Catholic religion in thofe flourifhing regions of which you are lord, and to your majefty an uninterrupted feries of happinefs and fuccefs!"*

Father Petre's dream of greatnefs thus clofed. What were the fecret motives of Innocent's refolute conduct, or the difficulties which he had explained to the nuncio, but which he was not willing, it feems, to commit to writing, have not tranfpired. The hiftorian, therefore, is left to conjecture. To the apprehenfion of the king, they, probably, appeared light, or he would hardly have perfifted in his application: but neither does he mention them, or attempt their folution, in his letters. The charge of ambition he alone inftances. He intimates, indeed, in the firft, and repeats it in the fecond letter, that the pontiff, perhaps, was influenced by fome *preformed* refolution (*confilium aliquod olim captum*): but this remains equally unexplained.

Innocent

---

* *Innocent's Anfwer*, Dodd, p. 513.

SUPPLEMENT.

Innocent, it is known, was no friend to the Jesuits, who, on account of some measures he had taken against them, in the first year of his pontificate, denounced him as a Jansenist, and ordered prayers for his conversion.* It might be some dislike of the society, or rather, I think, it was some more preponderating motive that could render the pontiff so obdurate to the warm entreaties of the king.

I should have noticed in its place, but a crowd of other matter intervened, that Dr. Giffard, on the 22d of April of this year, was made a second *apostolic vicar*, under what recommendation, or upon what new view of things, I know not. He was of the Giffards of Wolverhampton, a man of some learning, and of many amiable and christian virtues, and whom the king had lately chosen to be one of his chaplains and preachers.† The reader will also recollect that, when the first news came of Mr. Leyburn's appointment, Dr. Giffard accompanied the dean of the chapter to Whitehall to remonstrate against the measure, and against the very title of *vicar apostolic*, with which he now deemed it an honour, or a duty, to permit himself to be invested.

Dr. Giffard made an apostolic vicar.

---

* Hist. Eccle. an. 1676. † Dodd, p. 469.

vested. His title was *Episcopus Madaurensis*. It might be the real, or apparent, encrease of catholicity, that called, probably, for this accession to the mitre.

<small>The last year of king James.</small> We are come to the last months of James, the beginning of the year 1688.

Though he had advanced with wonderful rapidity, which little contradiction thwarted, to the accomplishment of his design, and, doubtless, with some success, yet neither the rapidity nor success kept pace with his desires. On this he published a second *declaration for liberty of conscience*, dated the 27th of April, of which the sentiments are admirable, founded on views of the justest policy, and the clearest deductions of reason. Speaking of the main object of the *declaration*, the king says: " We have resolved to
" use our utmost endeavours to establish liberty
" of conscience, on such just and equal foun-
" dations, as will render it unalterable, and se-
" cure to all people the free exercise of their
" religion for ever; by which future ages may
" reap the benefit, of what is so undoubtedly
" for the general good of the whole kingdom.
" It is such a security we desire, without the
" burthen and constraint of oaths and tests,
" which have been unhappily made by some
" governments, but could never support any:
" nor

"nor should men be advanced by such means
"to offices and employments, which ought to
"be the reward of services, fidelity, and
"merit."*—Nothing was ever more true; and
had the sanction of the legislature, and not the
royal will alone, established the venerable doctrine, the blessings of future ages had reposed
on their memories. Let some praise, therefore,
be given to the man, in whose breast such just
discernment could dwell, though the tendency
of his real views might be partial, and his
means of conduct arbitrary.

Not satisfied with publishing this *declaration*,
the king issued an order of council, enjoining
the bishops to distribute it through their dioceses, that it might be read, on certain days,
in all churches and chapels. What was the
conduct of the prelates, on this trying occasion, is well known. Seven of them petitioned
the king, to be excused from distributing the
declaration, " among many other considera-
" tions," they say, " from this especially, be-
" cause the declaration is founded upon such a
" *dispensing power*, as hath often been declared
" illegal in parliament, and particularly in
" the years 1662, and 1672, and in the be-
" ginning

---

* Rapin, p. 762.

" ginning of your majesty's reign."—They were summoned before the council; were committed to the tower; were tried in the court of *King's Bench*, on the 29th of June, for having uttered a *seditious libel*, for such their *petition* was styled; and were acquitted, amidst the shouts and loudest acclamations of the cities of London and Westminster.

Now, for the first time, the king beheld the precipice, to which he had been gradually approaching, and when to recede or advance seemed equally full of danger. He tried the army and the navy, and both, he saw, were disaffected, in spite of the Catholic officers to whom he had given commands.—Churchmen and Presbyterians united for their common security: Whigs and Tories were reconciled; and James received advice that a secret design was forming against his throne.—In consternation he consulted the bishops, what, in this emergency, was best to be done; and though the advice they gave, in an earlier stage of the business, might have saved the crown, it was now too late. The prince of Orange landed on the 5th of November, and the king, after a variety of events, abandoned by his friends, insulted by his enemies, finally withdrew to St. Germain's.

I must

SUPPLEMENT.

I must now observe that, in the preceding May, two more *apostolic vicars* had been appointed, father Ellis, of the order of St. Bennet, and Dr. James Smith.—Ellis was a chaplain and preacher to the king, and was consecrated at St. James's on the 6th of May, with the title of *Episcopus Aureliopolitanus*.*—Dr. Smith, at the time of his promotion, had been nearly six years president of the college in Douay; and it was, we are told, at the recommendation of Catherine, the dowager queen, who had become acquainted with his character, that he was raised to the episcopal office. The Catholic clergy had long considered him as a fast friend to their cause. He was consecrated in Somerset house, where the queen dowager resided, May the 23d, with the title of *Episcopus Callipoliensis*.†

Two more apostolic vicars appointed.

The kingdom was now divided into four districts. Bishop Leyburn resided in London, or the south; Dr. Smith went to the north; father Ellis to the western counties; and Dr. Giffard to those more inland. Of the last gentleman it may be remarked, that, on the death of Dr. Parker, the *royal* president of Magdalen college, he also, by virtue of the king's mandate, was admitted to the office, March 13. whence.

---

* Dodd, p. 467. † Ibid. p. 468.

whence, after a few months, he was displaced by the same arbitrary authority. On each of the vicars, agreeably to the first arrangement, was settled by the king, a salary of one thousand pounds *per ann.* payable from the exchequer, with a gratuity of five hundred pounds.* Before they departed to their respective stations, they addressed a *pastoral letter* to the laity of their communion, which breathes an admirable spirit of benevolence and wisdom, conveyed in a style of elegant simplicity. But this settlement, however inoffensive in itself, was not well received by the public, at a time when their ill-humour was afloat, and when much provocation, as I have shewn, had been given: wherefore, the bishops in the last advice which, on his requisition, they gave to the king, among other things, recommended, "That the four foreign "bishops, who styled themselves *vicars apostolical*, "be inhibited from farther invading the ec- "clesiastical jurisdiction, which, by law, was "vested in the bishops of the church of Eng- "land."†‡

---

* Dodd, p. 468.
† Rapin, p. 772.
‡ The reader who wishes to see an apology for many of the acts of this unfortunate monarch, may consult the *history* of
father

father Orleans, who drew his information from the mouth of the prince himself, with whom, he says, he conversed at St. Germain's as long as he could wish.—In an interview, at the same place, with Sir Edward Hales, mentioned by Dodd, p. 421, James owned, " that he came out of England by going too fast; " and hearkening to some Catholics, whom Sunderland made " use of for his own ends."

The *relation of the regulars*, which had been long silent, thus speaks of the reign of James: " To Charles succeeded that most " pious and ever to be remembered Catholic king, James II. in " whose reign, the cause of the innocent faithful, which had " long been oppressed, began to revive a little. For he, worthy " of eternal praise, made that cause his own, and, from the be- " ginning of his reign, was occupied with the care of establishing " it. He was willing, he was ardently desirous; he even com- " manded the public exercise of the true religion, for the gene- " ral good, and to the general joy; and in some cities he esta- " blished colleges and seminaries. He permitted priests, secu- " lar and regular, to frequent the palace: he procured the con- " secration of four bishops in the royal chapel; and for them, " as *vicars apostolic*, he divided the realm into four districts, " that each might severally govern the priesthood and the " flock."

" This measure, though every where applauded by good " men, the heretical bishops only, and the primate of Canter- " bury, and other Protestants, indignantly reprobated: and " the same primate, with eight other bishops of his own stamp, " dared to appeal to his majesty and wickedly to insinuate, that " the government of the provinces ought to be administered, " agreeably to the pretended laws of the country, the Catholics " to be ejected from their employments, their schools to be " suppressed, and the vicars apostolic to be deprived of their " jurisdiction. Not yet satisfied, they even pleaded for the " liberty to persuade the king (horrible to utter!) to embrace

" the

"the tenets of the Englifh reformation. But that invincible monarch, whom deceit and malice could drive from his throne, was here unconquerable; and he prefered rather to withdraw to another land, than to lofe that kingdom which exceeds realms and worldly treafures, committing himfelf and the prince his fon to the care of that Being, in whofe caufe he had fo glorioufly fuffered."

From

From the appointment of vicars apoſtolic in the reign of James II. to the preſent year, 1793.

THE reflections full of anxiety and foreboding alarms, that agitated the minds of the Catholics, I need not deſcribe, when they beheld the retreat of king James, and the maze of difficulties into which his enthuſiaſtic zeal, and the imprudent counſel of their friends, had precipitated them. The popular reſentment, as he retired, had riſen; and had deſtroyed their chapels in London and in other places. They contemplated the progreſs of the *Revolution*, proceeding in a firm and uniform courſe, that argued the capacity of the managers and their

The Revolution not unfavourable to the Catholics.

A a unvarying

unvarying purpofe, through a fucceffion of awful acts, to fome great and final iffue. Nor was it long, before this iffue became manifeft, by the fettlement of the crown, the folemn declaration of *rights* that accompanied it, and in thofe rights by the fanction of that eternal principle—*that all power is a voluntary delegation from the people, to be exercifed for their good by them to whom its exercife is entrufted.*

The evils which the Catholics had apprehended, did not befal them; and after the firft ferment was over, and the people faw that, with the flight of their late king, every meafure of his adminiftration was annihilated, had the Catholic party been difpofed cordially to accede to the new fettlement, they would have had little to fuffer from a prince who was never accufed of bigotry in religion, and whofe great ambition it was, from motives of perfonal aggrandifement, not to weaken by difunion, but by union to invigorate the arm of government. But the minds of Catholics, at that period, like the minds of many of their fellow-citizens, were fo obfeffed with the conviction, " that the power " of kings was derived from heaven, and that " the facred inftitution, therefore, was palpa- " bly violated in the perfon of the late mo- " narch," that they could not abandon his right to the Englifh throne, or even be contented paffively to fubmit to him, whom the nation

nation had chofen to be their governor. The beauty, therefore, the fublimity, the truth of thofe principles they were unable to comprehend, that the Revolution had confecrated, and which, when a few years more fhould be elapfed, their defcendents would learn to revere and to cherifh, as the Palladium whereby all that is dear and valuable in life can alone be maintained.

The reader, through the preceding reigns, has feen, from what caufes, the Catholics were difcountenanced and often punifhed with extreme feverity; while the popular hatred againft their religion grew, and from motives of policy, was, fometimes, encouraged: but, from this time, though the prejudice of the multitude remained, their governors faw in them a party *politically* difaffected, forming a branch of the great Jacobitical faction, and as fuch to be difcountenanced and repreffed. Some laws, it is true, in the firft, and in other years of William and Mary, paffed againft them, but their enaction was owing to particular circumftances, when the exiled king, for inftance, meditated fome attempt for the recovery of the throne, or when caufes of alarm real or imaginary, proceeding from the fame quarter, were excited. Had they furrendered their attachment to him they deemed their lawful fovereign, they might have retained

their

their religion, and have been permitted its practice, in eafe and fecurity. But, in the blindnefs of their loyalty, they fo far, even confounded faith and politics, as to deem a departure from either the fin of herefy.

From this time alfo, their own controverfy about the oaths of fupremacy and allegiance, which, as we have feen, had long engaged their attention, utterly fubfided; for why difpute about oaths, when the very fovereignty of the perfon was denied, who demanded thofe tefts of fealty? The oaths, themfelves, at the Revolution, had been altered; that of *allegiance*, to gratify the fcruples of the adherents to hereditary right; that of *fupremacy*, to eafe the confciences of the Proteftant Diffenters. The *prefent* difficulties of the Catholics were removed by neither change; otherwife they would have acknowledged, that the firft oath was cleared from every objection, and that the fecond was lefs complicated, being relieved from the whole *affirmative* claufe.

Government of the Vicars Apoftolic.

The vicars apoftolic, I have faid, had repaired to their refpective diftricts, little forefeeing the event that was foon to happen, and which, depriving them of the royal favour and of other benefits they might look to, would, at once, cut off their ample means of fubfiftence, and

SUPPLEMENT.

and reduce them to penury or the dependence of a precarious maintenance.—Bishop Leyburn was first committed to the Tower; but, on the assurance of his peaceful and inoffensive character, was soon afterwards released: and as his behaviour continued to be irreproachable, occupying himself in the discharge of his pastoral duties, he experienced little molestation from government, and temporary alarms soon subsided. It was only required that his place of abode should not be concealed.*— Dr. Giffard also had been apprehended; but he met with the same gentle treatment, as his unoffending conduct equally merited.†——Dr. Smith retired from York to a gentleman's seat in the country, where he lived in great estimation, practising the virtues, it is related, of the primitive ages.‡—— Father Ellis alone, from motives of fear, or from attachment to his royal master, retired with him to St. Germain's, which he afterwards quitted, and obtained a bishopric in Italy.‖

The mode of government, which these gentlemen permitted, by their means, to be introduced, was thus established; and has continued. It was an economy, in its obvious nature, most extraordinary and dependent, in which they

---

* Dodd, vol. iii p. 467. † Ibid. p. 469.
‡ Ibid. ‖ Ibid. p. 467.

who ſtyled themſelves biſhops, were but the delegated agents or ſtewards of another, while that other, the Roman pontiff, was himſelf the ordinary or immediate biſhop of the Engliſh Catholic church. This biſhop apportioned out to his delegates the *quantum* of juriſdiction, it ſeemed expedient they ſhould exerciſe, which he could recal, limit, or modify, as his own will or their conduct might direct. The agents were independent of each other in their reſpective offices, (which did but more evince the nature of the link that bound them to the Roman chair) " moving equally a-breaſt," it has been ſaid with ſome wit, " without any mutual relation, " coherence, or order among themſelves." Such a ſtate of inſubordination had not before been ſeen in the chriſtian church; where parts combine into unity by a beautiful and juſt gradation, each part poſſeſſed of its proper and eſſential energy, and one ſuperintending governor cementing, animating, rounding, perfecting the whole. A code of co-ordinate laws, denominated *canons*, had been adapted to this ſyſtem, whereby each part muſt be directed, and the whole governed. To the diſorganiſed or rather anomalous ſtate of things, of which I am ſpeaking, no primitive legiſlation could apply; nor did Rome wiſh it ſhould be ſo, " for all canons " are thrown out of doors or deemed inſignifi-
" cant,

" cant, when a government comes in that guides
" itfelf by the *placita curiæ Romanæ.*"*

The chapter, though fenfible of thefe deformities in the new government, which fome of their writers have ftrongly portrayed, judged it proper, as I have related, for peace fake, to *acquiefce*, when refiftance could but generate ftrife and encreafe the evil. Very early, therefore, after the entrance of vicar Leyburn, in a meeting of its members, December 2, 1685, they paffed a *refolution*, " That the jurifdiction of the chap-
" ter fhall be deemed to ceafe during the exer-
" cife of bifhop Leyburn's authority." But they fubjoined the enfuing claufe; " unlefs we
" perceive fuch an oppofition raifed againft our
" authority, as fhall manifeftly tend to its de-
" ftruction."† This they added from a well-grounded apprehenfion, that Mr. Leyburn had brought with him from Rome private inftructions to break down the authority of the chapter, as he fhould fee convenient, it having for many years exercifed *ordinary* jurifdiction, *fede vacante*, and ftill claiming the right, and therefore being the only obftacle, that ftood in the way of the paramount controul of the Roman court. In other refpects, they fubmitted with the

---

* *Serjeant's Papers MS.*
† *MS. Minutes of the General Affembly, held July 9, 1694.*

the *acquiefcence* of men to whom concord was moft dear, and in whom the love of order preponderated over every view of pre-eminence or power. But though the chapter ceafed to act, it did not ceafe to exift, meeting at ftated times, and regulating its own internal concerns.

Thus to the laity, moft of whom the infection of Jacobitifm had feized, to the clergy, who, by the expulfion of their king, faw all their fond thoughts of preferment and of the exaltation of their church at once diffipated, to the new fuperiors of that clergy, whom the fmiles of Rome muft, in future, nourifh, and not the more fubftantial favours of an indulgent court, opened the era of the Revolution. To the hiftorian, who confines his views, it is a barren period; but I will glean what I may be able, principally purfuing, as I have done, the little events of our church-eftablifhment, and with them connecting fuch incidental materials as may fall in my way.

King James,

When the attempt of James to recover the throne, and who with that intent landed in Ireland, had failed of fuccefs, and when fome laws, as I have mentioned, of a perfecuting tendency, had been enacted againft the Catholics, in the firft year of William and Mary, nothing more happened till 1693. In this year James meditated a fecond attempt which a *declaration* was to precede, dated St. Germain's, April 17. It contains

contains many curious claufes, evincing how much the lofs of a crown, or rather, perhaps, the hopes of thereby recovering it, could alter the tenour of a mind, habitually bigoted and unbending. He promifes, fhould he be received by the Englifh people, to maintain the Proteftant church as by law eftablifhed! To which conceffion, it appears, he had been induced by fome of the French bifhops and by fome doctors of the Sorbonne, and which opinion the Englifh divines that were with him acknowledged, *he might in confcience fafely follow*, though themfelves did not fubfcribe to it. He promifes to leave the *teft laws* in full force! The repeal of which, it feems, he now viewed as a matter of mere political confideration, in which confcience had no concern. He promifes to repeal all the Irifh acts, which he had made in that country while the Catholic parliament fat! He promifes, that the army which goes with him into England, fhall be new-officered with Proteftants, and that his whole court, on the king, the queen, and prince's fide, fhall be compofed of Proteftants!*—The fincerity of thefe promifes may be doubted, which the forlorn hope of his fituation had, probably, extorted: and in difcourfing with Sir Edward Hales on the fubject

---

* *Difcourfe between James II. and Sir Ed. Hales*, Dodd, p. 421.

subject of the *test*, James made an observation that shews to what his real views tended: " English *Protestants*," said he, " are very ob-
" stinate, if the things, they desire, are not
" granted; but if complied with, the easiest
" governed people in the world."*

Proceedings of the chapter.

The chapter, from the observation of some years, being now sensible that their plan of *acquiescence* must terminate in their own ruin, if something were not done to avert it, resolved to address the vicars, thereby to rouse them into action, or to learn, if it might be, what their views were. To be jealous of men *so* influenced in their thoughts, and *so* directed in their actions, was most natural. An *address*, dated November 16, 1693, was therefore sent to the three resident vicars; and that more attention might be secured to its contents, they accompanied it with a note to Dr. Giffard, in whom they had most confidence, reminding him of his former zeal in the common cause, and entreating his earnest co-operation. The substance of the *address* was:

" That the *dean* and *capitulars* having seri-
" ously reflected on the past attempts of their
" adversaries,

---

* *Discourse between James II. and Sir Ed. Hales*, Dodd, p. 421.

" adverfaries, and of the great interefts for-
" merly made againft them; and now forefee-
" ing, that, whenever providence fhall take
" their prefent fuperiors away, moft probably
" they fhould have thofe fet over them, whom
" their *adverfaries* fhould recommend, as having
" the power of *courts* to favour them; whereby
" a gate would be opened for all that mifchief
" to enter in, which has been defigned for
" many years; whence, by fubmitting, they
" muft confent to their own ruin, or elfe, by
" ftanding on the defenfive, run the hazard of
" great diforders, if not of fchifm:—Where-
" fore, they befeech them to take thefe things
" into their moft ferious confideration, and
" make fome provifion to prevent the evil;
" and therefore, fince the chapter was erected
" and confirmed by two learned and pious
" bifhops, with the advice of divers prelates
" and learned doctors, and with this exprefs
" claufe, that it fhould endure *until many bifhops*
" *being appointed in England, many chapters fhould be*
" *erected*; that they would either pleafe to erect,
" in each refpective diftrict, *chapters* to fucceed
" with *ordinary* jurifdiction; or elfe conclude on
" fome means whereby may be fecured to the
" prefent chapter its rights and privileges of *or-*
" *dinary* jurifdiction, nomination of fucceffive
" bifhops, &c. *fede vacante*, as bequeathed to it;
" for thus it was left as abfolutely neceffary for
" the well-being and prefervation of the body;
" nor

"nor can they lay it down without forfeiting that truſt repoſed in them, being falſe to their body, and to the oath they have taken for its ſupport, and alſo injurious to the memory and the whole proceedings of thoſe venerable prelates."*—It is ſigned by Dr. Perrot the dean and nine members, among whom is the Rev. *John Gother*.†

The Vicars anſwered: "That, as to the firſt point, the *erecting of chapters*, they ſhould be willing to comply, were the thing poſſible to be done; but, according to the preſent diſcipline, chapters will not be allowed, without leave and a confirmation from Rome; for though they did not diſown a *power of doing it in themſelves, as having ordinary juriſdiction*, upon which the former biſhops grounded themſelves; yet, as the practice is, they cannot do it, and that, whenever done, it will not otherwiſe be effected, than by the interpoſition of the king (James), which, at any time, would be ungrateful to the apoſtolic ſee, and now peculiarly unſeaſonable for his majeſty to propoſe.—As to the ſecond point, the *preſent chapter*, they would, according to the authority of all biſhops, leave at their deceaſe,

---

* *Tranſact.* p. 81. Alſo MS. copy of the *original minutes*.

† I make no comments on a name that is written on the tablet of all our hearts.

" deceafe, a vicar general with faculties for ex-
" traordinaries, for a *limited time*, during which
" if a new bifhop were not appointed, then
" they would not, by any act, prejudice the
" chapter, which might proceed as it thought
" proper.—Finally, that the *nomination* of bi-
" fhops was in the king (James), of whofe
" goodnefs they had no reafon to doubt, and
" to whom they might, with all freedom, make
" their applications; and that they, moft
" affuredly, would not prejudice his right."*

This anfwer, unfatisfactory and ambiguous, drew from Mr. Ward, the fecretary of the chapter, a treatife written with great force, wherein he proves firft the *neceffity* of ordinary jurifdiction, *fede vacante*, refiding fomewhere, call it a *chapter*, a *council*, or what you pleafe, as in all churches in general, fo more efpecially in the Catholic church of England.—2dly, that this is not *inconfiftent* with either a delegated epifcopal jurifdiction, or with the added title of *vicar apoftolic*.—3dly, that the *prefent chapter* is ftill the heir apparent of this *ordinary jurifdiction*, until each of the prefent vicars fhall erect or procure to be erected a chapter or fomething equivalent in each diftrict, in which may refide the ordinary

---

* *Tranfact*. p. 81. Alfo MS. copy of the *original minutes*.

ordinary jurisdiction after their deaths, *sede vacante*.—4thly, that the present vicars, unless they can procure such succession of ordinary episcopal jurisdiction *sede vacante*, as has been expressed, ought, at their respective deceases, to leave the present chapter, as they found it.[*]

But Mr. Serjeant, irritated by that expression in the answer, whereby the vicars insinuated that they possessed *ordinary jurisdiction* in the sense it was possessed by the two bishops of Chalcedon, with his usual fire and acuteness combated that assertion in a short *tract*, wherein he shews, by deductions from reason, and from facts antecedent to, concomitant with, and subsequent to the appointment of Mr. Leyburn, that the vicars could pretend to no *ordinary* powers, that they were *mere* delegates, stewards of the Roman bishop, amenable to his will, dependent on his beck. " As certain as it is," says he, " that bishops can erect chapters in " their own cities and dioceses, (which all the " world knows is most certain) so certain it is " (if the words of the vicars were really " meant), that they have power to do the " same; and yet they must not, or dare not, " do it, for fear of disgusting those very per- " sons that gave them this power. This is
" strangely

---

[*] *MS. Papers by* John Ward.

" ſtrangely myſterious: They have power
" given them under their hands to do this,
" and all power is eſſentially ordained for ac-
" tion; and yet this power is not to act, and
" therefore, in effect, is *no power*, but is *diſabled*
" from acting, which it could not be, but by a
" ſuperior power. And what power can that
" be, but its oppoſite power, the *extraordinary*
" power? Wherefore the extraordinary or *hu-*
" *man* is the commanding and over-powering
" power, and the *ordinary* (which is of divine
" inſtitution) is the poor, weak, ſubſervient
" power, and muſt not diſobey it; that is, the
" divine power has no power at all, but what
" the human will allow it: For the world
" agrees, that the *ordinary* power is *divine*, and
" the *extraordinary* human."*

The vicars, it is known, did but boaſt when they made the aſſertion; for had their power been the ſame as that which erected the chapter, (the canonical exiſtence of which they did not dare to controvert) what ſecret apprehenſion of diſpleaſing Rome or St. Germain's was to impede its exerciſe? Let it alſo be remembered, that theſe vicars, a few years before, had been members of the chapter, and ſtrenuous advocates

---

* *MS. Papers by* John Serjeant.

advocates of all its claims. But they now very pertinently obferved, that any attempt to eftablifh or introduce an *ordinary* authority would, at all times, "be ungrateful to the Roman fee." This caufed the paufe, and haraffed all their wifhes, which, at firft, I doubt not, were not directly unfavourable to the defires of the clergy. John Serjeant, however, very fhrewdly obferved, "that if the extraordinary power
"were permitted to get in a finger, ways
"would be found afterwards to bring in its
"whole body."

Under this impreffion, for Serjeant was now the foul of their exertions, the chapter, the following year, met in general affembly, and having, in their firft feffions, paffed fome internal regulations neceffary to ftrengthen their prefent independence and future permanence, they proceeded to the bufinefs of a fecond *addrefs* to the vicars, which was prepared and read. It ftated;

"That, whereas, in their anfwer to the
"*addrefs* of the laft year, the vicars had declar-
"ed that, notwithftanding their *ordinary power*
"of erecting chapters, they will not be allowed
"without leave and confirmation from the fee
"apoftolic, and that, therefore, according to
"the prefent difcipline and practice, they
"could not do it: The affembly, without a
"deep

SUPPLEMENT.

" deep fenfe of grief, cannot but reprefent to
" them, the ill effects that muft neceffarily fol-
" low in the refpective vacancies, (and how
" long they may continue no one knows) they
" muft leave at their deaths. The evils are,
" that, without a *ftanding ordinary jurifdiction*, this
" cannot properly be called a *church*; that it
" will be deftitute of all the advantages which
" fuch jurifdiction brings with it; that it will
" be without order, expofed to the encroach-
" ments of adverfaries, and the flowing in of
" foreigners; that the laity will be deprived
" of the facrament of confirmation, which, in
" the vacancy of fees, cannot be adminiftered
" without faculties from the ftanding ordinary
" jurifdiction, &c.—For the prevention of thefe
" and other evils, that their predeceffors infti-
" tuted a chapter for the continuance of *ordi-*
" *nary epifcopal jurifdiction, fede vacante*, to endure
" *donec pluribus in Anglia epifcopis Catholicis conftitutis,*
" *plura in Anglia erigantur capitula*; and therefore,
" unlefs this prefent chapter be fupported, or
" others erected, thofe dangerous mifchiefs
" muft fall on the clergy and laity.

" It is well known," they proceed, " that
" we were, divers times, forbidden by king
" Charles II. and his chief minifters ever to
" accept of a vicar apoftolic, as a title and
" authority underftood to be contrary to the
" ancient laws of this nation, and expofing

"English subjects to the danger of a *Præmunire*, and exclusion from the king's protection. Moreover, it is well known to you, what remonstrances we made to king James II. for preventing the admission of such a title and authority; and what good intentions he expressed for the obtaining an absolute ordinary for us. And finally, it ought also, as we humbly conceive, to be considered in what danger we still lie from the said laws, having a prince upon the throne not of our religion, and who we may justly fear, may be easily persuaded to the execution of them."

"This being the state of things, that, therefore, the dean and chapter of the English Catholic clergy now assembled, do, with all due respect, supplicate the vicars apostolic effectually to solicit the Roman see for the establishment of such a succession of *ordinary episcopal jurisdiction*, so necessary to this country above all others." "Or if you shall think fit," they conclude, "to accept of our concurrence also therein; we shall depute such members to attend you from time to time, as may be proper for the carrying on, and accomplishing so good a work"[*]
Dated July 13, 1694.

The

---

[*] *MS. Copy of the proceedings and acts of the chapter*, July 13, 1694.

SUPPLEMENT.

The dean, Mr. Ward the secretary, and Mr. Gother were deputed to wait on the vicars Leyburn and Giffard, who were in London, with this address.

The vicars answered: "That the *petition* of the assembly was most *reasonable*, and that such a supplication could not be offensive to the *see of Rome*, and that they would promote it, *when it should be judged a convenient time*."*

This convenient time never came. Even there are reasons for concluding that, during these very transactions, the vicars were meditating the utter suspension of all the powers of the chapter by a formal decree from Rome.

The English monks of the order of St. Bennet claimed peculiar privileges under the decrees of popes, and among them even a *capitular ordinary jurisdiction* in various provinces, which ceased not, they maintained, after the introduction of vicars apostolic. And it was this claim, it seems, that all along had rendered them so refractory to the jurisdiction of the chapter. The vicars complained to Rome, entreating the abrogation of a claim, which so obviously stood in the way of their spiritual admi-

Its jurisdiction suspended.

---

* Transact. p. 84.

niſtration.—The other regulars, at the fame time, in virtue of their refpective immunities, pleaded an exemption from the fame vicarial powers, and owned no obedience to them. Here was juſt matter for further complaints, which the vicars alfo carried to Rome, fupplicating that all the regulars, in parochial concerns, be fubjected to their controul.*

No mention is here made of the fecular clergy or of their chapter.—It muſt alfo be noticed, that it was precifely of thefe exemptions that the laſt biſhop of Chalcedon had complained; that to maintain them the regulars had refiſted; and that the court of Rome, long importuned on the fubject, had finally pronounced judgment in their favour: " Let all and every " of the miffionaries," it had faid, " ufe their " *privileges* and faculties, as they enjoyed them " before thefe controverfies."† But then (and here lay the bitter provocation) the biſhop of Chalcedon ſtrove to remedy the abufe by *his own episcopal* authority; and when he called on Rome to aid him, it was under the fignature of *ordinarius Angliæ & Scotiæ*. The vicars pretend to no fuch power, affume no fuch title: they humbly implore, and Rome refolves to fupport its delegates, that is, to fupport its own prerogative, though,

---

* *Two letters of the vicars*, Dodd, p. 528, 529.
† Brief *Britannia*, Dodd, p. 17, 158.

though, by the act, the decrees of former pontiffs, in the cafe both of the benedictins and the regulars, muft be fufpended.

Innocent, the 12th of the name, ordered a fpecial congregation to meet, before whom he laid the fupplications of his vicars. They difcuffed the fubject, and *decreed*, in regard to the firft point: " That, by the deputation of vicars " apoftolic into England, all jurifdiction what" foever of *chapters*, as well *fecular* as *regular*, of " all the churches of that faid kingdom, *did* " *ceafe* and *doth ceafe*;—but yet only while their " deputation or that of others fo deputed, at " any time, by the apoftolic fee, fhall laft: " *and not otherwife*."*—On the fecond point, they *decreed*; " That regulars, thofe of the fociety, " monks, and all others, be fubject, in all pa" rochial duties, to the vicars apoftolic in " whofe diftricts they may be placed."†—The decrees are dated October 6, 1695; and the pontiff, in the following year, confirmed them by an apoftolic fanction, dated October 6, 1696.‡

---

* *Decreta*, Dodd, p. 529.   † Ibid.

‡ Having ftated the cruel condition to which the Catholics were once more reduced, by the expulfion of their king, their moft loving father James, and the new laws then made againft them, the *relation of the regulars* proceeds to fay, " That, from " the appointment of vicars apoftolic that internal tranquillity

Whether the vicars, under hand, had urged the general decree; or whether the Roman court, availing itself of the fortunate occasion, involved spontaneously the chapter of the clergy in the same suspensive clause, is not distinctly ascertained. This, however, they have ascertained, that, by declaring the jurisdiction of the chapter to cease so long as there shall be apostolic

---

"had not arisen, which unexperienced men had expected; that, in 1694, a George Witham was deputed to Rome with complaints against the benedictins and regulars, (above-mentioned); that he obtained two favourable decrees, the regulars not being heard in their defence, and a single advocate only having spoken in the cause of the benedictins; that while these things were secretly transacted at Rome, it began to be rumoured at home, that the vicars were devising something against the regulars, under the specious pretext of their disobedience; that the superiors of the regulars, therefore, determined to write to the sacred congregation, and imagining that the business would not be terminated so soon or without their privity, that they, in general terms, exhibited many things against the pretended jurisdiction of the vicars over the regulars; that they finally urged the expediency of delay, that their agents might be sent to Rome, to represent the state of religion in England.—That, notwithstanding, the matter rested here, either because the vicars themselves were desirous to persuade the regulars, that they designed no innovation, or they were cautioned by others, lest should the subject be again discussed in the congregation, and their misrepresentations be detected, there would be an end of all their consequence, since nothing could be more evident than that the decree, they had procured, was not adopted to the state of the English mission." "This, at least, must be admitted," they conclude, "that the vicars studiously concealed their decree,

apoftolic vicars, *and not otherwife*, they have fanctioned its *canonical* exiftence; have acknowledged that its powers are only *fufpended*; and therefore, that it may *refume* their exercife, whenever the prefent extraordinary arrangement fhall ceafe. So true is the maxim of the law, *capitulum nunquam moritur*.

The clergy fubmitted to this decree; and from this time we hear no more of their chapter, than as a fociety nominally fubfifting by a regular fucceffion of members. They do well thus to perpetuate themfelves; for I view them as the ruins of a venerable inftitution, through whom has been tranfmitted the fame of men that would have dignified any caufe, and who, had their tranfactions been with any other court than that of Rome, would, by their perfeverant energy, have eftablifhed amongft us a form of ecclefiaftical government, independent and primitive.

The

" cree, never either publifhing or attempting to carry it into
" execution. Wherefore, by their own means, there was no
" mention of it, it being deemed inadmiffible in practice, and
" the regulars continued to enjoy their privileges for many
" more years, as will hardly be denied by any one."

And yet, as I have mentioned, the pope himfelf, in the following year, confirmed by a brief (which lies before me) the decrees of the congregation, at the exprefs defire of the vicars, and commands them every where to be *executed and obeyed.*

Treatment of the vicars by the Roman court.

The powers *delegated* to the vicars by the Roman fee were in themfelves ample, fuch as the archpriefts had enjoyed, and fuch as ordinaries exercife in their refpective diocefes; but then they are precarious, being revocable at will.— In 1696 the vicars, on account of many inconveniences, petitioned that their powers of *difpenfing* in certain cafes might be extended to a longer period. They had been granted, I believe, for five years. The facred congregation anfwered, "That it could not be done." —They had petitioned, that, without their approbation the regulars might not circulate their *indulgences*, as they too often did, to the prejudice of religion. "The fuperiors of thofe re-" gulars muft be heard on the fubject," replied the facred congregation.*

Thus does a foreign congregation, unknown to the prelates of former times, removed to the diftance of Rome, prefume to judge of the expediency of meafures; and treat the humble reprefentations of experienced and honourable men as the petulant expoftulations of fchoolboys!

The 11th of king William.

Nothing more occurs, of a public or private nature, in the concerns of the Catholics, till the 11th of William, when the *act* paffed *for the further*

---

* *Decreta Sacræ Congreg.* 26 Sep. 1696.

ther preventing the growth of popery. The clauses of that act were peculiarly severe, made without sufficient provocation for the severity; and when the manner in which it passed the houses, as recorded by Burnet, is considered, we are amazed that common humanity could be induced so wantonly to sport with the fortunes and happiness of its fellow-man. "Those who
" brought this bill into the lower house," says Burnet, " hoped that the court would have op-
" posed it; but the court promoted the bill; so
" when the party saw their mistake, they seem-
" ed willing to let the bill fall; and when that
" could not be done, they clogged it with
" many severe and some *unreasonable* clauses,
" hoping that the lords would not pass the act;
" and it was said, that if the lords should
" make the least alteration in it, they, in the
" house of commons, who had set it on, were
" resolved to let it lie on their table, when it
" should be sent back to them. Many lords,
" who secretly favoured Papists, on the Jaco-
" bite account did, *for this reason*, move for
" several alterations, some of them importing
" a greater severity; but the zeal against po-
" pery was such in that house, that the bill
" passed without any amendment, and it had
" the royal assent."*—And yet by this act,

thus

---

* *Hist. of his own Times.*

thus obtained, Catholics often suffered much, chiefly on account of the reward of a hundred pounds held out by it to informers.

Reign of Anne.

In 1701 king James died at St. Germain's; and in the year following, on the 8th of March, died William.

During the twelve years of Anne's reign, who now succeeded to the throne, the Catholics lived, as, since the Revolution, they had done, free from molestation, subject only to such restraints as former laws had imposed. To the queen they were, by no means, disagreeable: She recollected the loyalty they had ever shewn to her family; nor did their present attachment to her unfortunate brother James give her displeasure.—The profession of the same political opinions with the Tories, contributed not a little to procure them some esteem from that powerful party: it removed part of the odium that had been annexed to the name of Papist. Still, it is a truth which many facts have confirmed, that no Tory administration was ever sincerely disposed to lighten our grievances.— The Whigs continued hostile to them, not so much from any religious animosity, as because their politics threw some weight into the scale of their opponents.—The nation amused with the sound of victories, which on all sides, attended our arms, and engaged in political altercations,

cations, loft fight of other objects: Enthusiasm in politics had taken place of enthusiasm in religion.—The leading men of the Catholic party, though removed from the concerns of state, warmly espoused the Tory interest; whilst the multitude, now reposing from the violence of former oppression, enjoyed their present scanty allotment of ease, and occasionally indulged the vain reflection that, at the death of Anne, perhaps, their favourite prince might be called to the throne of his ancestors. In their turn, they hated the Whigs, whom they viewed as the instruments of the revolution; and though this event had procured to them their present tranquillity, it would have been criminal, they thought, to have entertained any favourable emotions towards them. Such was the temper of their loyalty; and, at that time, a Whig-Catholic would have been deemed a phenomenon, fit only to excite the detestation of some, and the amazement of others.

In 1706, upon a rumour of the growth of popery, attempts were made to bring in a bill, that should render more effectual the late act of king William. The bill, however, dropt; and an address was made to the queen, that she would order a return of all the Papists in England to be prepared for the next session of parliament. What was the issue of this return, I know not. But some years later, when the

queen's

queen's intention with regard to her brother was much suspected, and the cry of popery was again raised, a bill passed of the same tendency as the last. By it Catholics are disabled from presenting to benefices; and the benefices in their presentation are confirmed to the two universities, who may prefer bills in chancery to discover fraudulent trusts.* This was in 1713, the last year of Anne.

<small>The secular clergy accused of *Jansenism*.</small>

During the current of these years, as I have represented them, not untranquil, internal commotions, as usual, had disturbed the peace of Catholics. I shall briefly state the circumstance.

The reader, possibly, may know that, since the year 1641, great disputes, in regard to opinions, collectively from the name of Jansenius, termed *Jansenism*, had disturbed the general mind of the Catholic church. Jansenius was bishop of Ipres, who died in 1638, leaving behind him a ponderous manuscript, entitled *Augustinus*, in which he professed to deliver the opinions of the learned father of that name, on the mysterious doctrines of *grace* and *freewill*. The work was printed; and as what is least understood by theologians generally commands their greatest attention, so was it with this mighty

---

* 12 Annæ, cap. 14.

mighty volume. But I mean not to detail the progrefs of the controverfy it engendered, into which, for more than a century, and efpecially in France, all orders of men, the church, the court, the parliaments, entered with the inveteracy of the hardieft combatants. On the fame fubject when *other* controvertifts were once made to engage, it was faid, and the application is not diftant:

> Others apart fat on a hill retir'd,
> In thoughts more elevate, and reafon'd high
> Of Providence, foreknowledge, will, and fate;
> Fixt fate, freewill, foreknowledge abfolute;
> And found no end, in wand'ring mazes loft.
>
> Par. Loft, b. 2.

The hiftory of this controverfy is the hiftory, truly, of the *Egaremens de l'efprit humain*, in which, under the fpecious fhew of fupporting the integrity of religion and the caufe of truth, all the paffions to which man is fubject rufhed into action, and ranged unbridled. The Jefuits, in this warfare, were the champions of *free-will* againft the doctrines of Janfenius; while other orders, on the fide of *grace*, but not on the fide of the Belgian bifhop, whom the decrees of Rome had anathematifed, combated with equal ardour. But the controverfy, as it advanced, branched out widely, taking different afpects, and involing various matter. He, at firft, was a Janfenift who admitted the real doctrines of the fect; then he, who refufed to fubfcribe subscribe *unconditionally* to the decrees of Rome; he who *appealed* from those decrees to a general council; he, who, rejecting the doctrines, maintained that they were not to be found in the volume *Augustinus*; he, who wished to remain passive on the question; he, who could believe that a Jansenist might be an honest man; he, that did not admire all the maxims and manœuvres of the Jesuits; he, in fine, that was not a friend to their order.

As the English Catholics, particularly their ministers, were educated abroad, it may be conceived, how deeply they were sunk in the abyss of that interminable dispute; and that when they returned to England, they brought with them the animosity contracted in their schools. The reader will, likewise, recollect, that no cordial goodwill had ever subsisted between the English clergy and the Jesuits, the origin and progress of whose quarrels I traced. At this time, therefore, when other causes of mutual dislike had somewhat subsided, new matter of reproach was found in the Jansenistic controversy. The theological and moral principles, in which the clergy were educated, had rather a tendency to the side of Jansenism, (as all truth, in its human progress, converges, at certain points, to the meandering line of error); while the principles of the Jesuits, on the other hand, were thought to incline too much

to

to the exploded doctrines of Pelagius, and the loose maxims of some modern casuists. Thus was a ground established, on which the spirit of party could raise its structure of malevolent reproach, and insidious imputation. It was imputed to the clergy, that they were *tainted* with Jansenism. The calumny began first to be broached about the year 1706.*

The imputation originated, perhaps, in malevolence; perhaps, in wantonness. Be that as it may; the clergy resented the charge, and strove as seriously to repel it, by every effort, as if some secret consciousness pronounced against them, or they really feared the calumny. Rome that listens to every tale, as if to listen to tales befitted the dignity of her sacred congregations; and to whom every tale is carried, since carrying of tales has proved an introduction to favour; Rome, I say, was soon informed, that the hitherto fair fame of her English Catholic clergy was not free from the stain of Jansenism. As the report circulated, the vicars strove to stem its progress; and Dr. Smith from the north, in a *letter* to Rome, complaining of the groundless charge, exculpates his brethren, and attests their orthodoxy. Towards the

---

* *Secret Policy*, Lett. 19, 20, 21. A work written with too much acrimony, but which contains truth.

the close of his letter, he says: "One thing
"more I add, that myself, my colleagues, and
"my clergy are so desirous of peace and of a
"tranquil life, that we have ever passed over
"such sublime controversies, deeming them
"better adapted to the schools, than calculated
"improve the manners of our people."*

This was in 1707. Yet two years after, I find a list of charges transmitted into England from the holy Roman office. The charges were, "that many who were converted to the
"faith by the secular clergy, spoke irreverently
"of the pope, of the invocation of saints, and
"of indulgences; that many kept in their ora-
"tories the portraits of Arnald and St. Cyran
"(noted French Jansenists); that many books,
"either plainly Jansenistical, or nearly so, had,
"within the last years, been translated from
"the French, and printed; that a certain
"priest in the county of Durham instructing
"some scholars, read to them the *Provincial*
"*Letters*;† that he ridiculed indulgences, even
"that

---

* *Letter of Dr. Smith*, Dodd, vol. 3, p. 519.

† The *Letters* of the virtuous and eminent Pascal, *Sur la morale et la Politique des Jesuites*, begun to be written in 1656.
"Tout y est purité, dans le langage," says an excellent critic,
"noblesse dans les pensées, solidité dans les raisonnemens,
"finesse dans les railleries; et par-tout un agrément que l'on
"ne

SUPPLEMENT.

" that (of the order of St. Francis) termed
" *Portiuncula*, faying, that indulgences did not
" fatisfy the divine juftice for temporal punifh-
" ments, but were a relaxation only of cano-
" nical penances, as enjoined by the church."*

It is not eafy to be ferious in the difcuffion of fuch trafh. The clergy, however, affected a ferious air, and from London addreffed a long *Letter* to their brethren in the country, " in tef- timony," as they exprefs it, "of their innocence as to the afperfion of *Janfenifm*," dated Nov. 29, 1709. They had collected the opinions of the vicars apoftolic, of the fuperiors of the regulars, and even of the provincial of the Jefuits, all which they ftate, fhewing how unfounded the ac- cufation was.†

It could not be, while the clergy refiding in England were thus calumniated, that the college, in which many of them had been educated, fhould efcape uninjured. I related the rife and progrefs of that eftablifhment, (the college of

The college of Douay in- volved in the fame accufa- tion.

" ne trouve gueres ailleurs." Paral. des Anc. et des Mod. p. 121.
—He that has read thefe famous Letters will fubfcribe to the critique: he that has not read them, has loft a pleafure which their perufal only can compenfate.

  * *Copy of an Information*, Dodd, p. 519.
  † *Letter by order*, &c. Dodd, p. 524.

Douay)

SUPPLEMENT.

Douay) which afterwards continued to be the asylum of many distressed Catholics, and the principal nursery of our youth. Its discipline, under a succession of able men, had remained unrelaxed, its morals pure, its learning on a level with that of Europe, the principles of its religious instruction sound, unsophisticated, and genuine. Its present superior was Dr. Edward Paston.*

The accusation carried to Rome was, "That many and divers professors and scholars in that college publicly taught and learnt the false doctrine of Jansenius."†

His holiness Clement XI. in great irritation, commanded measures instantly to be taken to stop the spreading evil, signifying to the vicars apostolic, " that he should otherwise be necessitated to suspend the pension, or rents, usually allowed to the college, and convert them to other uses."§—The vicars exerted all their powers; the president of Douay and his professors were equally active; for, in addition to the menaces of the pontiff, it was likewise rumoured, that a plan was formed to expel the clergy, and transfer their college into other hands.‡ And of this

---

* Dodd, p. 479. † *Letter of Dr. Witham*, Dodd, p. 520.
§ Ibid. ‡ *Letter of Dr. Smith*, Dodd, p. 520.

this plan, and of the whole malevolent transaction, the Jesuits were said to be the contrivers and agents.*

Dr. Howarden, the ornament of the college, a man of uncommon abilities, but at whom the principal shaft, barbed by malice, had been aimed, was removed from his professorship; and soon a cloud of witnesses appeared, who attested the innocence and orthodoxy of the seminary. The first *Testimonial* was from the heads of the university and town of Douay, dated Feb. 2, 1708, who declare, " that the college of the secular clergy situated amongst them, had been remarkable, for above one hundred and forty years, for piety and purity of doctrine; for their singular erudition in Greek and Hebrew; for their studies of philosophy and divinity; for their exactness in discipline; and that they were equally enemies to loose morals, and affected severity."†—The court of St. Germain's, in 1710, after a minute scrutiny, make the same declaration, that the charge of Jansenism was a false and invidious calumny, as justice, they say, and charity, compelled them to depose.§—A visitation also of the college, by command of his ho-

---

* *Secret Policy*, Let. 21. † Ibid. p. 285.
Declaration & Testimonial, Dodd, p. 521.

Both acquitted.

Thus, in some suspence, the matter hung, for the truth of the adage, *calumniare fortiter, aliquid adhærebit*, was daily verified, till the Roman bishop, convinced by two formal subscriptions to all the decrees of his court against Jansenism, one by the vicars apostolic in 1710, the other by the superiors of the college in 1714,† commanded cardinal Paulucci to signify to the parties, that he was pleased with their obedience, and satisfied of their innocence.‡

The clergy, I believe, have never cordially forgiven this attack upon themselves and their college, which no provocation incited, or the semblance of guilt urged. And what must we think of the religion of men, whoever they were, who could wantonly assail innocence and the purest character of faith? I know not, under what casuistry it is, that the work of defamation is thus permitted: under what casuistry it is, that designs and motives, of every evil tendency, are thus imputed: under what casuistry it is, that erecting a tribunal in his own breast, a self-conceited mortal calls his fellow-creatures before

---

* Dodd, p. 480.
† *Subscription*, Dodd, p. 523.
‡ *Letters of Paulucci*, MS. and Dodd, p. 523

before it, and condemns or acquits them, as the current of bigotry, or of prejudice, or of falfe-piety may run. How truly humiliating to the honeſt pride of our natures is the hiſtory of all *religioniſts!* Arrogating to themſelves the office of heaven's vicegerents, even in its moſt myſterious ways, they pretend to be the champions of its truths, while they inſult reaſon, the faireſt of heaven's gifts, and expoſe, if they can, to ſhame, the deareſt bleſſings of man, probity of manners and innocence of heart!

In the following reign of George I. who came to the throne, purſuant to the *act of ſucceſſion*, in 1714, the ſtory of the Catholics is almoſt a blank, if we except the attempt raſhly concerted, in the enſuing year, to reſtore the pretender, in which attempt ſome few of that perſuaſion were unfortunately engaged. They ſuffered; and the Jacobitiſm of the party, awed by the ſevere leſſon, began to wane. The king was not their enemy. Unacquainted with our domeſtic quarrels, and therefore free from the prejudices they imprint, he could view in our religion no cauſe of jealouſy: but our politics threw ſome weight into the ſcale of a party, who were his enemies, and, from this conſideration only, he was hoſtile to us.

Reign of George I.

As I have often blamed the politics of Rome, willingly I would lower that cenſure, when an occaſion

Rome propoſes an oath of allegiance.

occasion offers. In 1716 it was signified to his holiness, Clement XI. that the English Catholics, by persevering in their opposition to the established government, exposed to ruin the cause of religion and their own domestic concerns. He, therefore, commanded a *declaration of allegiance* to be drawn up, to which the Catholics should subscribe; and which, by the nuncio at Brussels, was transmitted to the vicars apostolic. From the letter written by the nuncio on the occasion, it appears, that the matter had been some time in agitation on both sides the water, and that Rome, provided the cause of religion (as she, doubtless, interpreted that cause) were not touched, would permit an oath of complete fealty to be taken. In pursuance of this order, or intimation, or permission from Brussels, the heads of the Catholic ministry met, and modelled an *oath* agreeably to the pontiff's *declaration*. The oath was,

" I swear, and promise a true and universal
" submission to king George; and that I will
" attempt nothing in order to disturb the peace
" and tranquillity of the realm: Moreover I de-
" clare, that I will neither sue for, nor accept
" of, any dispensation from this oath."

Government, it is said, was willing to countenance the project; but it miscarried as other such projects had done. The undiscerning crowd

crowd of Catholics, wedded to their Jacobitism, represented the movers in the business as the foes to their religion, while the pretender's adherents so conducted their opposition at Rome, that his holiness, unwilling to offend a fallen prince, who had retired to his court for protection, interfered no longer. He left us, says my author, to the humiliating option, *qui vult decipi decipiatur.**

Though the oath be, undoubtedly, expressive of ample allegiance; yet the closing clause, it must be admitted, bears a suspicious aspect. It declares, that no *dispensation* will be *sued for*, or *accepted:* but it rejects not the *right* of granting such dispensation; as if the Roman court really possessed that right, but, in the present circumstances of the English Catholics, it were not *prudent* to exercise it.—And how opportune, it may be said, was the occasion, for disclaiming, with the dispensing doctrine, the monstrous prerogative also of *deposing* princes, had it been the will of Clement to give to the British court a satisfactory proof, that he had renounced the proud pretension. With a facility that politicians know, he permits his Roman Catholics to sacrifice at the shrine of interest the whole hereditary claim of the Stuart line, though that claim

by

---

* *Providential allegiance*, MS. by Dodd, p. 20.

by many was esteemed *divine*; while not a grain of a prerogative, obviously abusive and in practice subversive of all social order, will he surrender.—I must remark also, that this interference in our internal politics is to me a circumstance of extreme humiliation. He permits, or he forbids, us to swear allegiance to our sovereign, and he orders his nuncioes to signify the form of words we may adopt. I have lamented with my brethren that arrangement, which entailed dependence on us. " While our immediate " superiors, they said, are commissioners from " the pope, his will must be their rule, and " their will must be ours." Against this I protest.

<small>Dr. Strickland bishop of Namur.</small>

Still in 1719 another project was formed to favour the Catholics, to which, as it is related, the ministers of the crown cordially acceded. A committee of Catholics, therefore, met, and some progress seemed to be made. But the spirit of Jacobitism rushed in; their measures were disconcerted; and the project soon dissolved in air.* The principal agent in this business was Dr. Strickland, afterwards bishop of Namur, a man of parts and of singular enterprise, and whose intimacy with the king of England, had it been permitted to operate, might have

---

* *MS. Account of the transaction.*

SUPPLEMENT.

have enfured fome fuccefs. I have before me a letter, written by the doctor after his promotion to the fee of Namur, wherein, vindicating himfelf from certain charges, he briefly ftates fome principal incidents of his life in France, where he was educated; in the court of Staniflaus king of Poland, from whom he obtained the honour of the Roman purple, which he afterwards refigned; at Rome, where he acquired the efteem of Clement XI. and of the college of cardinals; at Vienna, which he thrice vifited, honoured by the emperor, and finally rewarded by him with the mitre of Namur; in the Britifh court, where he exerted all his influence in the caufe of his Catholic brethren, to reconcile them to their fovereign, and their fovereign to them, after the difaftrous events of the laft rebellion. The charges brought againft him were " that " he was an enemy to his religion, and inclined " to Janfenifm." So does malevolent bigotry always fhoot her darts. To the firft he ferioufly replies by enumerating the tranfactions of his life: the fecond provokes a fmile, but he repels the charge.

Some laws, even in this reign, were made againft Catholics.* In the firft year, the king had fignified his confent by a meffage to the commons,

Severe treatment of the Catholics.

---

* 1 Geo. cap. 50. cap. 55. 3 Geo. cap. 18.

commons, that the *two third parts* of the profits of the lands of popish recusants convict, which, by a law just enacted, were to be seized for such recusancy, might be applied towards suppressing the rebellion then lately made; and to the end the said two third parts might be the better known, commissioners were appointed to make proper enquiries. Dr. Strickland says, he was very instrumental in mollifying the execution of that severe act. At the same time, the commissioners were to enquire, what Papists had not taken the oaths, or in default thereof registered their names and estates, as another act prescribed. By which act, all moneys arising out of the said estates, were to be appropriated to the use of the public. On the 19th of February 1719, a report, signed by the commissioners, was presented, containing the names of the Papists who had registered their estates, and the yearly rent of the same, amounting in the whole to 384,950l. over and above large sums arising from time to time for fines payable by leafe-hold and copy-hold tenants.

Again, in 1723, the Catholics being accused of having, by favouring plots and rebellion, brought additional expences on the realm, a fresh burthen was laid on them. It was enacted that, in lieu of the said two thirds for one year (which, as I have said, had not been rigorously levied), and in lieu of other pains and forfeitures,

forfeitures, there should be raised, within the year, the sum of 100,000l. upon the estates of Papists, for the use of the public, over and above their double taxes, to be assessed in each county agreeably to a stated calculation.—The names of the counties and the sums to be levied in each may be seen in the act,* whence some estimate may be formed of the encrease or decrease of our religion since that period.

The thirty-three years of George the second's reign, which began 1727, exhibit no material change in the condition of Catholics. They continued in the same state of tranquillity, broken only by occasional alarms, unengaged spectators of those turbulent scenes, in which the nations of Europe were successively occupied. The rebellion of 1745 alone unfortunately intervened, to stem the progress of public favour, reviving against them the malevolence of some, and the prejudices of many. Few Catholics joined the rebel standard; but the cause was known to engage their wishes. In the *declaration*, published in the name of James III. by his son when he took possession of Edinburgh, among other singular clauses is the following: " We solemnly " promise to protect, support, and *maintain the* " *church of England as by law established* in all her " rights,

Reign of Geo. II.

---

9 Geo. cap. 18.

"rights, privileges, poffeffions, and immuni-
"ties whatfoever; and we fhall, on all occafi-
"ons, beftow marks of our royal favour on the
"whole body of the clergy, but more particu-
"larly on thofe whofe principles and practices
"fhall beft correfpond with the dignity of
"their profeffion. We alfo folemnly promife
"to grant and allow the benefit of a toleration
"to all Proteftant Diffenters, being utterly
"averfe to all perfecution and animofity on
"account of confcience and religion." The
prince in his manifefto goes further: "We
"come not, fays he, to impofe upon any a re-
"ligion which they diflike, but to fecure them
"all in the enjoyment of thofe which are re-
"fpectively at the prefent eftablifhed in Eng-
"land, Scotland, and Ireland. And if it
"fhall be deemed, that any further fecurity
"be given to the eftablifhed church or clergy:
"We hereby promife, in our father's name,
"that he fhall pafs *any law* that his parliament
"fhall judge neceffary for that purpofe."

The *declaration*, conveying the folemn promife of *maintaining* the eftablifhed Proteftant
church, was written, it muft be noticed, *at
Rome*; and the laft claufe of the manifefto, we
may prefume, had the fanction of the fame venerable cafuifts!—In neither of the inftruments
are the Catholics mentioned.

Some

Some internal concerns of the body require notice.—The brief of Innocent XII. which I mentioned, obtained in 1696, and which defined the submission due from the regulars to the vicars, either from the remissness of the latter who chose not to press an unwelcome authority, or from the reluctance of the former to obey, had not produced the desired effect. Unpleasant controversies, therefore, occasionally happened, as I find them particularly noticed in 1732, 1736, 1738; and complaints of the refractory disposition of the regulars, who still spoke of their immunities, and undervalued the episcopal jurisdiction, were carried to the nuncioes in Flanders, and sometimes to Rome. They endeavoured to establish a distinction between *faculties* and *approbation*. This, they acknowledged, they received from the vicars, who acted in the capacity of notaries appointed to examine and declare, whether the testimonials, they presented from their immediate superiors, were authentic and in due form: but their faculties or functionary powers, they insisted, were independent of that approbation, and received no validity from it. Under these circumstances of insubordination, a direct application was finally made by the vicars to the court of Rome, and that application, after some years, was crowned with success. The sacred congregation passed a decree, dated August 16, 1745, and Benedict XIV. the excellent

Controversy between the vicars and regulars.

cellent Lambertini, confirmed the fame by a pontifical brief on the second of the following month. The Decree is:

"That the regular missionaries in England, of whatever order they be, shall, in future, receive their faculties of administering the sacrament of penance, and exercising all powers regarding the cure of souls, from the vicars apostolic in their respective district; and that the same vicars may examine them, and for just causes (*legitimis causis*) totally, or in part, suspend them from the exercise of the said faculties, as likewise punish their misconduct, and ordain that they desert not, without their permission, the faithful once committed to their charge, nor pass the limits of the places assigned to them."*

Owing to various impediments, it was not till 1748 that the brief arrived in England, when the vicars took proper measures to carry it into execution and to enforce obedience. But the regulars were not disposed silently to submit. The decree, as was obvious, had been obtained without their participation, and they knew the temper of him who had been principally instrumental in obtaining it. Wherefore they requested, "that its publication and execution might be deferred, till they should
"have

---

* *Breve Ben. XIV. an.* 1745.

" have been heard in the Roman court." The requeſt was not granted; on which a *memorial* of great length was prepared, and difpatched with an agent to Rome. It contains a lift of reafons, rather fpecious, certainly, than found, why, without injuring the caufe of Catholics, the decree neither ought, nor can be, reduced to practice. But then the caufe of the Catholics, we muſt underſtand, is fuppofed to be involved in the nearer caufe of their own immunities.

They remind Benedict of the fupport that is due to his own fee and to the acts of his pre-deceffors. " By them," they fay, " it was
" conſtituted, that the regulars fhould enter
" England not *to be* approved, but already pof-
" feffing an approbation given by their own
" fuperiors, in the pontiff's name, an approba-
" tion that immediately flows from the holy
" fee, which no one can revoke, but that fee,
" or he who prefides over the Englifh miffion,
" the cardinal protector."—" Doubtlefs," they go on, " it is for the intereft of that fee to
" have many immediately fubject to it, that is,
" many of whom the pope is himfelf the im-
" mediate bifhop and diocefan. Since, there-
" fore, from the time of the reformation, all
" jurifdiction in England has devolved, *jure*
" *divino*, on the holy fee, and it has acquired,
" by the prefcription of two hundred years,
" the right to itfelf of immediate fubjection as

" to

"to an ordinary and diocesan; while England,
"on her side, has also acquired a prescriptive
"right of dependence on the same holy see: it is
"become expedient, that no derogation be made
"from that mutual state of jurisdiction and de-
"pendence, by the intervention of another au-
"thority; even it is proper, that of it some
"subsistent sign remain. But there can be no
"sign more proper, more useful, or more just,
"than that the regulars, who are the especial
"children and subjects of the Roman see, when
"sent into England, be approved by their su-
"periors under a commission from his holi-
"ness; for thence the vicars apostolic and
"others may learn, that the pontiff is theirs
"and England's diocesan."—" Nor can any
"event," they proceed, "so much diminish
"in England the authority of Rome, as the
"absolute subjection of the regulars, notwith-
"standing their privileges, to the apostolic
"vicars, especially as some of them so despise
"the Roman see, as very lately to have threa-
"tened with the vengeance of the penal laws
"certain regulars, if, as the canons ordain,
"they carried their cause thither."*—For these
and other reasons, they supplicate from Benedict a *repeal* of the obnoxious decree.†

But

---

* *Rationes contra Decretum*, MS.

† The *relation of the regulars*, which was written on this occasion, and to which is subjoined the above *memorial*, speaks of
the

But no repeal was obtained: even, a few years later, in 1753, to remove, if poffible, every occafion of difcontent, and to eftablifh a general fyftem whence peace and concord might flow, Benedict iffued a final *brief*, that fanctions all preceding meafures, and lays down *rules*, whereby priefts of every defcription, fecular and regular, muft be directed. To thefe *injunctions* all fubmitted; and the happy effects of a juft fubordination have been experienced. The mind of Benedict was above the little policy which could influence the councils of many of his predeceffors; and though, doubtlefs, he might wifh to cherifh the immunities of the regulars, as the main props that bolftered up

---

the *decree*, and of the vicars who procured it, with great afperity. "Notwithftanding the ftate of diftrefs," it fays, "in which all "miffionaries lived, it was the eternal defign of the vicars to "fubjugate the regulars to their will." The fame idea is often repeated in ftronger terms. It then dwells on the merits, on the labours, on the exemplary lives of the regulars, who in number even exceeded more than half of the four hundred priefts employed in England. The ambition, it concludes, of the vicars finally prevailed; and by mifreprefentation and furreptitious means the fatal decree found its way into England.

To this part of the *relation* the vicars replied, in a *letter* to his holinefs, refuting each charge, as it was eafy, and fubftantiating the urgent reafons on which they had founded their original application: but, for further information, they refer the pontiff to their agent, Dr. Stonor.

his prerogative, yet thofe props and the prerogative itfelf he knew how to value, when the peace of a venerable church was at ftake, as alfo a branch of his own power delegated to his Englifh vicars.

Bifhop Stonor.

I fpoke of one who, among the vicars, was principally inftrumental, I faid, in obtaining the *brief* of 1745. That was Dr. Stonor, *Epifcopus Thefpienfis*, and vicar apoftolic in the midland diftrict. The office he had exercifed fince the year 1716, fucceeding, I believe, to Dr. George Witham. He was of the Stonors of Oxforfhire, a gentleman of eafy fortune; and as his mind naturally nervous and penetrating, had enjoyed the advantages of an academical education in the fchools of Paris, he brought to his native country a ftock of learning which few poffefs, and the endowments of a fuperior character. But a certain harfhnefs, it appears, rendered thofe endowments lefs amiable; he was, befides, unbending in his purpofes when once they were formed, and imperious when their execution was refifted. This I collect from the narration of thofe who knew him, and more from many letters and papers he has left behind him. It was he, I obferved, who planned and conducted the late meafures for the overthrow of the immunities of the regulars; and they neither loved him when living, nor venerate his departed memory. Yet the point

point he aimed at, and finally accomplifhed, was, doubtlefs, agreeable to the fpirit of eccle- fiaftical difcipline, and the means he ufed were co-ordinate and juft. Viewing the independence of his mind, the comprehenfion of his thoughts, and his extenfive knowledge, I am furprifed that he never meditated the reform, the over- throw, if you will, of our own irregular church- government. The other vicars, fome of them at leaft, would have followed as he had direc- ted; and Lambertini himfelf, I doubt not, would have liftened to the propofal, and by a decree have fanctioned it.

The vicars contemporary with Stonor were bifhop Petre, and his affiftant Dr. Challoner in the fouth; in the north Dr. George Witham, father Williams, and after him Mr. Diccon- fon; and in the weft fathers Pritchard and Yorke.—Father Williams, I think, was an Irifh dominican friar; but by what means, he pro- cured the mitre of our northern diftrict, I do not find recorded. The circumftance, how- ever, fhews (for his appointment was generally unacceptable), that if the ear of the facred congregation can be obtained, or due intereft made, very common materials will form a vicar apoftolic. Yet, let me not be fuppofed to in- timate, that father Williams was not in his con- duct irreproachable, and in his manners conci- liating: I will alfo add, that he efpoufed the

The other vicars.

caufe

caufe of the clergy, and even co-operated towards the fuppreffion of the privileges of the men to whom he before belonged.*

Of bifhops Pritchard and Yorke the fame cannot be faid. The firft was of the order of St. Francis, promoted to his fee as early as 1715, the other a Benedictin monk. Thefe gentlemen had little connection with the other vicars: " It is, I believe, twenty years," faid Dr. Stonor, fpeaking of father Pritchard, " fince he has declined all correfpondence with " me, though by me moft humbly and earneft- " ly entreated to it." When, therefore, in 1748, it was propofed to them to co-operate in enforcing the brief of Benedict, they declined it, under the pretext, that, as they had not been advifed with in procuring the decree, fo neither would they attend to its execution, till they received further inftructions from Rome. Bifhop Stonor reprobates this conduct, in a letter to the nuncio, in the fevereft terms: " But " it is the elder vicar," he fays, " whom I " judge moft cenfurable, for Mr. Yorke, though " he has followed the direction of his princi- " pal, is, in my eftimation, a man of more " juft difcernment and of a more epifcopal " mind." Not fatisfied with witholding their co-operation,

---

* MS. Letters.

co-operation, father Pritchard with his colleague actively joined the oppofition, and addreffed a *letter* to each cardinal of the facred congregation, praying that their decree might not be enforced, unlefs under fuch reftrictions, as would amount to a repeal. The *letter* begins: " As vicars general are, and are ftyled, " the eyes of diocefan bifhops, fo may it be " allowed to us, who are vicars apoftolic, to " be called the eyes of the holy fee." They chiefly dwell on the two laft claufes of the decree, which ordain that, " without the permif- " fion of their refpective vicars, the regulars " quit not their refidences, nor pafs the pre- " fcribed limits." Of thefe regulations, they fay, the laity moft loudly complained, as an infraction of the liberty they had always enjoyed, of employing what minifter they pleafed, or of parting from him. They then propofe the modifications, I alluded to, the principal of which is, that fuch regulars as have been once examined and received powers from their own fuperiors, fhall only be required to prefent themfelves for approbation to the vicars.*

This, they muft have known, was the very circumftance that had lately caufed diffenlions,

---

* *Epiſtola Epiſcopi Myrinenſis*, MS.

and against which the clergy vicars had reclaimed. But every consideration, in their opinion, was to give way to those dear immunities they so highly valued, and to re-establish which they prayed, that a state of insubordination might be permitted to return, and with it a decent contempt of episcopal jurisdiction. But neither to the *memorial* of the regulars, as I have said, nor to this auxiliary *address*, did the sacred congregation or Lambertini listen.

Apprehensions of the clergy.

It had been apprehended by the wisdom of our clergy, before the establishment of vicars apostolic, that should regulars, as was very probable, ever find the way to the mitre, it would expose their cause to ruin. The event has not verified the justness of their fears, but it may be curious to know what were the grounds on which those fears rested. A paper I have before me, written about the reign of James II. states those grounds:

" 1. Because a regular is, by his very being
" such, so entirely at the devotion of the Ro-
" man court, to whose favour and not to
" Christ's institution he owes his essence, its
" continuance and advancement by exemptions
" and privileges, that to govern after the man-
" ner of an extraordinary authority, is most
" agreeable to his genius and interest.

" 2. That

" 2. That the example once introduced,
" the government of the clergy will never, in
" likelihood, be got out of the hands of regulars;
" but they will lord it over us by turns, they
" having more power at Rome than we, and
" the clergy's intereſt being ſtill rendered more
" inſignificant by this violation of their right of
" nominating, and their ſlaviſh ſubjection to
" one of their auxiliaries.

" 3. That the nature of a regular is to extend obedience almoſt to any thing; and ſo the
" clergy will be forced to obey *præter* and even
" *ultra canones*, which infringes their juſt liber-
" ties, and is the natural effect of extraordinary
" authority.

" 4. That he will be ſure to advance the re-
" gular intereſt of his own, and by conſequence
" of all orders, and ſo muſt neceſſarily depreſs
" the clergy in all thoſe juſt rights, which ſet
" them above the regulars.

" 5. In caſe a clergyman be a biſhop, the
" regulars can eaſily decline any encroachments
" upon them, by their exemptions and privi-
" leges: but if a regular be biſhop, the clergy
" have no way to right or preſerve themſelves
" againſt his injurious and prejudicial govern-
" ment; arbitrary or extraordinary authority
" being grateful to the modern temper of the
" high

"high court, the clergy's intereſt there ſmall,
"in compariſon of the others, whoſe generals
"reſide there, and the regulars (as we have
"experienced to our coſt in the archprieſts
"time) ready to ruin our credit, and conſe-
"quently livelihoods, upon every pretended
"defect of our obedience, however undue.

"Nor doth it all ſecure us here, in our cir-
"cumſtances, that, in Catholic times, many
"regulars have been biſhops, and careful of the
"clergy's intereſt. For then the clergy owning
"themſelves the ſole paſtors, the biſhops de-
"pending ſolely on the clergy, as to their elec-
"tion, revenues, &c. and in that open profeſ-
"ſion of religion and efficacy of the *forum exter-*
"*num*, the biſhops could only govern by canons,
"and a clergyman could defend his rights
"when invaded, by a fair trial in open courts,
"even againſt the biſhop himſelf. All which
"want in our condition in England, where, if
"the regulars can rule us *in virga ferrea*, we can
"have no defence againſt his ſuſpenſions, ex-
"communications, &c. carried on to diſgrace
"us. If he be a great courtier and addicted to
"the intereſt of the high court (Rome), we are
"not likely to be remedied there; ſo that we
"muſt defend our honour, be forced to have
"recourſe to foreign univerſities, petitioning
"them to decide the caſe ſpeculatively between

"us

"us and our enemies. All which was seen in the case of the archpriest."*

I have little more to add. The reign of George II. closed in 1760, and George III. ascended the throne. I have said, that the Jacobitism of the Catholics had been, for some years, on the wane; and from this time it so completely disappeared, as to make way for the repeal of part of the oppressive act of the 12th of William, in the spring of the year 1778. This was the first parliamentary favour they had experienced, since the suppression of their religion under Elizabeth; and I know not, whether, before this period, all circumstances duly weighed, their minds were in a proper temper to be admitted to indulgence.

Oath of allegiance in 1778.

In regard to the bill now obtained there was a circumstance which merits notice. An *oath* was annexed to it, to be taken, within a limited time, by all who would enjoy the benefits of the bill, which oath, in its principal clauses, was the same as that of James I. which Paul V. in 1606 anathematized, "as containing many things obviously adverse to faith and

---

* *Francis Fitter's MS. Papers*, a clergyman well esteemed at the beginning of this century, and whose indefatigable hand has transcribed and preserved many valuable papers.

" and falvation," which anathema he afterwards confirmed, as did Urban VIII. in 1626, and on account of which anathema, the Catholics at that time, and in after times, refufed to take the oath, thereby expofing themfelves to the odium of their fellow-citizens and the perfecution of the laws. The chief claufe objected to by the Roman court, and which, probably, drew its curfe upon the whole, was that which, abjuring the *depofing* doctrine as *impious* and *heretical*, pronounces it to be '*damnable.** In the oath of 1778, the fame doctrine is *abjured* without any qualification of its character or tendency. But it was the *doctrine* that Rome had laboured to fave, and as that in the laft oath was as *pofitively* abjured as in the firft, the phrafeology of epithets muft have been deemed immaterial. The fimple act of *abjuring* a propofition announces that propofition to be intrinfically *falfe* or in its tendency *pernicious*: and this admitted, the expreffions of deteftation that accompany it, do but declare the conviction or

the

---

* " It is obfervable, (fays an author writing in 1661) that at the firft publifhing of the oath, there were in every line and almoft particle of it pointed out by them (the new *De-fide-men* as he calls them) a feveral *herefy*: all which herefies are now at laft vanifhed, *excepting only one*, which is that by which there is enjoined a renouncing of that fo bruited *article of faith* touching the *pope's power of depofing princes.*"
—*Reflections upon the oaths of fupremacy and allegiance*, p. 61.

the feelings of him who takes the oath. He who took the oath of James, declared the *depofing doctrine* to be *impious*, that is, contrary to the found principles of morality, to be *heretical*, that is, in the language of the propounders, contrary to the written word of God, to be *damnable*, that is, to merit the ftrongeft abhorrence of language. He who takes the oath of George III. renounces the fame doctrine, and by implication loads it with the fame weight of imprecation. What is *falfe* in the fenfe of that propofition, is falfe in all its concomitant analogies, that is, is *impious*, is *heretical*, is *damnable*. At all events, in 1778, that tenet was *abjured* by the Catholics of England, clergy and laity, which, in 1606, a pope of Rome had forbidden to be *abjured*; and by the act it was declared that the *briefs* of pontiffs, in fome cafes, were unbinding and nugatory. For *truth* herfelf does not vary; and her maxims in all ages are the fame.*

Thus the event happened.—By a repofe of many years, we had loft fight of the difputes of

---

* It is true, as I have before ftated, the oath of James was rejected not *merely* for its renunciation of the depofing power; and, within a few days, have been fhewn me fix weighty objections, as they are called, whereby an intemperate author pretends to demonftrate that no catholic, even now, could take the oath of James without *prevarication* and *perjury*. Of thofe fix
weighty

of our ancestors, and many of us hardly knew what animosities the oath of James had excited, or that it had been censured by Rome. Viewing the object, therefore, with a coolness of reflection unwarped by prejudice, we saw the deposing doctrine in its true light, and were anxious to repel from us all the odious consequences it presented. It was fortunate too, that the hurry with which the bill passed at the close of a session, did not allow the punctilious and sophistic to brood over their own minds, in which, had there been leisure, they would have found, I know, an ample store of quirks and quibbles, on which to build that cobweb structure that shall perplex the ignorant, and disturb the timid, while themselves glory in the vain ingenuity of their shrewdness, and proclaim the triumph of a success, that has saved religion, they say, and morality, and the integrity of faith. And also fortunately, we then possessed the venerable Dr. Challoner, whom long experience had taught the truth of the observations I have just made; and whose advice, therefore, when he was consulted, was, to proceed

---

weighty reasons, the 1st, to my apprehension, is most ludicrous, of the three following the second only is adhered to by the enemies to the oath, the 5th is sophistic, and the last could only weigh on a mind warped by quibbles. Such a mind, for aught I know, even in the face of evidence, might expose itself to *prevarication* and *perjury*.

SUPPLEMENT.

ceed with as little noife as poffible, and bring matters to a fpeedy iffue.

The tumults of 1780 which the paffing of this bill excited, though a momentary evil, contributed to accelerate the further emancipation of the Catholics. The malevolence of many feemed to have evaporated in the explofion; and goodwill and a more general forbearance took poffeffion of the public mind.

It is unneceffary I fhould ftate the circum- cumftances that preceded, or accompanied, our late application to parliament. Already they are fo amply recorded in a variety of publications, that they ftand not in need of my co-operation to give them perpetuity. However, to complete the fketch I have in view, I fhall, as briefly as may be, exhibit fome general outlines.

More recent events.

In a country where oaths have been fo multiplied, as to excite little attention and lefs folicitude, our oath of 1778 had not, in the removal of prejudices, produced the effect that was expected from it. It was, therefore, deemed expedient, by fome other method, to attempt the falutary work; and in a full and explicit enunciation of our tenets folemnly to declare, what our civil and political principles were. This was done in 1789, by an inftrument

ment termed a *protestation*, which the Catholics almost unanimously signed, and which was presented to the public. The effect it produced, combined with other general causes, was sudden and extensive.—At the time, the draft of a bill was preparing, for our further relief from many aggrieving statutes: on which it occured to some persons in power, that nothing, probably, could better serve our cause than to annex a new oath to the bill, that should be modelled agreeably to the clauses of the protestation. To this the Committee, who had been entrusted with our concerns, acceded, and an oath was framed.*

Thus far all was well.—Among ourselves an accord of sentiments prevailed, to which for years we had been strangers, and which augured an encreasing flow of happiness. The charges brought against our faith by our fellow citizens we had replied to; and they believed us. A second time we had renounced the *deposing power*, calling it *execrable* and *impious*, and with it that grand foundation of all the abuses which have depraved the prerogative and power of Rome, the *personal infallibility* of her first pastor. When prejudices shall be thus removed, what obstacle, we thought, can long delay our complete emancipation?

---

* *Letters of the Cat. Com.*

emancipation? And though this event (which in the temper of men's minds cannot be) fhould ftill be diftant, yet of a partial indulgence we are fecure, while our own internal peace, the beft fource of happinefs, will amply compenfate for every remaining evil. So we reafoned.

In the fummer of the fame year 1789, the new form of oath, as modelled on the *proteftation*, was circulated, that, its contents being maturely weighed, it might be ready to accompany the bill into parliament. I admire the candour, but not the prudence of the Committee. They had been compelled, it feems, by circumftances which they could not command, to depart from the *letter* of the proteftation in wording the oath.* Here was the firft evil. The fecond was, in permitting the oath thus worded to lie for months before the minds of fome men, fuch as I defcribed them, punctilious and fophiftic. Thefe faw in it a departure from the inftrument they had figned, a departure obvioufly *verbal*, and which, by means of a little torture eafy to be practifed, might be conftrued into a formidable deviation. The committee might alfo have been aware, though the fignatures to the proteftation were general,

that

---

* *Letters of the Com.*

that among them some would be found who, ruminating on the act, might review it with horror, as it reprobated certain principles which they had once been taught to venerate; and, therefore, that they would eagerly seize the present occasion, if not to withdraw their signature, to magnify its precipitancy at least, and to censure in the oath what too hastily they had professed in the protestation. The committee might likewise have been aware, that the few who had refused to sign the *protestation*, would now be loud in vindicating the measure of their singularity, and by proving that both instruments were alike, endeavour to shew that they both merited equal execration.

It is, therefore, to me most clear (and I saw it at the time) that the committee should never have consented to the smallest departure from the protestation, conscious of the characters of the men with whom they had to deal; and that if, without their consent, the alteration was to be made, then should they at once have stated the fact, and have left the oath to make its own way. But in a consciousness, from their own view of things, that nothing had been done *materially* to affect the sense of the original clauses, they boldly committed the oath to examination, asserting its congruity with the protestation, and thus provoked the scrutiny and the cavils of sophisters. Little had they imagined

imagined that men who, a few months before, had signed their names to an instrument, would refuse to the same the more solemn pledge of an oath, wherein, with a trifling deviation as they conceived it, the same errors were renounced, the same truths admitted.*

The controversy that now took place was acrimonious and stubborn, in every point most minutely resembling that which the oath of James had excited. It even seemed, after the lapse of almost two hundred years, that the same men still existed to combat, and that their generation had not passed away. To men of reflection, however, the thought was melancholy, that with the *tenets* of our faith our *opinions* also had been stationary, that is, our reason had not been progressive, and that we too nearly approached to that race of beings which naturalists, from their unvarying character, have defined to be *imperfectible*. The beaver

---

* I am informed that *many* priests, with the *vicars* Walmesley and Douglas at their head, have *recently* withdrawn their names from the *protestation*, (the original of which is deposited in the British *Museum*) and that the deed is recorded in an authentic instrument, termed a *Counter-Protestation!*—Are we, therefore, sure that there may not also exist a *counter-oath?*—When our enemies, as I thought them, used to proclaim that *no form of words could bind us*, I indignantly repelled the charge. In future, I and others must be silent, hang our heads, and blush.

constructs his house of clay as beavers always have done; and the owl hoots to the moon, and builds her nest, as the parent owl, that Noah harboured, built her nest and hooted.

The vicars apostolic, in this discordance of opinions, imprudently, I think, censured the oath, forbidding it to be taken, and more imprudently did not assign their reasons for the censure. The days of passive obedience are gone; and it is the weight of evidence, not the mere mandates of authority, that can now ensure submission. The committee, some of them peculiarly enlightened and inquisitive, all of them cool in discernment and steady in conviction, were roused by this intemperate act, which no friendly intercourse had preceded, no attempt to conciliate, or to modify or expunge what in the oath had excited their zeal; and on this occasion, they published their first *letter.*

The opposition which the censure of the vicars raised, soon became formidable; and no means were omitted to impress on the minds of the multitude the alarming thought, that the oath of the committee, if not intentionally so designed, was at least so worded as to endanger the faith of him that should imprudently take it. The press, meanwhile, groaned with publications, which, on both sides, indicated

cated some ingenuity; but which, on both sides, indicated more animosity than love of truth, more display of sophistry than honest zeal, more inveteracy of party than a wish to instruct by candour and mutual concessions.* And so it ever is in controversy, and more so when that controversy is religious. At first men take sides from various motives, of some private resentment, it may be, or of a laudable emulation, or of a personal attachment, or of a thoughtless indifference, or of a sincere zeal. But soon, as the passions warm, every inferior consideration gives way, and the spirit of party alone predominates. Then does the perception become distorted, the medium of view dark and troublous, and objects change their magnitude and figure. The progress of a disputatious mind, through all its gradations, from indifference to warmth, from doubt to certainty, from hesitation to conviction, and from opinion, in religious matters, to what it calls faith, may be distinctly traced. Nor does it

---

* And yet, as is acknowledged by the latest writer against the oath and its inveterate enemy, *the terms only of the oath were objectionable*, and a *few verbal alterations*, which, however, he says, were *essential*, would have *relieved his conscience*. It was, indeed, cruel to oppress a mind so delicate, particularly as that oppression seems to have deranged its *native candour*; for now he sees in the oath of the committee all the horrors of the French *civic oath*, and by that name, still somewhat generous in spite of oppression, he often calls it!

pause

pauſe here: A more pernicious affection has grown up with this mental proceſs, I mean, a diſpoſition of malevolence, (which the poſſeſſor miſtakingly fancies to be the holy fire of the ſanctuary) that imputes to his adverſary motives of conduct which that adverſary never entertained, thoughts, reflections, meanings, purpoſes which ever were moſt foreign from his mind.

The controverſy, of which I am ſpeaking, laſted, without intermiſſion, from the cenſure of the oath by the apoſtolic vicars in October 1789 to the ſpring of the year 1791, when the bill paſſed, and the oath, which the Iriſh Catholics had taken, was ſubſtituted in lieu of the oath of the committee. But, in truth, the controverſy did not end here, though the oppoſing party had gained their wiſhes, and might have triumphed in the ſucceſs: for too much ill-will, too much of all the paſſions that debaſe our nature, had been excited, at once to fall back and ſubſide into a calm.

Caſe of Mr. Wilks. A clerical member of the committee, whoſe endowments are above my praiſe and whoſe virtues gave a luſtre to his miniſtry, the Rev. Joſeph Wilks, by perſevering in the diſcharge of a public truſt impoſed on him by the Catholics, after the vicars had cenſured the oath, and his own biſhop with two new colleagues had confirmed

confirmed that cenfure, drew on himfelf the animadverfion of his ecclefiaftical fuperior. This fuperior was Mr. Walmfley, the fenior vicar apoftolic, formerly a monk of the order of St. Bennet, and who, through the progrefs of the conteft, had ftood confpicuoufly forward, in zeal as ardent, and in means as inventive, as if he had been ferioufly convinced that the integrity of his religion were really at ftake. " I " defend the caufe of religion, which you are " attempting to injure;" he publicly declared in a *letter* to the committee. And yet each member of that committee valued whatever was valuable in his religion as much as did the fenior vicar, and was equally difpofed to maintain it. When an expreffion, fuch as I have quoted, drops deliberately from a man, in fuch circumftances as we then ftood, whatever may have been his previous character, or high his prefent ftation, his fentiments lofe all claim to deference, for he has proclaimed himfelf a partifan, whom no moderation guides, or cool difcernment guards againft the intemperance of paffion. And to words fo irritating which often circulated, and to conduct in himfelf and others, fometimes refentful, fometimes arbitrary, may, I think, be afcribed that warmth which the committee occafionally betrayed, particularly in their *appeal* and *proteft*, thofe barbed arrows that no friendly hand has yet been able to draw from the fides of the vicars apoftolic.

Mr. Wilks was *suspended* from all his parochial powers and ecclesiastical functions in the city of Bath, and within the district of Mr. Walmesly; " because," says the censure, " he " had refused to submit to the ordinances of " the apostolic vicars."—Many deemed the sentence arbitrary, unwarranted by the mild spirit of Christian discipline, and contrary to established forms. But the reader will recollect the passages I quoted against the episcopal government of regulars; " The nature of a re- " gular is," says one passage, " to extend obe- " dience almost to any thing; and so the " clergy will be forced to obey *præter* and even " *ultra canones*, which infringes their just liber- " ties, and is the natural effect of extraordi- " nary authority." He confounds *monastic* with *canonical* subordination. Mr. Wilks, however, was himself a regular, whom certain ordinances, I know, of the brief of 1753, particularly guard against oppression, which his brethren, we may presume, will not permit to be violated.*

It was imagined that the Catholic clergy, with the spirit of their ancestors, would have been roused to screen their delegate from oppression; for Mr. Wilks, doubtless, they viewed

as

---

* Page 15, 16.

as their especial representative in the Catholic committee; and it was for the conscientious discharge of that trust, they knew, that he now suffered. The Catholic clergy were not roused to screen their delegate from oppression. They left him to his fate; and talked—and talked.— A mock reconciliation afterwards ensued, which was soon followed by a second censure, or a substraction of powers; *because* when the story of the reconciliation was circulated in a manner that reflected on the probity of Mr. Wilks, he judged it proper to tell an unvarnished tale.

Thirteen clergymen only of the county of Stafford, (whose conduct shall not be omitted in a history that has recorded the prowess of their predecessors, and particularly the act of the thirteen worthies in their *protestation of allegiance* to Elizabeth),* thirteen clergymen only of the county of Stafford felt the injury offered to their delegate, and resolved to make his cause their own. They had viewed with pain the infliction of the first censure, to their apprehension, *unjust* for want of matter, *illegal* for want of form, and therefore in itself *null*; and they had trusted, that a general *remonstrance* would have been signed against the measure. A reconciliation, however, took place between

Mr.

Is supported by a few of the clergy.

---

* See p. 69.

Mr. Wilks and his superior; when welcoming, as they thought, the return of peace, to it they sacrificed every other interest, and suspended all resentment. The peace they had welcomed was an illusory appearance; for, in a few weeks, they understood, that Mr. Wilks was again deprived of his parochial powers in the city of Bath, and in the western district. On this they prepared an *address* to the Catholic clergy of England, which they signed, and circulated.

In this address they endeavour to shew, from the rules laid down by canonists, that the last punishment inflicted on their delegate was *arbitrary*, *unjust*, and *uncanonical:* for no *citation* had preceded the sentence; in it was no *expression of the cause*, unless in vague and undeterminate words; the sufferer had been guilty of no *grievous crime*, attended by *contumacy*. These three articles they specifically examine.* And having stated what is their belief in regard to the rights of *episcopacy* and the *priesthood*, they lament that perturbed situation of things, which will not permit us, *in all cases*, to be governed agreeably to the rules of other churches, and close, in their own names, and, as far as may be, in the names of the Catholic clergy of England, in their own behalf and in behalf of their successors,

---

* *Address to the Catholic clergy.*

ceffors, with a *folemn proteft* againft the meafure.—The *addrefs* is dated Jan. 26, 1792.

The clergy of Staffordfhire had flattered themfelves, that, as the rights of the priefthood were obvioufly involved in the prefent queftion, to vindicate which from oppreffion and to impede the eftablifhment of a dangerous precedent, was the leading motive of their conduct, they fhould be actively joined by the fecular clergy of all the diftricts. Again they were miftaken. In the fpring an *anfwer* was publifhed to their *addrefs*, figned by thirty three names, chiefly from the weftern diftrict, a motley congregation, among whom a few of the old fecular clergy were thinly fcattered. This I notice; becaufe as long as the regulars plead an exemption from epifcopal jurifdiction, and are governed by their own laws, fo long we admit not them as judges of what may or may not be the rights of the fecular priefthood, of what is or is not, in our eftimation, oppreffive and uncanonical. Thofe exemptions are maintained in the *tract* before me. Mr. Wilks, it is true, is a regular, but we viewed him, I have obferved, as our delegate to the committee; for the difcharge of our truft he fuffered; and therefore, it was our duty not to defert him. He was the delegate alfo from the regulars; and they will fay why, in his regard, they permitted even their own exemptions and the rules

They are oppofed from the weftern diftrict.

rules of his order, to be violated. Unfortunately for him, he espoused that side of the question which many of the regulars, some particularly, reprobated, and the sentence against him came from a brother's hand.

<small>The answer from the western district examined.</small>

The *answer* to the *address* is a remarkable composition, not from its style which merits praise, but from its artifice and affected candour that merit censure. To the school, whence much of it flowed, I could point with certainty.

We had most unaffectedly styled ourselves the *Catholic clergy of the county of Stafford*, to designate who we were.—The *answerers* cannot allow the appellation; it establishes, they say, a collective capacity unknown to them; and they tremble, if it be admitted, for the peace and welfare of their church!

Speaking of the first censure on Mr. Wilks, we pronounced it to be *unjust*, *illegal*, and therefore *null*. The *nullity* of such censures is maintained by all canonists, and particularly by him we quoted. But we did not say, that submission was not often due to an *illegal* sentence, from motives of subordination and the danger of scandal.—The *answerers* impute this assertion to us; and they do it, to enforce a grave admonition founded on the most ludicrous conceit. We had exposed ourselves, they say, (by

a

a declaration we never made) to the horrid imputation of admitting " the ninety-firft *propofition* among the hundred and one of the noted Pafchafius Quenell* condemned by the church!"—*Rifum teneatis.*

We had faid in regard to that cenfure, that an *appeal* to a *fuperior tribunal* was in actual force, when the *inferior judge* (bifhop Walmefley) pronounced it.—The *anfwerers* afk with feeming furprife, having given the definition of an *appeal* and the formalities that attend it, if we mean the act of *proteft* and *appeal*, figned by the committee, in the month of February, 1791? —We meant that precife *act*, becaufe it fpecifically *protefted* againft and *appealed* from thofe encyclical letters,† or *ordinances of apoftolic vicars*, for *non-fubmiffion* to which, as the words of the cenfure pronounce, Mr. Wilks was fufpended. He was the victim, it feems, to the collected refentment of the venerable triumvirate.‡ What
formalities

---

* Quefnell, a man of many virtues and of great learning, was an honeft *Janfenift*, who died in 1719, anathematized by Rome, and perfecuted, for the excrefcences of a wild imagination, by kings, priefts, and Jefuits!

† *Second letter*, p. 30.

‡ A writer whom I wifh not to notice, but who on this fubject, I prefume, is well informed, has very lately declared, that the *ground-work of the cenfure* on Mr. Wilks was 'the *requifition of the bifhops* made *March* 8, 1791. March fhould be February, or the fuppofed *ground-work* of the cenfure will have been eleven days *pofterior* to it. The cenfure is dated February 19. But is
the

formalities he neglected, or what formalities, in this curious act, they adhered to, he and they muſt explain.

Now comes the grand diſplay of theological reſearch.—We had ſpoken of the withdrawing the *parochial faculties* of Mr. Wilks, in the ſecond ſentence, as of the canonical cenſure of ſuſpenſion; we had denominated it ſuch; and to it as ſuch we had applied the rules of canoniſts.—The *anſwerers* are aſtoniſhed. The ſubſtraction of faculties, they ſay, is no cenſure, becauſe it is not the taking away of that to which the prieſt had any *right*, but merely the withdrawing of a commiſſion that was *freely* delegated, and may as *freely* be witheld. And of this kind, they add, are the miſſionary faculties of prieſts in this kingdom, ſubject to the " arbitrary and un- " qualified pleaſure of our biſhops." They then quote their canoniſt to ſhew, that biſhops are endowed with this diſcretionary power.

I admit the reaſoning, in the ſenſe of the canoniſts; but I deny its application to England. And this is the eſſential error, to uſe their own language, that pervades their whole argument.

---

the accurate man alſo aware, that the biſhops he ſpeaks of were thoſe of London and the north, for oppoſing whoſe *Requiſition*, he will hardly, I think, maintain, Mr. Wilks, the ſubject of another ſuperior, could be *canonically* ſuſpended. Yet this he equivalently aſſerts.

argument. They confound two things that are palpably diftinct, that is, the fituation of the priefthood in this country, and that of auxiliary or itinerant regulars and priefts abroad. From thefe, undoubtedly, what has been *freely* given may be *freely* withdrawn, nor by the act is any injury done to them, for the law fuppofes them otherwife provided for; nor is any injury done to the people, who otherwife enjoy the benefit of their immediate paftors. But here, the moment faculties are withdrawn, all means of fubfiftence are at an end; and the flock is without a paftor. I will allow, from an irregularity that the times have introduced, that our cures are not ftrictly *parochial*, and that the powers of our miniftry, by an *abufe* which acquiefcence has fanctioned, are *delegated* to us. Still we are not in the ftate which canonifts defcribe, and to which ftate alone their reafoning applies. Wherefore, in a juft appreciation of our peculiar circumftances, it fhould be faid, rather that we refemble a parochial clergy, and are entitled to its rights, than the precarious miniftry in queftion. And our vicars, I will add, if they reafoned juftly and valued the honour of our church, would endeavour to ftrengthen this arrangement, and to give it all poffible validity; and not aim at an arbitrary jurifdiction over men, who bear the burthen and heat of the day. Their own commiffion, it is true, is *delegated*, and revocable at the will of his holinefs; but

fhall

shall one abuse sanctify another? Besides, as I have elsewhere observed, the inferior priesthood of this country has existed in an unbroken succession, from the times of their Catholic ancestors, and oppression from penal statutes and the prejudices of men, not a regular system of altered discipline, has entailed dependence on them. With the clergy then alone, in my estimation, rests the choice of withdrawing their acquiescence from a system irregular and abusive, and of vindicating to themselves the canonical rights of a parochial ministry.

But as things are, it will be said, can the substraction of faculties, with any propriety, be termed a censure?—Most certainly it can: for it takes from the incumbent not his *jurisdiction* only, to which, it is by some pretended, he had no *right*, but also his *benefice* or means of subsistence. Now the censure of *suspension* is generally defined to be, "an ecclesiastical punishment, whereby a clerk is deprived of the exercise of his *order*, or his *jurisdiction*, or the use of his *benefice*." It deprives him also of another possession more valuable than the other three, that is, his good name.—Let me then ask, whether we are really so debased in our condition, as to have no *title* to a *maintenance*, none to *reputation*; but that these may be sported with at pleasure, under the plea that our missionary faculties, with the exercise of which our bread

bread and fame, in this country, are connected, were a commiffion voluntarily delegated. A regular abroad has his commiffion withdrawn, and he retires to his convent; a fecular prieft has his patrimony. Once for all I will obferve, that the rules of canonifts, perhaps, neither apply, nor were they meant to apply to our condition; or if they do they rather eftablifh than weaken our parochial capacity. But there is a *fpirit* as well as a *letter* in the law; and though the letter may not always fpeak in our favour, the former does, and by this we fhould be guided. Agreeably to this fpirit, no paftor can be removed from his charge, without having been guilty of fome crime that rendered him unworthy of it; nor lofe his means of fubfiftence, or be injured in his fame, at the difcretionary, perhaps, the wanton or refentful will of a fuperior.

Nor is it a new claim we make. The old clergy of this kingdom, at all times, maintained it, and it has been made the rule of practice. We were therefore authorifed to fay as we did, " Whenever an inftance of the contrary prac- " tice has happened, the general voice, we know, " has pronounced it to be arbitrary, oppreffive, " and irregular." Truly, it makes me fmile, to read in the *anfwer* many paffages inculcating almoft a blind obedience to epifcopal mandates, and that from men, the majority of whofe anceftors,

cestors, if not themselves, have resisted, in defence of idle immunities, the *canonical jurisdiction* of bishops, in all times, and in all seasons. I will refer them to an authority they profess to respect. When the brief of 1745 decrees that regulars may be suspended from *their faculties (ab exercitio facultatum)* by their respective vicars *for lawful causes (legitimis causis)*, is that, I will ask, to erect an *arbitrary* tribunal? And bishop Stonor in explaining to his clergy the brief of 1753 says:
" If he, against whom a complaint is lodged,
" be a secular, let all things be done according
" to the *general rule* of ecclesiastical discipline."

The remaining pages of the *answer* chiefly regarding the personal conduct of Mr. Wilks, I leave them to his discussion when he shall be returned, if ever he be permitted to return, from exile. One passage only calls for notice.—We had observed from the canonist we quoted, that the judge who should violate the formalities to be observed in the infliction of censures, " is
" himself, *ipso facto*, to be suspended from the
" services and offices of the church."—The *answerers* rebuke us, as we meant the text to apply to the vicar who had, *uncanonically* we judged it, suspended Mr. Wilks, and they refer us to a statute which exempts *bishops* from the penalty.— We knew that statute; but we did not know that *vicars apostolic*, in the eye of the law, were *bishops*, particularly as a layman may be raised to
the

the dignity: And Benedict XIV. in his brief of 1753, addressing himself to these vicars says, " but, at this time, there are *no bishops* in Eng- " land."*

To the *answer* is subjoined an invaluable *letter* from Cardinal Antonelli, president of the congregation de Prop. fid. to the Right Rev. Charles Walmesley, in approbation of the con- duct he had pursued towards Mr. Wilks. It shall have a place here, as a standing monu- ment of that interference in all our concerns, which I have deplored, and of our utter depend- ence on a foreign court. The style, as the edi- tor observes, is most flattering.

" *Most illustrious and most Reverend Sir, as our*
" *Brother.*"

" Your Grandeur's dispatches of the 18th
" of October of the foregoing year afforded sin-
" gular satisfaction to their eminences, the fa-
" thers of the congregation; in as much as they
" not only informed us of the present success-
" ful state of religion in the kingdom of Eng-
" land; but that you had subdued the boldness
" of the missionary Joseph Wilks, who, in con-
" junction with others, had protested against the
" encyclical letters of the apostolical vicars con-

---

* Page 20.

"demning that known form of oath propofed
"for the Catholics. Your conduct in compell-
"ing that perfon, by means of ecclefiaftical pe-
"nalties, to return to his duty, and make the
"neceffary recantation was fo approved by their
"eminencies, the fathers of the congregation,
"that they judged it fuitable to decree to you,
"for fuch behaviour, their juft and honourable
"congratulations."

"I am your Grandeur's Brother,

"*L. Card. Antonelli, prefident.*"

Rome, *March* 10, 1792.

CONCLUSION.

Reflections on our prefent fituation.

THROUGH a period of two hundred and thirty four years, from the beginning of Elizabeth to the prefent time, I have exhibited a fhort, but accurate, view of the fufferings, the troubles, the diffentions, the hopes, the fears of a fociety by their enemies termed *Papifts*, by themfelves *Catholics*, and whom Providence, by an intervention almoft miraculous, has preferved from utter extinction. They are the venerable ruins of a majeftic church, that once filled the extent of our ifland, that civilifed its rude inhabitants,

habitants, planting in their minds the feeds of virtue, and with them the feeds of Chriftian faith. The perils they have gone through were many; and they may now look back from the port, and recount them; for by the ftatute of 1791, the grievances that oppreffed us moft are removed. Our fituation being thus really and relatively meliorated, new duties have arifen with the change, becaufe we have acquired new powers, and new means of exertion. The proper ufe of thefe means, and the exercife of our powers, will give us additional confequence in the eftimation of our fellow citizens, and render us deferving not of further indulgence only, but apt alfo to the difplay of a more dignified conduct in the participation of common rights. When oppreffion weighed us down, and a general difcountenance damped exertion, the efforts of the mind were languid, and no profpects opened to fuccefs, or even invited to enterprife.

The fituation, in which we now ftand, fhould, therefore, be maturely weighed, and every meafure be adopted that may be beft calculated to multiply its advantages and to develope its energies. It would furely be abfurd, when obftacles are removed, to fit down as liftlefs and unconcerned, as when barriers, furmountable by no effort, lay heaped before us. And I know of no reflection better fuited to lead us right, or to point out what fhould be avoided, and what embraced, than that which our own hiftory prefents to the reader's mind. That hiftory tells him, what were the impediments, the ftatutes of the realm laid in his way;—of thefe ftatutes he knows which are removed: that hiftory tells him, what once were the prejudices of the multitude, againft which it was not poffible to advance;—he knows that of thefe prejudices the heavier weight is difpelled: that hiftory tells him, how unceafing were the internal diffentions that corroded the peace, and deadened the exertions of the community, and it tells him what were the certain fources of thofe diffentions;—he knows that means are now before him, whereby all thofe fources may be dried up, never, as far as human forefight can calculate, to flow again: In a word, his own hiftory will be a fure monitrefs, if he liften to her counfels; and with that view, I laid the page before him.

Education fhould be adapted to it.

I ftated the origin, and I followed the progrefs of our foreign feminaries, the eftablifhment of which I deplored, as they were not adapted, I thought, to the genius of Englifhmen, as they created a dependence on the Roman court which operated fatally, and as they foon began, and continued to be, a popular and plaufible, if not a well-grounded, pretext for fufpicions and hurtful imputations.

They

They alfo, by engendering partial interefts and partial views, were almoft the fole and original caufes of the bad fpirit that divided us. But if, at all times, thofe eftablifhments were productive of *fome* evil, and never productive of *all* the good that might have been obtained at home, why fhould they be longer fupported, when the very motive of their foundation, namely, the fuppofition that they would not be permitted at home, fubfifts no more? It is true, a provifo of the laft act prohibits the endowment of fchools and feminaries; but a repeal of the claufe might be eafily obtained, or a fpecific act for the purpofe, if judged more expedient.

I know not what it is, but the prejudice of habit, that can attach us to our foreign education. When abftractedly confidered, we deplore it, as our anceftors did, as a grievance: but no fooner is a propofal, however remote, made for its fuppreffion, than the grievance is converted into a bleffing, on which the very exiftence of our religion is faid to depend, and which, on no confideration muft be furrendered. And what is that education fo exclufively advantageous, that nothing can compenfate for its lofs? And how is the exiftence of religion connected with it?—The *education*, I admit, were education nothing more than a fchool of moral virtue, is not, was not, at leaft, blameable;

but

but if education be taken, as it should be, in its comprehensive acceptation, as combining a system of universal instruction, I will be bold to say, that, as it was practised in our foreign seminaries, it was extremely defective. However, defective or perfect, it will be enough to shew, that *as much* at least may be done at home; for then the other considerations, whether of economy, of native character, of patriotic propensions, of the acquirement of the language and habits of Englishmen, will throw into the scale a preponderating weight.—And as to *religion*, I am amazed the objection can be urged by any man who knew what our situation was. He would know, we were secluded from the citizens of our towns, and that of the practice of religion we only beheld its shews and pageantry, which had better been hidden from us. But why, let me ask, should not religion be taught where it will be practised, and in the language also and the usages of that practice? It is a worthless compliment to the evidence of our faith, to imagine, that its existence, or even its lustre, must depend on climate or the influence of walls.

At all events, be it allowed, that those establishments, in their origin, were dictated by dire necessity, and that they were productive, in their progress, of great good, being conducted by wisdom, and animated by the purest views. But are they adapted to our altered and improved

proved ſtate? — We aſſociate freely with the world, where other manners and other learning, of a more refined and miſcellaneous character, are neceſſary, than what we formerly imported, learning that was confined and ſcholaſtic, manneis that were uncouth and repulſive. I ſhall ſurely be underſtood, to ſpeak only of ſuch learning as improves and exalts, of ſuch manners as, by embelliſhing, give a charm to virtue.

In diſcharging the public offices of religion, we are now expoſed to obſervation; for our chapels are open, and curioſity, if not devotion, prompts many to enter.—We can, therefore, no longer, with credit to our miniſtry, be neglectful, precipitate, or heedleſs as many formerly were; but a deeper ſenſe of religion will be impreſſed from attention to its offices, and more dignity, more recollection, more external piety, at leaſt, will accompany the ſervice. I will add, (and here reſts the chief importance,) from the circumſtance of the publicity of our ſervice, our own language muſt be more cultivated, and a greater facility of expreſſion and perſpicuity of elocution acquired, than at a diſtance from our own country, and in the habits of ſpeaking dead or foreign languages, were poſſibly attainable. Could there be a greater abſurdity than to cultivate that tongue leaſt, which afterwards muſt be the vehicle of our thoughts? Or in how low an eſtimation, muſt even religion and its ſacred truths

truths have been held, when no care was taken to qualify their ministers to recommend that religion by a display of its evidence, and to imprint those truths by enforcing their sublimity or their moral excellence? The error lay in the plan of education; nor could it be well surmounted.

A scheme proposed.

We have abroad, in different countries, in France, Flanders, Germany, Spain, Portugal, and Italy, houses of education. Few of them are rich: the revenues of some are principally drawn from the countries where they are established, being the donations of former charities, and therefore not to be removed: but the chief property of most is vested in the English funds or in English securities. To judge from the spreading torrent of politics, not in France only but in other countries, which no combination of kings will be able long to stem, great changes, in a few years, must take place on the continent of Europe. But in the view of such changes, what prudent Englishman will not, before the day, look to his own country for an asylum, the land of tranquil liberty, which no innovations will convulse, if its governors, learning prudence from the misfortunes of others, shall make a timely reform by an alleviation of every grievance and a suppression of every abuse. Had our countrymen, settled in France, whom an early notice, I know, warned, practised this salutary

salutary measure, they would have avoided many evils, and have secured much property that must now be lost. I will, therefore, suppose, if the choice be not in time spontaneously made, that events of no distant period will dissolve our foreign establishments, dissipate their revenues, and disperse their members. If advice can be necessary, I advise that prudence, from this moment, direct their counsels, and energy invigorate their resolutions.

In this state of things, the probable issue of which no obstinacy will controvert, three measures of an interesting magnitude present themselves. First, to draw into this country whatever property can be withdrawn from our foreign establishments, and that as expeditiously as may be;—Secondly, to concentre all our strength; —and thirdly, to adopt such means as, with the sanction of parliament, shall be thought most conducive to the establishment of one or more houses of education, on the broadest basis and on the most enlightened plan. Thus will a foundation at once be laid, on which may be secured the sacred interests of religion, education prepared for our youth, the seeds planted that shall improve our general character and exalt it, and finally good be drawn from evil, unanimity from discord, strength from divided weakness.

But is our schemer aware, will the reader say, of those differences of orders, monks, Dominicans,

minicans, Franciscans, Carmes, which have hitherto subsisted, and do subsist, whose interests are various, whose views diverge, and whom no event, it seems, can ever call together? Is he aware, that the disciples of Ignatius, though deprived of their former name, and by a papal mandate, released from every tie of the institute, are not less, than they were, an insulated body, whom former jealousies seem to animate, or whom, at least, no common interest has hitherto seemed to lead to a cordial union with their elder brethren? Is he aware of all the dissentions, controversies, bickerings, which, from whatever causes they may have sprung, have generated a repellancy of character, that the lapse of many years, and the efforts of candour and benevolence, will not be able utterly to eradicate?

Of all this the schemer is aware, and therefore does he prescribe a remedy to the evil. He will dry up the very source, and cause a purer stream to flow, whence harmony shall spring, and its attendant blessings, success and happiness.—I admit the existence, and the discordant views ascribed to them, of our different orders. But they have seen their closing day in France, and, in other countries, the same fate will soon attend them. Where then lies the difficulty of sacrificing distinctions that will be but ideal, and of throwing into a common treasury

treasury, on the noblest of motives, their remaining wishes, and such property as may survive the wreck?—The ex-jesuits, animated by the laudable example, will be induced, I am sure, to follow it.—And as to the general causes of division, when variety of colours and appellations, when scholastic disputes, when domestic views, when mutual jealousies which occasioned them, have ceased to operate, we may look for a reunion of sentiments and the preponderating influence of worthier motives.

I therefore propose, from a conviction of its expedience, and the ease that will attend the execution, the measure of forming establishments at home, on the basis, I have suggested, of one grand and comprehensive plan, that shall annihilate every former distinction, and views of party, consolidating all our property into one mass, and our different orders into one body of secular clergy.

A second measure, not unconnected with the first, is also before me.

The reader will recollect the origin of our church establishment: he will recollect how adverse it was to the wishes and efforts of the clergy, and how reluctantly they acquiesced in the arrangement. He will also be sensible of that dependence on the court of Rome which it entailed on us; and how indecorous in itself and

Evils of our church government.

SUPPLEMENT.

and inconfiftent with the free fpirit of Chriftian difcipline, and the dignity of a venerable church, that dependence is, and has been. But if the clergy, more than a hundred years ago, on the cleare convincement of its expedience, ftrove to procure a regular hierarchy, when their fitu tion was fuch as I defcribed it, full of perils, uncertainty, and troubles, what fhould our thoughts and language be? I am difpofed to allow, from the characters of the men raifed to the vicariate, that many of the evils did not enfue, which the clergy had predicted; and that, from the ftate of oppreffion under which our fathers lived, the e ablifhment of an ordinary epifcopal government would have brought with it, perhaps, no peculiar advantage. But was the abufe for this lefs flagrant? And why were we to be fingled out as a rickety and degenerate race of Chriftians, whofe back-ftrings the pontiff only muft direct or his facred congregation? It might be, and the friends to abfolute monarchy fhould patronife the meafure, it might be, that, the whole church could be equally well governed by pontifical lieutenants, deputed with co-ordinate and revocable commiffions. Yet the primitive inftitution fhould not, therefore, be annulled: and why then annulled in our regard?

I drop all confideration of any irregularity in the firft appointment of our vicars apoftolic,
and

SUPPLEMENT. 461

and of all the good or evil which, in the courfe of a hundred years, the arrangement has produced.—But when long ufages have fanctioned a meafure, it will be more prudent, fome may think, to retain it, than by attempting a change to rifk the evils of innovation.—I would fubfcribe to the caution, were thefe evils certain, or were not what is meant to be reformed itfelf a palpable abufe, and invariably productive of, or itfelf accompanied by, evils. I will enumerate thefe evils as they exift in 1793.

But firft, that the government by *vicars* is *abufive* will hardly, I think, be denied, when the inftitution by Chrift, as we conceive it, of ordinary epifcopacy is admitted, from which that of vicars is a plain, and not a *neceffary*, deviation.—Its evils are: Firft, *dependence* on the Roman court, or rather, on one of its congregations.—So entire is this dependence, as to the vicars whole commiffion and its exercife, that the *placita curiæ Romanæ* are the fole rule of their conduct, of which conduct and of all perfons and concerns fubject to their infpection, they are bound, at ftated times, to give in an account. It is pretended, I know, that the vicars poffefs fome powers which ordinaries have not, and therefore that advantage and even an additional dignity are annexed to the office. The circumftance of thefe *extraordinary* powers only the more ftrengthens their dependence, point-

ing

ing to the sacred congregation, as to an indulgent parent that commands even the gratitude of its votaries.

Secondly, an *arbitrary* mode of governing: The vicars, themselves dependent, and subject to an *arbitrary* controul, affect a pre-eminence of jurisdiction above the ordinary rules of discipline, and maintain that they are accountable only to their sovereign lord, for their words and actions, in their vicarial capacity. " Because you maintain principles *that I disapprove*," said the senior vicar to Mr. Wilks, " I declare your missionary faculties to cease." " Nor was I bound to give any reason at all," he afterwards observed, " either by ecclesiastical law or practice of the mission;"* grounding this arbitrary declaration on the *placita curiæ Romanæ*, that as his own powers were revocable at will, so were those of his clergy. He can, therefore, force a beloved pastor from his flock, reduce him to penury, and blast, as far as may be, his name, under the prerogative of despots, *tel est notre plaisir!*

Thirdly, The want of *subordination* or of a *metropolitan* head.—The four vicars, it has been long ago observed, go equally abreast, without any mutual relation, coherence, or order among them.

---

* *Pamphlet of the Mediators*, p. 17.

them. And though the arrangement may answer well the purposes of dependence, for which it wa established, it has no resemblance, we may safely pronounce, in the Christian church, where all the ministers link into unity by a just gradation. Some head seems essential to every government, where the levelling principle of *liberty and equality* is not admitted; and that headship is as necessary to the due administration of the governors, as to the well being of the governed. Where governors for their actions are only accountable to a distant master, liable to be imposed on by false representations, and judging from report, how perturbed, how loose, how precarious, how feeble must such administrations be. Besides, where all are equal, there is no tribunal of *appeal*; no remedy for the redress of grievances; no regulating power when the master-wheels of the machine are themselves deranged. A metropolitan in every church has been established, as essential to its government. But with a glance it may be seen, why we are thus disorganized. It is that Rome may be our hand, our foot, our eye; that in her we may live, and move, and have our being.

Fourthly, their *election* without the consent of the clergy they are sent to govern.—This is the master evil, because by a prudent choice we could, in part, provide against the evils I have

have enumerated. But the flock, in the maxims of the Roman court, was made for the paftor, not the paftor for the flock. Hence, not only is our confent not afked, or our wifhes explored: even vicars have been appointed notorioufly adverfe to the exprefs and known defires of the clergy. Nothing remains to complete the degrading infult, than that Rome fhould give us an Italian, that Italian a layman.

But let it not be fuppofed, however fevere I may be againft the principle, and the occafional or poffible application of it, that I mean to infinuate the moft diftant reflection on thofe venerable men who have been called to the office. I revere the evangelical virtues of fome; I admire the learning of others; and the piety of all, I believe, was examplary and genuine. From them, therefore, has the employment, which, from its oppofition to the found maxims of antiquity, I deem abufive and degrading, received a luftre; and in this only I think them cenfurable, that Mr. Leyburn, the firft vicar, did not refufe the extraordinary miniftry, and that his fucceffors, while, from motives of fome public utility, they fubmitted to the charge, did not, at the fame time, enter their folemn proteft againft it, as humiliating to their church and fubverfive of the order of the hierarchy. Certainly, if in any department of life, the fentiments of men fhould be collected as a guide a guide to the choice of officers to preside over them, in none is it so neceffary as in that of religion, where mutual confidence muft be found, and reciprocal returns, or the great benefits of inftruction and advice, reprehenfion and praife will be loft or much obftructed. I have heard of vicars who, in a codicil to their wills, bequeathed their extenfive flocks as a part of their live ftock, recommending the man of their private choice to the favour of the facred congregation.

Thefe are the moft prominent evils of our church eftablifhment; and they are abundant. The experience of them has long excited murmurs, and recently application was made, by fome gentlemen of our late committee, to the vicars themfelves, " that they would exert their endeavours to procure, that in future the eccle-fiaftical government in this country, may be fettled according to the known rules and canons of the Catholic church, by which the clergy may poffefs the rights of a parochial clergy."*—I admire the zeal of thefe gentlemen, but not, in this inftance, their wifdom: for when was it known, that men ever ferioufly undertook the reform of abufes, whence the eminence of their own ftations is alone derived?—

Propofals for its reform.

---

* *Pamphlet of the Mediators*, p. 13.

The vicars, as was natural, anfwered, "that the fubject required the moft mature deliberation; that they will give it their very ferious attention, and report their opinions thereon in the courfe of three months, tho' they fear that fuch a meafure is not practicable under the prefent circumftances."* The three months are gone, and they have, doubtlefs, reported their opinion. I have never afked what it was, as I know it muft be comprifed in the laft line of their anfwer: "The meafure is not practicable under the prefent circumftances."

I would not willingly propofe a meafure that fhould give pain, much lefs that fhould have a tendency to lower that refpect which is ever due, I think, to rulers, and who, though they may feel gratification in the exercife of power, muft ftill experience uneafinefs and many afflicting cares. But I have fhewn how abufive the government of our church is, and what are its evils. Will it be faid, that they are not of a magnitude to call for redrefs? Will it be faid, that what our anceftors *acquiefced* in, we fhould not attempt to *reform?*

Our vicars have faid, "That they fear the meafure is not practicable under the prefent circumftances."—May I afk on what that fear is grounded? What view they have taken of

---

* *Pamphlet of the Mediators,* p. 18.

of these circumstances? What portion of serious attention they gave to the subject, which required, they acknowledged, the most mature deliberation? For, in my estimation, their fear is without cause, and the present circumstances are most propitious. At what time, were the prejudices of the public less inveterate; the dispositions of government more favourable; the pretensions of Rome less overbearing; our own condition more flattering and secure? But our vicars, I know, some of them, are haunted by idle apprehensions. They permit men to obsess their ears, who alarm them with the tale, of designs formed against episcopal government, of attempts to introduce the *constitution civile* of the French assembly, of machinations for the overthrow of the whole jurisdiction of Rome, of a settled plan to weaken, and then to exterminate the faith of our ancestors. Such things have been told them; and, at a time, when credulity is proclaimed to be the test of patriotism,* can we be much surprised, if our vicars took the

---

* "There are seasons of believing, as well as of disbelieving; and believing was then so much in season, that improbabilities or inconsistencies were little considered. Nor was it safe so much as to make reflections on them." So observed bishop Burnet, speaking of the times of Oates's plot; and as we seem to live in a season (the beginning of 1793,) when *believing* is equally in fashion, may it not be inferred, that there is a certain rotation in human events, and that mankind will again be involved in all the chaos of former errors and former ignorance?

contagion, and believed what they heard? Under the impression of those horrors, vain as the dreams of the morning, it was, that they returned their answer: "We *fear* such a measure is not practicable under the *present circumstances*."

Character of bishop Talbot. Let it not be thought, that I involve all the vicars in this censure, if a censure it may be called; or that when I spoke of arbitrary conduct and a disregard of the rights of the priesthood, it was my intention to cast a general blame. One,* at least, there is who merits no such censure, no such imputations. He is prudent, beneficent, mild. His peace is not alarmed by jealousies, nor the forebodings of credulity; for in the evidence of religion he sees an anchor, in the professions of honest men a sufficient security, and in the general aspect no cause for fear. In him his clergy witness no pageantry, no needless display of power. They obey from duty and the impression of filial love; nor do they know they have a ruler, but by the experience of those generous and parental acts which station empowers that ruler to perform. We beheld, through the progress of the late controversy, his wisdom matured by years, under the reproaches of party zeal his forbearance, at all times his love of peace ardent and unshaken.

Convinced

---

* Uncle to the present Earl of Shrewsbury.

Convinced then, that the present circum- *Plan for a re-*
stances are as adapted to the reform we medi- *form sketched.*
tate, as the most sanguine mind could have
wished, what remains to be done? The vicars,
we may be assured, will never confess the time
is proper; or, should they be prevailed on to
carry a supplication to the foot of the pontiff,
so hesitating would its language be, so courtly,
so unimpressive, that the sacred congregation
also would be induced to " *fear* that the mea-
" sure was not practicable under the present
" circumstances."

The clergy, who feel the grievance most,
are most adequate to its reform. They are
versed in the history of other ages: they know
what their discipline was, what abuses deformed
that discipline, and what means the sages of better days would have used in the correction of
those abuses. From them they will have learned a manly firmness, unabashed by the obstacles
of frowns or menaces, tempered by mildness
and the forbearances of an untired patience.
Were I to speak to them of violence, they
would condemn me; of secret combinations,
they would not listen; of artifice, they would
repel the insidious proposal. They shall undertake the reform then in their own way, and,
if my advice can prevail, they shall accom-
plish it.

I advise

I advife that, in each diftrict, a few meet, impreffed as I am with the importance and expedience of the meafure; that they difcufs the fubject in an accurate and comprehenfive manner, taking in all its views, its relations, and its various bearings; that they commit to writing a fketch of their thoughts; and that the vicar apoftolic be immediately waited on.

To him they will communicate thofe thoughts, entering more at large on the fubject; and having liftened to his queftions, his objections, his difficulties, and replied to them, they will entreat his co-operation and fupport, ftating that they earneftly wifh for both, as the beft aids to their plan, and the vouchers of their moderation and unambitious views. I will not fuppofe, that the vicars can decline this honourable call on their miniftry and their profeffions of attachment to ecclefiaftical difcipline.

The fame fketch of thoughts muft then, by letter, be communicated to each clergyman in the diftrict, with an intimation of what has been done, and of the vicar's wifhes to co-operate. It would be well, therefore, that his fignature, or fome unequivocal expreffion of his intentions, accompanied thefe letters.

The fentiments of the body being collected from their anfwers, it will only remain to pre-

pare

pare the form of a *supplication* to be presented to his holiness; and this form must also be previously submitted to general infpection, and particularly to the examination of the vicar, if he has not himself been the principal author of it. The form, when approved, or returned with fuch criticifms as may add to its accuracy and complete the whole, will be ready to receive fuch fignatures as may be judged moft proper to eftablifh its validity, and make it fpeak the univerfal voice of the diftrict.

The *fupplication*, without the circumlocution of empty phrafes, fhall ftate, what, from the time of its facred inftitution, is and has been, in regard to epifcopal government, the difcipline of the church; when and how it happened, that a government fo well adapted to the exigences of a chriftian people, was fufpended in the kingdom of England; how unceafing, for many years, were the efforts of the clergy to bring back the falutary inftitution; that Rome, ever deaf to their prayers, finally forced on them vicars apoftolic, contrary to the exprefs defires and the known reclamation of the fame clergy; what are the evils of a vicarious government; that the clergy, notwithftanding thefe evils, from motives of a laudable fubmiffion, had acquiefced in the arrangement; that now we are no longer the oppreffed people that we were, and that our altered ftate calls for a more regular and independent

pendent eftablifhment; that a government by vicars apoftolic is no longer agreeable to us, and that we pray for its fuppreffion, and the reftoration of an ordinary epifcopal hierarchy.

Rome will liften to this *fupplication*, and grant it's prayer: The childifh objections from want of fees will be removed: The vicars apoftolic, by an eafy tranfmutation, will be raifed into bifhops of diftricts, unlefs they prefer their Afiatic appellations, and the care of imaginary flocks : Chapters will be erected in each diftrict: Our church will be reorganized: And with it will return the bleffings of a renovated christian fociety.

The directions I prefumed to fuggeft to one diftrict, muft be underftood to belong to all. They will correfpond by an eafy communication of opinions ; the fame plan will be eftablifhed; and one *fupplication* formed upon a decided and unequivocal enunciation of fentiments.

I have propofed the free expreffion of my thoughts; and in this I have done my duty. My brethren will weigh them in their wifdom, and approve or reject of them what portion they may pleafe. I have pointed out the evils in our foreign education and in our domeftic economy; and I have attempted to fhew by what means thofe evils may be furmounted,

and

and their fources converted into fources of improvement and felicity. Eftablifhments or modes of life that were once, perhaps, not fo unadapted to our circumftances, at prefent, when thofe circumftances are altered, fhould no longer be retained. This I wifhed to imprefs, and with it the important leffon, that there is a flow in human events, on an active attention to which our own fuccefs depends, and the progrefs of future generations.

Here alfo I clofe the fketch, perfect as I could make it, of the *hiftory* of the troubles of my own fociety. And fuch, generally, is the hiftory of man. But a dayfpring opens before me, and I will not cloud it, as is the practice of prophets, with any vifionary forebodings of untoward events from the inveteracy of habits, the prepoffeffions of a fancied excellence, the general errors of education. Rather let me indulge the hope, that a fociety which has furvived the preffure of an unexampled feries of ftorms, is deftined for a happier duration, that in that duration it will gather ftrength, and in that ftrength profper.

THE END.

O'Shaughnessy Library
College of St. Thomas
St. Paul, MN 55105

**WITHDRAWN
UST**